Operations of the Polish Army During the 1809 Campaign in Poland

Prince Jozef Poniatowski

By General Roman Soltyk
Translated & Annotated by
George F. Nafziger

Account of the Operations of the Army
Under the orders of
Prince Józef Poniatowski
During the 1809 Campaign in Poland
Against the Austrians

Preceded by a notice on the life of the Prince
Enriched with a Portrait and a Map
By Roman Soltyk

General of Polish Artillery,
Papal Nuncio to the Diet of Poland,
Decorated with the Military Cross of Poland and the Legion of Honor

Author of
Poland or Historical and Military Account of the 1831 Revolution and of
Napoleon or Memoir of the Account of the 1812 Russian Campaign

Paris
Publisher and Military Library of Gaultier-Laguionie
(Maison Anselin)
Rue et Passage Dauphine, 36
1841

Printed in the United States of America

ISBN 978-1-945430-37-4
Library of Congress # 2017952468

Published by The Nafziger Collection, Inc.
PO Box 1522, West Chester, OH 45069-1522

E-mail: Nafziger@fuse.net
On-line Catalog: http://home.fuse.net/nafziger

In conjunction with
Winged Hussar Publishing, LLC
1525 Hulse Road, Unit 1
Point Pleasant, NJ 08742

Email: Hetman@wingedhussarpublishing.com
https://www.wingedhussarpublishing.com

Note on Translation:

The language of the author is tainted with his nationalism, but was generally clear and straightforward. It has been translated closely to what was written, with a few exceptions. On those occasions where the author waxed eloquent and a close translation was not possible, the spirit of his words was maintained. For the facility of the modern reader, the phrasing has been modified so that all references to "us" and "our" have been replaced by "the Poles" or "Polish" and "enemy" with Austrians, in order to ensure clarity in the reader's understanding. In a few occasions, the author made references to people by their titles; i.e. "the Major General" or the "Prince de Neufchâtel" specifically. Since the modern reader may not be familiar with those individuals, who, in this instance, were the same individual, Marshal Berthier, I have taken the liberty of using Berthier's name. There were a few other such instances where similar changes were made.

Notice by the Publisher (Original)

General Soltyk, in confiding the publication of his work to us, thought that we should neglect nothing to bring out the merits of his work. However, as the role of editor forbids all praise, we set ourselves to fix the public attention on the material addressed by the author. The account of the 1809 campaign is not a simple recitation of the events of the war; it is a reasoned critique of the operations of the Polish Army, disputing its territory and its liberties from the Austrian Army foot by foot. It is the latter description of this campaign which is presented today, and perhaps the sole subject which links the historical period of the fall of Poland with the end of the 18th century and the wars of the empire.

One is not less flattered to find a sketch of the life of a hero who had tied his destiny to that of France, and whose name is, and shall, for a long time, be venerated by us.

Notice by the Author

My goal in writing this work is to describe the operations of the Polish Army in 1809, to retrace the works and the efforts of the Poles, ably directed at this time by Prince Józef Poniatowski. I served for several years under the orders of this illustrious chief. He honored me with his particular good will while I got to know and appreciate him. Having original material, which I joined to my memoirs, the souvenirs of those of my compatriots who had assisted in the scenes that I wished to describe, nothing kept me from accomplishing this goal, to which I have consecrated all my available time.

However, to the end that I advance my work, I recognize that the account of the 1809 campaign is not sufficient in itself to make Poniatowski well known. Before this campaign, the prince had taken an active part in great events, while later he also did great things, and acquired the skills that caused Napoleon to choose him for important commands and to elevate him to the rank of Marshal of France. It is, therefore, necessary to look both forward and backwards, and to give the reader a glimpse of the life of which I shall trace one major episode. This is what I have done in the biography which precedes the account of the 1809 campaign.

My work finished, I decided to publish my manuscript in French, happy to be able to, by this feeble homage, demonstrate my gratitude to the noble nation which receives us in our exile with such cordiality, and which does not cease to give us indications of its greatest sympathy.

General Roman Soltyk

Roman Soltyk

Account of the Operations
Of the Army
Under the orders of
PRINCE J. PONIATOWSKI
During the 1809 Campaign in Poland
Against the Austrians

HISTORICAL NOTICE ON
PRINCE Józef PONIATOWSKI.

The Poniatowski family did not appear on the political scene until the beginning of the 18th century. At that time, they produced several distinguished personalities, among others Stanislaw Poniatowski, Colonel of the Guards of the King of Poland Stanislaw Leszczynski, the companion of Charles XII, king of Sweden. Stanislaw Poniatowski had several children. In 1764 one of his sons was elected King of Poland and reigned under the name Stanislaw-August. Another was a lieutenant general in the service of the Emperor of Germany and married Theresa Kinska, of an illustrious Bohemian family. To this union was born a son, Josef Poniatowski. It is this man whose story we will sketch.

Prince Josef Poniatowski, born in 1763, grew up and was raised under the protection of his uncle, the King Stanislaw-Augustus. He was educated with great care under the direction of his mother, a woman of great merit, and he excelled in his studies, manifested always with a marked preference for military studies.

The national history offered him a good example to follow. He avidly read the accounts of the brilliant feats of arms that immortalized Tarnowski, Chodkiewicz, Zamoyski, and Sobieski. His strong personality swelled up with a desire to imitate them. He realized that Poland could only raise itself by military action and he abandoned his penchant to predilection. At the age of 16, he requested that the King allow him to enter the Polish military. The Polish Army was then quite small, and its organization very poor. It had been reduced, over the past half century, to 24,000 men and its training was not strong. It had lost its warlike spirit that had previously distinguished it. Poniatowski was not able to acquire, in its ranks, the theoretical knowledge and practices by which alone it is possible to educate a good officer. The King, his uncle, decided to send him to Vienna and to have him take service in the Imperial Army, which was renown for its discipline and for it instruction, in which many Poles of note served.

Józef entered the service of the Emperor in 1779 as a cavalry officer. Filled with zeal and energy, he threw himself into his studies of the military art and soon earned the favor of the Emperor Józef II. His advancement was rapid. In 1787 he commanded a dragoon regiment with the rank of a lieutenant colonel. At the head of this unit, he took part in the campaign against the Turks that occurred in that same year. The young Poniatowski seized this opportunity to distinguish himself and to give proofs of both his courage and talent. He was wounded at the siege of Sabacz, was subsequently made an aide-de-camp to the Emperor, and promoted to colonel of cavalry. Field Marshal Lascy, one of the illustrious soldiers of the century, who commanded the Imperial Army, recognized him his talent, grew to hold him in affection, and trained him in the principals of army operations. As a result, Józef became a capable and trained officer. His destiny was promising: nephew of a king, favorite of the Emperor, colonel at age 24, and the future reserved for him brilliant success.

Poniatowski was one of the most handsome men of his time. His skill in military exercises was astonishing. He distinguished himself equally by his courage and his presence in danger. Full of enthusiasm and animated by a noble ambition, no obstacle was capable of stopping it. His heart was excellent, and in perfect harmony with his straightforwardness and the purity of his principals. One can say that he had faults and they found their source in excess, as did his qualities. He was always courageous to the point of being reckless, enthusiastic to the point of rapture, generous to the point of profligacy. He was like a knight of ancient times. If he had been born two centuries earlier, perhaps he would have been better understood and better appreciated than in the present, where a calculated cold and guilty egotism seemed to tear the soul and crush the spirit of heroism. Happily, Poniatowski appeared in a nation where the influence of the times was less felt. In Poland he was looked upon as a hero.

The King, Stanislaw-August, had been placed on the throne by the intrigues and the influence of the Empress Catherine of Russia. The Empress supported the candidacy of her protégé with 40,000 troops she had massed under the walls of Warsaw. Her influence, already great in Poland, grew still further during his reign. Called upon to play an eminent role, Stanislaw-August was endowed with the qualities that could bring one great renown. He joined to them a spirit that was fine and penetrating and a character that was soft and affable. His manners were distinguished and his speech easy. He was at home in the government and the salon. However, he was far from possessing the high sentiments and the indispensable force of spirit necessary for his important mission. He had neither the habit of public affairs nor the high capacities which were needed for the state of Poland, which, agitated within and threatened externally, could not be saved except by a leader who could, at the same time, regenerate it and defend it. Under such a king, Poland was to be delivered to all the hazards of events.

The Empress Catherine II did not fail to profit from the state of these circumstances, and took steps to exclusively direct the destiny of Poland. It was easy for her to work towards this goal because Prussia was her ally and Austria did not have the political power to block her ambitious projects. In order to better assure her power, she took care to foment the hostilities between parties that continued to divide the nation and kept them in a permanent state of hostility. Not content to stir up discord between the Protestants and the Catholics, she also deflected the ideas of the innovators, who wished to walk with the illustrious men of the century, while she at the same time supporting the partisans of the ancient order of things, who opposed all reforms and the exorbitant rights and oppressions of the nobility, in its turbulence, its misinterpretation of the laws and shamelessly acted against the public good. However, within the ranks of this nobility were men marked as superior by their talents and character, who put the interests of the country above the privileges of their social position and sought reforms that would renew the state. At the beginning of the reign of Poniatowski, the efforts of the reformists appeared about to be crowned with success. A few notable changes were made to the fundamental laws of the republic and the Empress did not oppose them. However, soon politics changed. A new diet, elected under her influence, abrogated the modifications which had been decreed, and the oppressive power of Russia once again grew. In vain a few influential senators, such as Graetan Soltyk, Józef Saluski, Winceslaw and Severin Rzwuski sought to oppose this shameful oppression.[1] They were arrested in the capital in 1767 and sent as prisoners to Kaluga. The indignation produced by this outrageous act of violence was tremendous. The friends of the imprisoned patriots armed themselves. A bloody war erupted. The patriots fought under the flags of the Confederation of Bar and the partisans of Russia fought under the flag of the King. The Empress, who supported the latter, profited from these circumstances to establish her troops on the territory of the republic. The efforts of the confederates could not give them victory. Despite the arrival of a few French officers and the diversion produced by the war against Turkey, they succumbed in the battle, resulting in the first partition of Poland. In 1772 Russia, Austria and Prussian divided the provinces of Poland between them. This violent act, without parallel in the annals of the world, was executed in peace, without the result of a war by the dividing powers against Poland, and in the face of other powers who had an interest in the existence of an independent Poland. The territories and population of the republic were reduced by a third.

The exceptional richness of its soil, the warlike nature of its people, and the prestige of its ancient victories caused the Polish Republic to aspire to a distinguished place among the great powers of Europe. The diet held every four years, convoked in 1788, began a new epoch for Poland. The reformists found themselves in the majority. At their head was Adam Czartorski[2], Ignace and Stanislaw Potoçki, Stanislaw Soltyk, Stanislaw Soltan, Julien Niemdcewicz, Józef Wybicki, and finally, the most devoted of them all, Stanislaw Malachowski, Marshal of the Diet. The reformist movement was so strong that the king was obliged to associate himself with them. He then took part in the drafting of the new constitution, which was prepared in secret. This new pact reinforced the power of the King, establishing a hereditary throne, abolished the veto, accorded rights and immunities to all classes, and abrogated the abuses of the government. It was proclaimed, without regard for the displeasure it brought the Empress Catherine II of Russia, on 3 May 1791.

Poland liberated itself from the odious Russian yoke and reclaimed its independence. The king acceded to this great national act, but without conviction and grudgingly, because he believed that this decisive act would deprive him of the protection of, and earn him the enmity of the Empress Catherine of Russia, who was very interested in maintaining Poland impotent or in anarchy. The reformists sought, then, to make another alliance. The ambition of Russia, its conquests in the east, and its exclusive preponderance of influence in Poland had caused Prussia and Austria to come together to oppose further increases in Russia's power. The King of Prussia, Frederick-Wilhelm, appeared to seek a friendly relation with Poland. An alliance was concluded with him, a deceitful alliance that reserved a cruel deception for Poland. However, the Empress Catherine, after making peace with Turkey in early 1792, declared herself against the Polish reforms. It became necessary to prepare for war against Russia, but it was very difficult to bring together the resources necessary in a country so long torn asunder.

The fight was, therefore, unequal and difficult to sustain. However, there lay in the republic an enemy more redoubtable than its external enemies. This enemy were those who were against the reforms and who had submitted to an imposing majority, but continued to act in

---

[1]Soltyk was the Bishop of Krakow, Zaluski was bishop of Kiiow, Venceslaw Rzewuski, Palatinate of Krakow, and his son Severin, Staroste of Dolin.
[2]Father of Prince Czartorski, who found himself exiled at this time.

the shadows and secretly awaited the Empress. The leaders of this party, such as Felix Potocki, Francis Xavier Branecki, Alexandre Sapieha, and Severin Rzewuski[3], were driven by ambition and perhaps, at the same time, by their love for the ancient constitutional liberties. In addition, among this group were men who had been bought by the Russian court, and sadly, men of influence. The King was guilty of weakness in lending an ear to their insinuations and he was successively drawn into their intrigues. His hesitations, his weakness of character, and perhaps his ill will, paralyzed the efforts of the Polish Diet and destroyed the effects of its best actions.

Prince Józef continued his service in the armies of the Emperor. A second campaign against Turkey was about to begin and it promised to increase his glory, but the King recalled him to Poland to assist in the organization of the 100,000 men that the Diet had ordered raised. The Prince obeyed, and, upon his arrival in Warsaw in 1789 and contributed to the raising of new formations. However, prior to turning to this effort it was necessary for him to prepare for war with Russia. Prince Józef was called to command the Army of the Ukraine, which had no more than 14,000 men. This army was to defend central Poland against a force of 60,000 Russians under the command of Kakhovsky. In addition, his forces were spread out in many widespread cantonments. The remainder of the Polish army, some 55,000 men, was unable to enter the line and most of them were not even formed.

The Diet was dissolved at the end of May and the King was invested with almost unlimited power. A council of war was called in Warsaw by Stanislaw-Augustus before sending the two army commanders to their commands. Prince Józef expressed his opinions in this council with frankness. He declared that it was imprudent to begin a war with such a small army.[4] He requested that the king engage a foreign general to command who was more capable than he. He declared that he was prepared to serve in command, but was convinced that, with the available forces, it would be difficult to expect a happy outcome of the campaign or even glory for the future commander. The King rebutted his concerns about insufficient military resources, stating that it was the duty of every Pole to defend his country and then, in a word, ordered Prince Józef to obey. The campaign plan that was developed was well-considered. It was decided to not defend the very extensive borders and the Armies of the Ukraine and Latvia were ordered to unite at suitable locations, then to coordinate their activities, and maintain themselves in constant communication. Prince Józef's army was to be reinforced by a levy of Ukrainian Cossacks destined to operate on the Russian borders, and a division of 6,000 men under Prince Michel Lubomirski. The artillery and munitions necessary would be sent to him and the king would hold himself ready to march at the head of a reserve division of 8,000 men. Finally, it was observed that the Prussians had promised an army of 30,000 men that would cooperate with then at the beginning of the campaign. Prince Józef chose the city of Polonne as the place for his magazines of provisions and munitions and the city was quickly fortified.

THE 1792 CAMPAIGN

With all the measures decided, the prince placed himself at the head of his troops. His arrival was none too soon. The Russians had penetrated into the territory of Poland at four dif-

---

[3]Rzewuski had been put at liberty by the Empress after five years of captivity in Kaluga. He then changed his allegiances and engaged himself under the flag of the Russian partisans.[The Targowica Confederation - ed.]

[4]These details are drawn from one of the Prince's documents, entitled: *My Souvenirs on the 1792 Campaign against the Russians.*

ferent points. Their march was so rapid that the Polish were not able to complete the unification of their forces nor implement their defensive plans. The levy of Cossacks did not occur. The delivery of the artillery and munitions was delayed. Polonne was abandoned before it could be fortified. Prince Lubomirski did not unite his division in time, the king was persuaded not to join the army, and what was even worse, the Prussians did not life up to their commitment to send their forces to the support of Poland.

In Lithuania, the Prince von Württemberg, who secretly favored Russia's aspirations, did not move and presented only a feeble resistance to the troops under Krechetnikov as he advanced. He was replaced, but too late to make a difference, by General Judycki.

In the Ukraine Prince Józef drew together his forces. He succeeded, then, in withdrawing them into the interior of Poland, but his troops were ill-organized, having neither a general staff, nor a logistical service. The prince, seconded by Generals Kosciuszko and Wielhorski, both of whom were extreme patriots, made prodigious efforts to support the army, but they were completely surprised and the army withdrew precipitously. This withdrawal was not without glory for the Polish Army. On the 15th of June a serious battle occurred. It occurred before the dikes of Boruszkowce. The Polish rearguard fought valiantly, but was obliged to withdraw through a long defile in the face of the enemy, where it lost a large number of its forces and nearly all they army's baggage. General Wielhorski commanded the Poles on this disastrous day. Despite his ability and his courage, he was not able to balance fortune and was obliged to cede.

Since the opening of hostilities the Russians marched in three columns. While the central Russian column followed the withdrawal of the main body of the Polish Army, the two others sought to turn it. Kakhovsky, aware of the valor of the Poles, did not wish to run the risks of a battle and avoided all serious actions, contenting himself to harass the Poles as they withdrew. Finally a general engagement occurred on 18 June. During this day the Russians directed their principal effort against the Polish center. However, hammered by the Polish artillery, which they could not overcome, they withdrew with heavy losses. Their left was entirely broken and they were forced to withdraw their entire line.

The Polish victory was complete, but Poniatowski was unable to profit from it because he lacked the ammunition necessary to continue the battle and he feared the arrival of the other Russian columns on his flanks as they continued their turning movement. He was forced to content himself with observing them as he was unable to detach sufficient forces to contain them. In this situation the Polish general estimated his losses at 4,000 men. After remaining on the battlefield for a few hours, he withdrew to Zaslaw and then to Ostrog, where he remained for two days in the presence of the entire Russian Army, suffering from their cannonade without being able to respond because he lacked the ammunition.[5]

The prince crossed the Bug, where direct orders from the king ordered him to stop. However, the Bug could not long stop the Russian's progress. Its bed is fordable almost its entire length in the summer and the front was too extended to be defended by an army of 24,000 facing the forces of Kakhovsky. At the same time the Army of Lithuania had withdrawn on Brzesc and was followed by superior forces that sought to bring it to battle near Mir.[6] Passage over the Bug was forced by the Russians at Dubienka on 18 July. Kosciuszko, who commanded at that point, used all his skill and warrior spirit. However, he was forced to cede to the Russians, fighting for every foot of ground while inflicting heavy casualties on the Russians.

---

[5] In his Memoirs, the prince says that they had only eleven shots per cannon.
[6] General Zabiełło commanded the Lithuanian forces at this time, having replaced Iudycki.

With these events, terror struck the souls of the inhabitants of the countryside. The anti-reformists formed a confederation at Targowica. Beginning on May 14th they began organizing a military force under the protection of the Russian Army and followed in their baggage train. The king then defected to the pro-Russian party and abandoned the cause of the patriots to throw himself under the protection of the empress and changed his colors. He detached himself completely from the perfidious alliance with the King of Prussia, who had contented himself with counseling him to a rapprochement with the empress.

Because of these changes, nothing had been prepared to lay the groundwork for a vigorous defense. If it had, despite the reverses early in the campaign, the war could have been continued along the Vistula with a chance of success. In effect, the Russians, weakened by their marches and battles, and having been forced to leave numerous garrisons along their lines of communications, now advanced on Warsaw with an army of 70,000 or 80,000 men, while the Polish Army, destined to defend Warsaw now contained 40,000 men with the troops that Zabiello brought from Lithuania. And these forces could have been augmented with levies drawn from the provinces on the left bank of the Vistula, which had not yet been invaded by the Russians.

In this situation, if the line of the Vistula could have been fortified with a few good bridgeheads, it would not only have stopped the Russian advance, but at the same time given the Poles favorable opportunities to assume the offensive. With the army of the Empress contained to its front and its rear harassed by bodies of partisans that would intercept its communications, it would soon find itself lacking sufficient food and munitions and would be forced to retreat. However, none of this was done. Discouraged by the initial failures, the king acceded on July 23rd to the Confederation of Targowica, while the national army was ordered to retreat behind the Vistula and take up positions at Kozienice. It was then disbanded by royal decree and reorganized. This newly organized army had partisans of the pro-Russian faction placed at its head. The patriot generals, among them Prince Józef Poniatowski, resigned their commissions. They were grief stricken, these noble champions of Polish independence, and nothing speaks to it better than a letter written to the king by Prince Józef, from the camp at Markuszew, shortly before the army was dissolved.

Sir,

If I can find words to express the despair of my soul, I shall not fail to do so my the conviction that Your Majesty has joined with men held in public scorn, who traffic in the blood of their compatriots and who have been called to dictate the law to men who have offered their lives to your Majesty and who breath only for the glory and happiness of their motherland. Your Majesty has not recognized that it is better to die with honor. That a total defeat, with honor, is preferable for the nation to an existence besmirched with intrigue, treason, disorders and anxiety! Yes, Sire, it is better to sacrifice and all of us. What cruel pity that now covers us with ridicule and shame. Wielhorski and Mokronowski utter to Your Majesty our unalterable desires. We know to respect the law and the king; but it is with regret in our hearts that we can no longer count ourselves among the defenders of our country. One will say of us at least, "*They have fought with honor and they have withdrawn without reproach.*"

All resistance had become impossible and it was necessary to submit to the inevitable, but hope had not been banished from the hearts of the army's commanders. They emigrated from Poland to find the means to renew the struggle. Except, before the dissolution of the army, with dignity of the best sort, they wished by a solemn act to give to their illustrious commander proof of their esteem and devotion. This was the goal of the following address:

> We recognize all your immovable courage and your attachment to each of your subordinates, which you have manifested during the present campaign. We wish to render homage to your prudence and your noble character, which brought honor and respect to our arms. We assure you of our eternal recognition, of our respect and our affection, which shall last as long as virtue and justice are honored among men. So that this homage of our sentiments might be known to the entire world, we have decided that there shall be struck a medal representing on one side your profile and on the obverse the inscription *"Miles imperatori."*

This address contained the signatures of the army's generals and those of the superior officers, the subalterns, and of a soldier from every unit.

After the sad outcome of this war, Prince Józef Poniatowski was pressed by the king to remain in Poland, but no consideration could bring him to share the shame of his uncle and the abasement of his country. He went to Vienna where memories of his youth drew him.

The second partition of Poland was completed in 1793. Prussian and Russia wee enlarged with several of its provinces and there all that remained of the republic was a phantom existence. Reduced to a third of its former territory, deprived of its natural boundaries, left with an army incapable of defending it, governed by a king who has bowed his head to the law of the victor, it remained occupied by Russian and Prussian troops who placed garrisons in sits principal cities and the capital itself, where the Russian ambassador ruled. For Poland there remained two paths to follow: to take up arms or to submit to foreign oppression. The national dignity left only one choice and an insurrection was secretly resolved upon. The nation prepared itself in silence.

A people as valiant and as in love with their country as the Polish people that are placed under a foreign yoke will not long submit before rising in force to break free. Patriots inside Poland and those abroad waited and planned their insurrection. The former had gathered to this end in Warsaw and Wilno. The others, living in France and Italy, planned among themselves and followed events in Poland. However, they lacked a leader to direct their great enterprise. The King Stanislaw, who had the criminal weakness to sanction the Diet of Grodno in 1793, which caused further spoliation of Polish provinces, was not lost on the Polish people. Prince Józef, who despite his personal merit and patriotism, and despite having no blame, was enveloped in the disgrace of the king. In other circumstances he would have surely been the choice of the nation, but in these sad times, unjust suspicions enveloped him. He was, it was said, too close to the throne to not be influenced by the royal atmosphere. This was an error on the part of the popular judgment.

Happily Poland possessed a distinguished man of military talent and a vast knowledge of politics, a proven man of virtue. At a young age,[7] he was capable of enduring the harshest work. He had acquired high military renown in two hemispheres:[8] this man was Thaddeus Kosciuszko. The memories of the previous war recommended him to the public opinion of Polish people in 1794 and he was unanimously designated for the supreme command. After a few

---

[7]Kosciuszko was at this time 48 years old.
[8]He had served with distinction under Washington, in the United States, during the war of independence, and, as

delays necessitated by circumstances, the moment was judged favorable and Kosciuszko moved to Krakow where he put himself at the head of the city's garrison, 1,000 Polish troops, and was declared *naczelnik* or dictator by the people on 24 March 1794.

The Polish army at this time consisted of 24,000 troops, but they were scattered about the country in many different garrisons and closely watched by the Russians and Prussians.

THE CAMPAIGN OF 1794

Kosciuszko had only a short period in which to organize his forces. He hastily united a weak division, which consisted of, for the most part, peasants armed with scythes. At the head of this corps, consisting of less than 4,000 men, he advanced on 1 April to engage a Russian division of 6,000 men commanded by Denisov and defeated it on 4 April at Raclawice.[9] During the course of the same month, Warsaw and Wilna rose up, vanquished and expelled their Russian garrisons, and recognized the authority of Kosciuszko's dictatorship. During the month of April and through May Kosciuszko profited from the general enthusiasm for the insurrection, which propagated itself in most of the Polish provinces occupied by the Russians. With an activity characteristic of him, Kosciuszko did everything. He constituted a government, raised an army, handled public affairs, and directed the war operations. He soon commanded an army of 26,000 regulars and 34,000 irregular levies. However, the Russians and Prussians, alarmed by the Polish progress, drew together their forces: 75,000 Russians and 45,000 Prussians, successively, moved against Poland.

In June the coalition assumed the offensive; Kosciuszko fought at Szczekociny on June 6th an army twice the size of his own. Forced to withdraw before such superior forces, he withdrew in good order to Warsaw without his enemies following him closely. Nonetheless the Prussians occupied Krakow. Finally, an army of 36,000 coalition forces, with the King of Prussia at their head, advanced and besieged Warsaw on 13 July.[10] For seven weeks the Allies struggled in vain to take the capital, which was defended by 18,000 regular troops supported by an armed population.

Greater Poland was inspired to an insurgency by the other Polish provinces. The communications of the besiegers were threatened and the Allies decided, on 6 September, to raise the siege. The Prussians, under the orders of their king, withdrew via Piotrkow in the direction of Breslau and the Russians, commanded by Fersen, moved up the Vistula to its junction with the Pilica, crossed that river and moved on Kozienice on the Vistula. Later they raised a bridge to cross the river and rejoin Suvorov, who, at the head of a division of the Army of Turkey, was moving to their succors, and was at that time on the Bug River. At this time the Lithuanians undertook an unequal struggle against several diverse Russian corps that operated on that side and made excursions on the Dvina and the Berezina, but the Russian forces grew constantly and forced them wit abandon Vila on 12 August. The Lithuanian Army withdrew to the Bug, fighting the Russians all the way. The principal engagement occurred near Krupczyce on 18 September under Suvorov and Sierakowski, with the engagement going to the advantage of the Polish

---

we have seen, during the 1792 campaign in Poland.

[9]Kosciuszko, who often marched at the head of Polish peasants, wore their uniform, lived frugally as his soldiers, and was accessible to them all. He was a man of the people and the Polish peasants called him, "our Thaddeus".

[10]Warsaw had a population of 110,000. Its defenses consisted of a weak line of works constructed in 1769 when the plague had ravaged the countryside. However, Kosciuszko had successively reinforced them during the siege and constructed a further 105 entrenchments of diverse sizes.

general. However, the following day, Sierakowski, not securing his rear, was turned and taken in the flank between Terespol and Brzesc by the Russians. This forced him into a precipitous retreat in which he lost all his artillery.

After the lifting of the siege of Warsaw, Kosciuszko found himself forced to deliver himself to the duties of ruling the country. By his nature, dictatorial, he power with which he was invested resulted in a simple and strong action, but it soon resulted in opposition in a country accustomed to a constitutional form of government. Kosciuszko had to overcome those obstacles and constantly enforce his authority, but with a gentle and conciliatory character, he was repelled by acts of severity. He was obliged to support many personal disagreements, which dripped with resentment. It was only on the battlefield that he recovered his serenity. Persuaded that the future of Poland was to be found only in victory, he frequently repeated to those in his councils on various governmental issues where the recommendations were divided, "It is necessary to fight and fight yet again, and vanquish the enemy."

A new enemy now menaced the insurrection. The Austrians had sent a division to occupy the Palatinate of Lublin, under the pretext of covering their frontiers. Kosciuszko detached to that front 3,000 men under the orders of General Poninski, who he charged with simultaneously observing the Vistula and delaying Fersen, who was on the right bank of the Vistula, from crossing the river. Poninski defeated the Austrians at Jozefow and forced them to withdraw back into Galicia. He then moved to Bobrowniki, on the Wieprz, in order to resume his mission of observing Fersen. After having detached a division to watch the Prussians, Kosciuszko resolved to unite his forces between the Bug and the Vistula in order to prevent a junction of the two Russian corps that found themselves separated by these two rivers. This capable general sought to be able to engage each force separately. The opportunity appeared to him for a decisive action. For the first time he would be able to engage the Russians with nearly an equal force. His plan was good, but his implementation of it was foiled when Fersen audaciously crossed the Vistula near Maciejowice with 12,000 men. The superiority of his artillery did not permit Poninski, who had about 5,000 men under his orders, to dispute the crossing very long.[11] This operation was executed rapidly and Kosciuszko did not have time to rally all his available forces. He advanced at the head of 7,000 men against Fersen who occupied a position near Maciejowice, with his back to the Vistula. Kosciuszko saw the opportunity to throw him back into the river, placed himself before the Russians, prepared for battle and counted on the arrival of Poninski the following day. However, Kosciuszko was too confident in his ability and took a rash risk. He deployed his forces with an impassable swamp behind him. The anticipated junction with Poninski did not occur and during the course of 10 October the Polish troops were defeated and nearly annihilated. The destruction of the Polish corps was a catastrophe, but the fatal blow for the national independence was the capture of the dictator, who was taken prisoner at the moment when he attempted to rally his troops and send them back into combat. Kosciuszko, surrounded by the enemy and covered with wounds, refused to accept quarter and fell nearly lifeless into their hands.

This unexpected catastrophe threw the ranks of the patriots into chaos. Citizen Wawrzecki replaced Kosciuszko as generalissimo, but he was not a soldier.

Suvorov gathered 24,000 men before the Praga where Wawrzecki had united 14,000 men in the feeble entrenchments. This army, deployed with the Vistula to its back, having only a single bridge across with which to effect its retreat. It was a huge error to accept battle in this

---

[11]Poninski had 22 cannon and Ferson had 94

position. If the Polish had chosen to cross the Vistula and occupy Warsaw they could have continued the fight. However, Suvorov attacked Praga, forced their entrenchments, and destroyed nearly their entire army during the night of 3rd/4th November. Twelve thousand citizens, who inhabited this suburb, were massacred, as well. The few survivors of the defense of Praga withdrew into Warsaw where they joined the garrison. However, they were disheartened by their reverses and were incapable of sustaining a new siege. On the 8th Warsaw capitulated and fell to Suvorov.

The forces that remained to the Poles were united near Radoszyce, below the Pilica. Wawrzecki, Dąbrowski, and the other commanders held a council. Some wished to march westwards across Germany and join the French republicans on the Rhine, but this bold project was quickly abandoned because of the low morale that dampened their spirits. The army disbanded and a few individual commanders went to France. These soldiers would later form the Polish Legions in the French Army that distinguished themselves during the wars of the revolution and for a while kept alive, the sacred flame of Polish patriotism.

It remains to us to describe the part that Prince Poniatowski had in this memorable struggle. As soon as the news of the insurrection in Krakow reached him in Vienna his heart soared with joy and opened itself to hope. He did not hesitate to join the revolutionary army. He found Kosciuszko in late June near Warsaw. Prince Poniatowski, with the humility that so characterized him, offered his services to the dictator as a volunteer under his orders. Kosciuszko, who appreciated his loyalty and patriotism, did not hesitate to give him an important command. During the siege of Warsaw he gave Poniatowski the command of the right wing of his army. He was charged with defending part of the wall of the city that ran from the Vistula to the Vola. The prince set himself to his task with great activity and the great ability for which he was known. Every day was marked with new engagements. It was learned that the weaknesses of the newly constructed fortifications had been communicated to invaders. The newly constructed entrenchments on the sand hills, near Poniatowski, known as the Swedish Batteries, were attacked in the night and carried. They were two far from our lines to be supported. The Prussians occupied the village of Powonzki simultaneously. However Prince Józef rushed forward and immediately retook it. Public praise was heaped upon him. All reverses, however, were imputed to treason and as the prince had momentarily lost the position, there were some murmurs against him. Soon, however, they died out and Kosciuszko continued to give Poniatowski his confidence, to which, on all occasions, he responded with dignity.

After the raising of the siege of Warsaw, Prince Józef was detached to Bzura at the head of 3,000 men to observe the Prussians, who were withdrawing. He maintained communications with Dąbrowski, who Kosciuszko had sent into Great Poland. It was there that he learned of the successive disasters of Maciejowice, Praga and Warsaw, the captivity of Kosciuszko, who was taken to St. Petersburg and locked in the citadel, and the total loss of the Polish cause. His weak corps was in no position to offset the balance of events. He withdrew on Radoszyce and underwent the fate of the other Polish forces. He then took the road to Vienna and established himself in Austria. There he was completely independent and was able to await the most propitious moment. However, he did not look to take service in another army, Austrian or French, not wishing to draw his sword except in the service of his country.

Poland was then definitively dismembered by Austria, Russia and Prussia and wiped from the map of Europe. The king was forced to leave Poland and went to Grodno, abdicating there in 1795. In 1797 he was in St. Petersburg where he continued to live a life of shameful opulence. Despite his family and emotional attachments to his uncle, Prince Poniatowski did not wish to follow him into exile and continued to live in Austria. In vain Catherine proposed to him that he enter her service and threatened him with the confiscation of his properties if he refused to submit. He preferred, however, to expose himself to the empresses vengeance and he lost his estates in the Russian territories.

King Stanislaw of Poland died in 1798 and Prince Poniatowski received an immense inheritance consisting of the possessions of the King in Prussian Poland. In these vast domains he found superb villas embellished with exquisite taste by the king who had cultivated the arts and sciences, galleries of paintings, libraries with hand selected books, statues and expensive objects of art. Lazienki, the royal park enclosed in its walls numerous elegant architectural works and was situated within the walls of Warsaw, was the most remarkable of all for its magnificence. It was there that the Prince received Louis XVIII, the King of France. This exiled prince remained at Lazienki for several months and the Polish people paid their respects and homage to him. He was to them an analogy to their own sad situation. Poniatowski responded with dignity, under these circumstances, to the sentiments of his compatriots. However, Prussian politics soon forced Louis XVIII to leave Warsaw and he established himself in Mittau, in Kourland.

Prince Józef preferred, above all his other estates, Jablonna, which was two miles from Warsaw. He worked to contribute to the happiness of his peasants, to whom he had extended kindnesses with great liberalness. For the eight years that followed his return to Poland he spent the summers in Jablonna. While there he meditated on the future of his country. In the winter he lived in his mansion in Warsaw where he held court, giving magnificent parties, and drew together the elite salons of the capital. This was a characteristic trait of the Prince that he could modify his behavior to match the demands of the moment. In war, his morals were austere, his table frugal, and he abandoned the luxuries and conveniences of live, and none of the generals of his army surpassed his strict observance of the duties of command service. However, in peacetime, to the contrary, he loved his luxuries, the magnificence, and himself into his pleasures with abandon and an ardor that came close to indolence

However, political events advanced rapidly. The French Revolution had defeated its interior and exterior enemies. This great political commotion had brought forward men of great capacity in France. Napoleon Bonaparte surpassed all of them with his genius. He shined equally on the battlefield and in the council chamber.

Favored by circumstances he rose from a simple *sous-lieutenant*[12] to the rank of First Counsel and, in 1804, received the imperial crown of France. Under his government the French Empire consolidated itself daily, and with each successive victory Napoleon enhanced his power. If Louis XV, plunged into the shameful sensual pleasures, had made no effort to prevent the first partitioning of Poland, if the Governments of Louis XVI and the Republic, constantly torn by interior disturbances or occupied with defending itself against an exterior enemy, had been unable to come to the support of the Poles between 1788 to 1794, it was believed that Napoleon would seize the first opportunity to set right the failures of his predecessors and reconstitute the independent state of Poland as a most faithful ally of France. The hopes of a great number of Poles turned to Napoleon. They were justified by his genius and his manifest interest in maintaining his crown. In 1805 these hopes seemed to acquire some basis. Napoleon went to Moravia, won a substantial victory at Austerlitz, and his victorious troops pushed to the frontiers of

---

[12]In the French system, a sous-lieutenant is the equivalent of a 2nd Lieutenant and is the lowest commissioned officers rank.

Poland when the Treaty of Pressburg put an end to the war.[13]

In 1806 Prussia engaged imprudently in an unequal fight with Napoleon. It saw its army annihilated at Jena and the entire campaign was nothing but a string of disasters for Prussia and triumphs for France, who planted the imperial eagles on the banks of the Warta. Napoleon arrived in Posen on 25 November. He was received with great joy by the population of Great Poland, which rose in mass to throw off the Prussian yoke. The emperor, no doubt, had the best intentions for Poland and he wished to re-establish its ancient boundaries, but this proved difficult. Prudence did not permit him to attack the three partitioning powers at one time. It was necessary to suspend his blows on one side while striking the other, and he closely defended the interests of his empire. He encouraged, therefore, upon his arrival in Poland, the insurrection that spread progressively through the land, but without giving the Poles any firm indications of his future intentions.

The French army advanced on the Vistula. The Prussian troops were, at that moment, leaving Warsaw. The King of Prussia, fearing the disorders, which would accompany a popular insurrection, sought to put power in the hands of an influential Pole who could limit the disorders with his popularity. He turned his sight towards Prince Józef and proposed to him control of the government of Warsaw and the surrounding territory. Poniatowski, imbued with a sentiment that can be readily understood, ejected the repugnance he felt at the thought of taking power from the hands of a foreign monarch and a usurper. However, wishing to be useful to his fellow Poles, he accepted the proposition of the King. He was named governor of the capital of ancient Poland. It was in this quality that Prince Józef was called upon to receive the advanced guard of the Grande Armée commanded by Murat, during his triumphant entry into Warsaw, and he shared, on this occasion, the joy of all his compatriots. However, at the same time, with exquisite delicacy that characterized him, Poniatowski wrote to the King of Prussia to explain to him the motifs of his conduct, dictated by his patriotism. Murat witnessed to the Polish his sympathy, but did noting to indicate the intentions of the emperor regarding the political existence of Poland and contented himself with instituting an administrative commission in Warsaw.

The enthusiasm of the inhabitants of Great Poland and of Mazovia increased. They all ran to arms to battle the enemy and the prince shared their sentiments. In his high position, however, prudence dictated that he act with reserve. Before acting he had to know the intentions of Napoleon towards Poland. Napoleon arrived in Warsaw on 19 December and was surrounded by the most illustrious persons of the country. Wishing to profit by the general spirit of the nation to form an army which could serve him as an auxiliary, Napoleon sought to put at its head an eminent person and first turned his sight on Kosciuszko, who had left the prisons of St. Petersburg and gone to America,[14] then had gone to France where he was living at that time. However, Kosciuszko had developed an antagonism towards Napoleon which generated a defiance, no doubt drawn from his republican principals, instructed in the school of sadness, and appreciating his just influence over the Polish nation, demanded first positive assurances on the part of the Emperor. He wished that the independence of Poland, within its ancient bound-

---

[13]There was at this time a party in Poland that sought to put Alexander on the Polish throne. At its head were the Princes Czartoryski. This party, which was not very strong, was not without influence in the country, and had some chance of success. Prior to the battle of Austerlitz their projects seemed close to attaining their goal. The Czar sought to detach from his empire the Polish provinces, which had been incorporated into it. Prussian Poland was to rise and Poniatowski was to put himself at the head of the insurrection, but a rapprochement between Prussia and Russia ended these pointless dreams.

[14]It was the Emperor Paul I who set him at liberty upon his ascension to the throne.

aries, would be proclaimed first. Napoleon, who had to deal with Austria, could not pretend to advance this cause. Kosciuszko rejected his propositions, as a result, and said haughtily, "that having once decided the hopes of his co-citizens, he did not wish to expose them to a new catastrophe." Napoleon's sight then turned towards Prince Józef, who, swept up with the general spirit of the moment, was much easier to rouse. Napoleon formally invited him to assume command of the Polish army, which he was going to form under his protection. However, Napoleon gave no positive assurances as to the reestablishment of Poland and had no desire to convoke the national diet, so he contented himself with naming a governing commission, at the head of which he placed the marshal of the last diet, Stanislaw Malachowski. Poniatowski thought it his duty to accept the propositions of the emperor, because he thought it indispensable to quickly form an army, which would contribute powerfully the outcome of the war on which the future of Poland depended.

At that point Poniatowski became the principal representative of the interests of Poland near Napoleon and he accomplished this task with great dignity. The efforts were, at this time, with regards to the Polish population, prodigious. Not only did the land, newly liberated, have to furnish the French army with all the logistics necessary for its support, but it also provided three legions under the commands of Dąbrowski, Zajączek and Poniatowski with 27,000 men.

Poniatowski frequently consulted with the emperor and had discussions with him regarding the interests of his country. He supported his opinions with a frankness and directness that was characteristic of him. He raised between them principals that were points of important disagreement. Napoleon wished that the newly raised troops should raise the French cockade. Poniatowski, however, supported the necessity of their wearing the national cockade and he commented that it was necessary "to give a tacit recognition Poland." Napoleon eventually ceded to the prince's opinion.[15] Soon the new regiments, in the middle of flying Polish flags, advanced to reinforce the Grande Armée and to second its efforts.

Shortly after the occupation of Warsaw a Russian army advanced to support Prussia. The war expanded and continued despite the bad season. The Allies attempted to drive the French army back over the Vistula. Battles followed at Pultusk and Golomin, and the bloody battle of Eylau.

Hostilities ceased for a while and the two parties used this period of repose to reorganize themselves for the resumption of fighting.[16]

In springtime the skillful maneuvers of Napoleon prepared for the decisive victory of Friedland, which decided the outcome of the struggle. The Allies then withdrew behind the Niemen. An armistice was soon concluded and a final peace was signed on 7 July 1807. The hopes of the Poles, who fervently desired the reestablishment of Poland to its ancient boundaries, were realized only in part. Napoleon could not force Austria to restore its portion of Poland and momentarily thought it best to manage Russia. He did not dispute the acquisitions that it had made in the three partitions of the ancient republic, and he increased the size of the government in Bailystok, which was detached from Prussia. Only Prussia was forced to give back all its possessions in Poland. From the majority of these lands Napoleon formed an independent

---

[15]This was a white cockade

[16]Alexander, who dreaded Napoleon's progress in Poland and sought to balance his influence by the formation of his own Polish army. He promised the reestablishment of a regenerated Poland under his scepter. He sought to raise this army under General Kniazewicz, who lived around Wolhynie, but this veteran of the Polish legions refused to cooperate in a civil war and the project was abandoned.

state, governed by a constitution and known as the Grand Duchy of Warsaw. He gave sovereignty of it to the King of Saxony, whose ancestors had ruled in Poland earlier. The Poles were far from satisfied, but soon new events, the news of the wars fought by France against the Allied powers and above all the confidence Napoleon's genius reinvigorated their faith from their momentarily chilled zeal and rallied them to the French cause with complete confidence and a devotion without bounds.

After the establishment of the duchy all branches of the administration of the country were promptly organized and the formation of the army was pressed forward vigorously.

Poniatowski continued to manage the military affairs of the duchy in the capacity of minister of war. He completed the formation of the three legions that were planned. They consisted of troops of all arms with a uniform organization, but each had a chief, a general staff and a different uniform. This division of the army became inconvenient because of the rivalries between Zajączek, Dąbrowski and Poniatowski, who commanded them. It was as if the communal love of country did not exist within the ranks of the noble fraternity. This, however, changed with the aspirations that inhabited the troops and with the prompt implementation of instruction in the Polish army. In the year 1808 the Grand Duchy of Warsaw provided three infantry regiments and an artillery battalion for service with the French Army in Spain.[17] Three other regiments were formed concurrently organized to garrison the Prussian fortresses occupied by the French. A cavalry regiment was formed and sent into Westphalia. In 1809 only 15,000 troops remained for the defense of the Duchy along with 2,000 Saxons stationed in it. These troops were not immediately available for the defense of the duchy when hostilities erupted with the Austrians. At that time a levy of 8,000 conscripts joined the Polish ranks, but these men were not sufficiently trained to be employed in the campaign.

When Austria prepared for the war it counted on the support of England, on the discontent of the Germans, and on the reduction of available forces to the French as a result of the employment of a considerable army in the peninsula. There remained to Napoleon about 300,000 French and Allied troops to respond to the aggression. Austria deployed 330,000 regular soldiers and a further 100,000 Landwehr to oppose him. The Austrians took the offensive on all points: in Italy, in Bavaria, and in Poland. Thirty-three thousand men were designated for the conquest of Poland. This army was formed with veteran troops and commanded by the Archduke Ferdinand d'Este, brother of the empress. The Polish were taken by surprise, as were the Bavarians and the Italians. At the opening of the offensive, the defensive preparations were far from complete. It was critical for the Polish to avoid a general engagement. From the beginning the Polish army could be destroyed by Ferdinand. Poniatowski needed to temporize, to drag out the war, and to profit from the patriotism of the inhabitants of the duchy as well as Galicia to organize an insurrection, which, behind the Austrian lines, would strongly support the operations of the main Polish army.

CAMPAIGN OF 1809

Towards the middle of April, Ferdinand advanced at the head of 33,000 men, marching on the capital of the duchy, which Poniatowski would not abandon without a fight. On 19

[17]Editor: These were the 4th, 7th and 9th Infantry Regiments and the 3rd Foot Battery. Equipping these units had been a problem and the French provided them with uniforms and all necessary equipment. Because of the difficult financial situation in the Grand Duchy these units were entirely financed by the French Army. They would be withdrawn from Spain in late 1811 and joined the Grande Armée to participate in the invasion of Russia in June 1812. They remained in Germany during the campaign and in 1813 they were in garrison in Spandau.

August a battle occurred at Raszyn, about two miles from Warsaw. The position of the main body of the Polish army was covered by a marshy river, but its advanced guard stood in front of the battle line and occupied the village of Falenty and the neighboring woods. It found itself, as a result, exposed to the initial shock of the Austrian attack. Ferdinand, impatient to bring the Poles to battle, neglected to deploy his army and to reconnoiter the Polish positions. He launched his attack around two o'clock in the afternoon against the Poles at Falenty with his advanced guard supported by a few battalions of infantry that arrived successively on the battlefield. The Austrians supported their attack with the fire of several batteries, to which the less numerous Polish artillery was only able to feebly respond. Nonetheless, the battle was hot. The Polish resisted desperately, but by five o'clock they were forced to retire to Raszyn.

The archduke then launched his attack against Poniatowski's army, forcing his way across the river that covered their position on three points. However, his principal efforts were directed against the Polish center, which was covered by the village of Raszyn. Possession of Raszyn was hotly disputed. The Austrians eventually captured it, but they were unable to move out of the village because of the heavy cannister fire from the Polish and Saxon batteries that fired on them for over an hour. As night fell, the Austrians withdrew behind Raszyn and the Poles maintained their positions. The cannonade continued, on one part of the line or another, until nine o'clock in the evening. On that day the Poles lost 1,400 men *hors de combat*, and the Austrians, who fought in the open, were estimated to have lost 2,500 men. Poniatowski, had no more than 12,000 men under his command and it was further weakened by the departure of 2,000 Saxons, who, according to orders from the Emperor, were sent back to Saxony, judged it appropriate to withdraw to Warsaw for the night and to rally his troops there.

The result of this battle, bought by the valor of the Polish troops who spent hours in battle, was that the Austrians were obliged to sign a convention that permitted Prince Józef, who could no longer maintain himself in Warsaw, to evacuate his arms and military supplies to Modlin and then evacuate his army to the left bank of the Vistula.

At that point the goal of the campaign was accomplished and the first efforts of the Austrians were rendered fruitless. The Austrians attempted in vain to cross the Vistula and they were thrown back with losses to the left bank. Poniatowski[18] was able to continue the campaign with advantage. He was covered by the Vistula and he used that advantage to execute a bold move. He moved his army into Galicia and surprised the isolated detachments of the Austrian army, dispersed its recruits, took the fortresses of Zamość and Sandomierz, seized the Austrians depots and magazines, and called the population to arms, who then responded in great numbers. From the Bug to the Dniester, all the country rose in revolt. At the same times the lieutenants of the prince, Dąbrowski and Zajączek, organized new levies within the Duchy, on the two banks of the Vistula and the Polish were able to take the offensive on all fronts. Ferdinand, who counted on forces being raised in northern Germany, and especially on the cooperation of Prussia with whom they had entered into secret negotiations and who had moved troops to the frontiers to threaten Thorn, and in this manner lost precious time. All their hopes were dashed. The insurrections in northern Germany were smothered and Prussia, terrified by Napoleon's victories, refused to declare against him.

Poniatowski's progress in his rears unnerved Archduke Ferdinand. He withdrew and abandoned Warsaw. Poniatowski, master of the important position at Sandomierz, was able

---

[18]The prince was at this time both the political and military chief of Poland. He unified in his person the dictatorial power that alone could save the state in great political crises.

to march ahead of Ferdinand and cut him off from Krakow and threaten his retreat. Though he had not yet acquired the skill and the confidence in himself that he would later gain on the battlefields and though he was unwilling to abandon the inhabitants of the right bank of the Vistula to the vengeance of the Austrians and the ill-will of the Russian army, which was advancing on the Bug as an ally of Napoleon and whose secret intentions were known to him, he remained inactive on the San, exposing his communications to Sandomierz to be intercepted, which, though defended by a brave garrison under the orders of General Sokolnicki, he could not resist very long. Dąbrowski and Zajączek closely followed the Austrian retrograde movement, but isolated as they were and marching at the head of newly raised levies, they could not undertake anything definitive to relieve the fortress. Ferdinand, who had united his forces between the Vistula and Piliça, sought to profit from his central position to successively attack the isolated Polish divisions. However, he executed his plan weakly and was unable to strike decisive blows. Zajączek was, it is true, pushed back and joined Poniatowski on the San. Dąbrowski was also forced to recross the Piliça. Sandomierz was reoccupied by a capitulation after a heroic defense by the garrison[19] , but during this no Polish corps was destroyed nor cut up.

The prince, attacked by the Austrians on 12 June at Wrzawy, foiled the enemy's efforts, despite their superior forces. Two hours after noon the Austrians started their attack on the Polish division, who occupied, before the San, a position covered by dikes and the village of Wrzawy. The Austrian attacks were impetuous, but the Poles vigorously repulsed them and the Austrians suffered heavy losses to the batteries of advantageously positioned Polish artillery. Towards evening as the Austrian attack rallied, the Poles threw themselves on the Austrians and bent back their lines. One Polish company advanced too far in its pursuit of the Austrians and was sobered by the Austrian chevaulegers. The day ended with a cannonade that lasted into the night and during which the two sides held their respective positions. The following day Poniatowski remained on the battlefield, but during the night of the 13th/14th he recrossed the San over a pontoon bridge that had been erected to assure his retreat. The bridge was lifted up and removed once his forces had effected their passage.

In the meantime, the other Austrian corps, for the most part new levies, had reoccupied the part of Galicia that extended from Leopol towards the Dniester, and occupied themselves with raising new forces in those regions. However, a Russian corps of 35,000 under the command of Prince Galitzin arrived on the San and on the side the capable movements of the Polish partisans, who harassed them without cease, forced the Austrians once again to cross this river and abandon Leopold and the region around it to the Russian troops. Galitzin's army appeared to promise Poniatowski powerful cooperation, but it was a false hope, as Galitzin did not wish to take the offensive and refused to cross the Vistula. The two commanders then developed a new campaign plan. The Russian army would act on the right bank of the river and the Polish army would cross to the left bank to attack the archduke and preserve the duchy from a new invasion.

Poniatowski crossed the Vistula at Pulawy while Sokolnicki and Dąbrowski crossed at Piliça and moved to join Poniatowski at Radom without the Austrians seeking to block their union. The Archduke was then recalled and replaced by General Mondet, who succeeded him in command of the Austrian corps. Mondet then began to withdraw his new command into Austrian Silesia and sought to close with the main Austrian army under the Archduke Charles,

---

[19]Solonicki concluded an honorable capitulation with the Austrians by which he was able to withdraw his troops behind the Pilica

who was at that time preparing for a major engagement. Poniatowski followed the Austrian movement and battered their rearguard. On his size, Galitzin, after reoccupying Leopold, which had momentarily fallen into the Austrians' hands, advanced slowly down the high road to Krakow without encountering much resistance.

As Poniatowski appeared before Krakow the Austrians decided to evacuate the city and wished to delay its occupation by the Poles with negotiations to establish a capitulation by which it would be surrendered to the victors while at the same time sent word to Galitzin, who detached a division from his army to Krakow to take possession of the city. Prince Poniatowski, taking his rights, ordered the Polish advanced guard to enter the city, by force if necessary, and the Russians did not to think to oppose him after this order was issued.

All the time the Poles divided their conquests with the Russians and the troops of the two nations jointly occupied Krakow.

The prince was received by the citizens of Krakow as a liberator and he had the glory of delivering the ancient city where the ashes of the ancient kings of Poland resided, and which enclosed the monuments that attested to the grandeur of a nation that was once the most powerful state in the north.

While these events were occurring in Poland, the operations in Italy and Germany, which had begun so favorably for Austria had turned to Napoleons advantage. After his victory at Rattisbonne and the capture of Vienna, the emperor had sought to cross the Danube. His first effort was unsuccessful and the two armies remained inactive for some time. The opposing commanding generals converged their forces on the Danube. The Austrian Army of Italy withdrew into Hungary and that of the viceroy.[20] A second effort to cross the Danube succeeded completely and resulted in the singular victory of Wagram. The army of the Archduke Charles withdrew into Bohemia and everything seemed to presage the total destruction of the Austrian monarchy. However, it was not in Napoleon's political agenda to destroy the empire, he sought only to weaken it and to detach from it territories to augment the holdings of his allies.

An armistice, concluded at Znaim on 12 July ended hostilities. A peace treaty was signed in Vienna on 14 October. The Grand Duchy of Warsaw received New Galicia and the circle of Zamość, which had been part of Old Galicia. The Russia Empire received the area of Tarnopol[21], detached from the latter province. The remainder of Austrian Poland continued to be part of the empire of Francis II.

Thus, in three months Poniatowski had not only stopped the progress of the Austrians down the Vistula, but had also reconquered a province of 2,000,000 inhabitants.[22]

The campaign completed, the rebuilding of the cadres of the army of the Grand Duchy now claimed the attention of the minister of war. Poniatowski attacked this task with zeal. The Polish army had increased to 60,000 men during the 1809 campaign and now it received a new and uniform organization in which the old legions were abolished. It also perfected its instruction and discipline.

[20]Editor: Eugene Beauharnais, Viceroy of the Kingdom of Northern Italy, stepson of Napoleon, and natural son of Józefine.

[21]Today, Ternopil.

[22]The services rendered by Poniatowski in this campaign were compensated by Napoleon and the King of Saxony and the Grand Duchy of Warsaw. Napoleon sent him the Grand Cross of the Legion of Honor and a sword etched with his cipher. Frederick August sent hi the Grand Cordon of the Military Order of Poland, to which he attached

Napoleon then began planning his campaign against Russia, to throw them back in the north and to reestablish a powerful Poland, always armed and ready to defend the eastern frontier of his empire and keep the Muscovites out of Europe. To this end he had to depend principally on the active cooperation of Poland, bring about the rearmament of Poland, and assign an important role in the coming campaign to the Poles. The Poles were the best acclimated to the region and had a substantial interest in the outcome of the campaign, far beyond that of any other nation whose troops would form the Grande Armée. Despite this, Napoleon was confident in his armed forces and limited the augmentation of the Polish Army, bringing it to an effective strength of 70,000 men and provided the financing for one third of them.

Before acting in an almost entirely unknown country and since he did not possess an exact map, Napoleon sought to consult on this important subject with Poles who knew the area and principally with Prince Poniatowski. He wrote Poniatowski about his campaign plan. The prince gave him all the information desired, as well as counseling him to unite the Polish troops on the Bug and then to employ them to conquer the provinces of central Poland in order to put the immense resources of that land at his disposal.[23] In addition to the products of its fertile soil, it could furnish Napoleon with 100,000 men and 100,000 horses. This conquest would realize another important goal, that of a rapprochement with Turkey. The conquest of this land would raise the courage of the Ottomans and bring important support to the French cause. However, Napoleon did not judge it convenient to detach such a considerable force to that flank. He believed he did not require the resources that Poniatowski's plan assured him. His decision, in this circumstance, was driven by other political and military considerations, and he resolved to establish his line of operations via Kowno and Wilna, on Smolensk and to support his left wing on the sea. Facing him the Russians supported their right wing on the Baltic and extended their 200,000-man army south to the Styr in an overly extended position. This decided Napoleon to focus his principal efforts on the center of their line. Finally, Napoleon, marching at the head of 400,000 men[24], believed he was able to overcome all obstacles and that the probability of success was in his favor. The difficulty, however, was the subsistence of all his forces. One can reproach Napoleon for not having better organized his supply services in this campaign, because it was the lack of supplies that proved to be the principal cause of the subsequent disaster.

1812 CAMPAIGN

The beginning of hostilities coincided with the opening of the Diet of the Grand Duchy of Warsaw, which was confederated and proclaimed the reconstitution of the Kingdom of Poland. On his side, Prince Poniatowski oversaw the final preparations for the campaign. According to the orders given by Napoleon, the troops of the duchy, as well as several regiments that served as part of the French Army[25], the Polish troops were divided between several different corps of the Grande Armée, with the exception of three infantry divisions and a light cavalry division that were organized into the V Corps, some 35,000 men under the command of Prince Poniatowski.

---

a stipend of 1,000,000 francs on the newly reconquered territories.

[23]Editor: The author is speaking of the Ukraine.

[24]Editor: In fact, the Grande Armée contained over 600,000 men when it invaded Russia.

[25]Editor: These regiments were known as the Vistula Legion, which had four infantry regiments, as well as the 7th and 8th Lancer Regiments.

Napoleon moved his principal forces against Kowno and Olitta. The V Corps entered into Lithuania via Grodno and formed part of the right wing of the Grande Armée under the command of the King of Westphalia, Jérôme Bonaparte. The forces under his command included the VIII (Westphalian) Corps, the VII (Saxon) Corps, and the IV Reserve Cavalry Corps composed of French, German, and Polish cavalry. This imposing force, around 80,000 men, and supported by 30,000 Austrians who crossed the Bug at Drohiczyn, were to operate against the Russian 2nd Army of the West, under the command of Bagration.

From a position near Wilna, Napoleon hoped to delay the junction of the 1st and 2nd Russian Armies of the West as the 1st did an eccentric movement towards the Dzvina. He detached 30,000 men under Davout to cut off Bagration's retreat. He was certain that if his orders were executed exactly, the 2nd Russian Army of the West, pressed by superior forces, would be forced to surrender or throw itself into the Ukraine. However, the King of Westphalia marched slowly. His troops, since the beginning of the campaign, lacked sufficient food and were not able to closely pursue the Russians. Bagration profited ably from all the obstacles presented by the countryside to delay his pursuit. Davout was unable to stop his retreat alone. He was constrained, after an indecisive battle at Mohilov, to allow him to cross the Dnieper and to join, under the walls of Smolensk, his army with the 1st Army of the West under Barclay de Tolly. United, these two armies withdrew into Smolensk to escape Napoleon's pursuing forces. When Napoleon was furious when he learned of the delays in Jérôme's advance, the lack of success in his first operations, and the ambush and defeat of his advanced guard at Mir. He determined that Jérôme should leave immediately and return to his capital.[26]

The right wing of the Grande Armée remained without a commander for several days until Poniatowski was invested by Napoleon with this important command. It was impossible for him to make up for the lost time, but he promptly executed the orders he was given. Napoleon, who did not admit to insurmountable obstacles, did not absolve the prince of not meeting the objectives of his plan. However, soon after, he realized his error and Poniatowski was returned to Napoleon's good graces and demonstrated this by the union of the V Corps with the main army before Smolensk.

Napoleon prepared for an attack on Smolensk, where the Russian armies had stopped and which they proposed to defend. Smolensk was the key to western Russia. It was important that Napoleon take and occupy it. On 15 August he arrived at Smolensk and launched an attack on the citadel of Smolensk with Ney's corps. The attack failed. The following day Napoleon consolidated 150,000 men around the city and renewed his attacks with vigor.

In the order of battle Poniatowski's corps formed the right. On 17 August, in the morning, a brigade of Polish cavalry, supported by a battery of horse artillery, attacked the Russian cavalry defending the suburbs of Smolensk and drove it into the city. The infantry of the V Corps, divided into four columns, moved against the suburbs and chased the Russians out, despite their strong resistance, and established themselves in the suburbs. The Polish artillery contributed strongly to this attack with their sustained fire. The Poles lost, 500 killed and 700 wounded in this attack. The other corps rivaled the zeal of the V Corps and made substantial progress.

---

[26]Editor: Actually, Napoleon had given Davout a letter authorizing him to relieve Jérôme should it seem appropriate. When Davout implemented the letter, Jérôme was insulted by his brother's (Napoleon) lack of faith and quit his command without permission.

During this bloody day, which terminated with the occupation of Smolensk's suburbs, the Polish troops were unable to penetrate through the city's walls until a breach was broken in them after several hours battering with field artillery. The city was set afire at many points by our projectiles and the suburbs, occupied by the Poles, were totally destroyed by the resulting fire.

The French prepared to renew the attack the following day, but the Russians, fearing for their lines of communications, withdrew during the night and after a murderous battle that occurred on the 18th at Valoutina-Gora they began their march on Moscow.

Napoleon resolved to pursue them, hoping to force the battle he ardently desired. The French resumed their march in three columns, the main one advancing down the main road to Moscow and the other two followed parallel roads. Poniatowski's corps formed the right column. He found nothing before him but Cossacks, so he had no serious engagements. However, this route forced him to take long detours because it did not move directly on Moscow and in order to keep up with the main column he had to march his forces especially hard.

Happily, Poniatowski was able to maintain the discipline in his troops. There were no marauders and the countryside was not stripped. This wise conduct kept the inhabitants in their homes and they provided good intelligence for the Poles. They also provided food and forage in abundance, which kept the V Corps in good condition.

During this time Kutusov replaced Barclay de Tolly in command of the Russian army. He sought to announce his ascension to command with an engagement and decided to give a general battle to defend Moscow. He chose a strong position on the main road before Mojaisk. When Napoleon learned of this he ordered his lateral columns to close on the main road. Because of this order Poniatowski took part in the engagement of 5 September that was the prelude to the great battle that was to follow. During this day, the Polish corps cooperated with the advanced guard of the Grande Armée commanded by Murat, King of Naples, and contributed to the capture of the redoubt near the village of Scheverdino which was the key to the Russian position, and which was carried by Compan's division.

The following day was employed in preparing for the coming battle. Poniatowski remained on the right of the line of battle and had a decisive operation confided in him. At the beginning of the battle he was to attack the left of the Russian army, which contained only 11,000 men under its flags.[27]

On 7 September, at 5 o'clock in the morning, the Polish corps began its march to turn the woods, which supported the left of Kutusov's army. He advanced down the old road from Smolensk to Moscow in order to attack the Russian's extreme left. A strong battery supported his movement with its fire. The village of Passerevo, occupied by the Russians, was taken. The V Corps continued its offensive movement as Poniatowski directed three infantry battalions to attack an ancient mound covered with brush that was covered by a force of Russian infantry. This attack was executed in skirmish order and was strongly supported by artillery fire. A lively fusillade began along the line and because of the superior strength of the Russians, continued until noon, preventing the Poles from making any notable progress. Poniatowski ordered his infantry to redouble its efforts to occupy the mound so strongly defended by the Russians. The Poles eventually seized its summit, but could not maintain themselves there and contented themselves with occupying the brush that covered their side of the mound. The Polish artillery

---

[27]Since the crossing of the Dnieper the V Corps had been weakened by the detachment of Dąbrowski's division, which blockaded Bobruysk.

fire continued to pound the summit.

Things remained stationary until 2 o'clock in the afternoon. At that time Poniatowski, seeing the lack of success in the center, directed a new attack on the Russian position. His infantry, formed in column, attacked the mound frontally while his cavalry turned its left. This movement was successful and the position was finally carried. The Russians vainly attempted to retake it, but they were repulsed with heavy losses and pursued by Polish troops. The Russians lost heavy casualties during the day's action, but the Poles took few prisoners because the cavalry had sabered the fugitives without mercy.

During this memorable day, Napoleon's army triumphed over all obstacles and achieved a significant advantage, but the victory would have been more successful, but for a fault in the order of battle. In effect, Kutosov's army had token a position that eminently favored Napoleon's plans. His center and left faced Napoleon's army as it straddled the road from Smolensk to Moscow. However, his right, which was refused without reason, had no enemy to engage. Napoleon's plan was to destroy the center and left before the right could intervene. He deployed his army so as to attack by echelons, by his right, and planned to engage his army corps as progress was made. The importance of the mound that Poniatowski's V Corps was to carry was key to the success of the battle, but the 11,000 Poles charged with this operation were not sufficient for the task. They could not obtain marked advantages and were obliged to stop their march before renewing their efforts because of the superior number of Russians facing them. The other echelons engaged themselves successively before the Russian left before it could be forced from its position. The attack became a parallel attack instead of an oblique attack and the principal efforts were directed against the center of the Russian army, which occupied a formidable position covered with ravines and fortified with several redoubts. These different obstacles impeded Napoleon's progress from what had been intended in the initial plan and gave Kutusov time to redeploy his right and to use it to support that part of his army, which was heavily attacked. The bravery of the troops and the good dispositions of the corps commanders overcame the Russian resistance. The center of the Russian position was forced. Numerous French artillery crowned the heights occupied at the beginning of the attack by the Russians and spread death in their ranks. Fifty thousand Russians were laid low on this bloody day, while Napoleon's army lost 18,000. This was certainly a good result. The Russian troops, discouraged and thrown into disorder by their tremendous losses, withdrew and were not able to offer any resistance as Napoleon marched on Moscow.

The Grande Armée occupied this ancient Russian capital on September 14th and Napoleon counted on that to give his troops the rest that they so well deserved. However, this repose was soon destroyed by the incineration of the city.

In abandoning Moscow, the governor, Rostopczin, had made preparations for its complete destruction. Several hundred criminals, supported by the Russians themselves, had set the city afire the night after the French troops arrived and returned over the next several days to make sure the job was complete. The greatest part of the houses of Moscow were made of wood and three quarters of this great city were consumed in less than a week. This blow, inspired by despair, was equally disastrous for the Russians as it was for the French. They destroyed the center of their commerce and industry, but at the same time they deprived the French of much of the resources that would have supported them in Moscow. Despite this there remained sufficient resources to support the French for many months and the fertile country around Moscow would have furnished the indispensable forage necessary to support the army's horses. If

Napoleon had resolved immediately after the destruction of Moscow to fall back on Smolensk the burning of Moscow would have been of little importance. However, his confidence in his luck and in the success of negotiations undertaken with the Russian government caused him to remain around Moscow too long and exposed his army, deprived of winter clothing and poorly acclimated, to a complete disaster.

Poniatowski's V Corps, which was designated to form part of the advanced guard under the command of Murat, King of Naples, had only passed through the suburbs of Moscow and moved on Pahra where it joined the troops there under Murat's orders. It was designated to observe Kutusov's army. Kutusov first advanced in the direction of Kazan, then took up position on the road to Kaluga, covering the fertile country, extending from there into central Russia, from where he could draw tremendous resources and recruit to fill up the ranks of his army. Murat followed the Russian movement and the advanced guard was engaged in several engagements. One of the most important was that of Tscherykov. The V Corps commanded by Prince Józef was the only force engaged at Tscherykov and the success in this battle belongs to Poniatowski alone.

On September 29th Poniatowski moved, by the woods, on the village of Tscherykov. His cavalry supported by the horse artillery, marched in the lead. As he extended from the woods, he found himself faced by a Russian cavalry corps that was quite superior to his cavalry. The cavalry of both sides charged repeatedly and the result was decisive. However, during the engagement the Russian infantry had the time to deploy parallel to the high road from Moscow to Kaluga. The V Corps took position facing the Russian army. After reviewing the Russian position, Poniatowski attacked the village of Tscherykov, which supported the Russian right wing. The Russians were chased from the village and it was set afire as they left. Shortly later the copse of woods that was nearby was cleared of the Russians by the Poles. However, the Russians maintained their position in the woods that covered their center. Poniatowski launched his infantry against it, supporting their attack with his artillery and drove the Russians from it. The Russian cavalry division then moved against the Polish left, but it was driven back with losses. Nonetheless, the Russians rallied and attacked the Poles along the entire length of their line. Their principal efforts were directed against Tscherykov, but they were repulsed everywhere.

The Russian attack on the woods was equally unsuccessful. The Polish troops occupying it were briefly enveloped, but broke free with a bayonet charge. Every time they were driven back the Russian infantry rallied. The engagement was very lively and the Russians lost heavily, until they broke and withdrew from the battlefield. The Russian lost around 1,000 men as casualties and a further 500 prisoners, all of whom were wounded. The Polish lost 160 men dead and 300 wounded.

After the battle, as Poniatowski returned to his headquarters, followed by his staff and an escort of 50 men, at nightfall he encountered a strong column of Russian infantry flowing out of a wood. They were not recognized as Russians until there was no time to withdraw. A single volley at this range would have been potentially deadly to the Prince, putting his life in great peril. He had no choice but to launch an audacious blow to escape this dangerous position. Resolved to the audacious, the prince and his tiny escort charged forward into the Russian column, driving it back and even taking a few prisoners.

By virtue of the victory at Tscherykov the V Corps, as well as the advanced guard, was able to gain several days of rest. The Russians, in order to avoid any major engagement and in order to lull Napoleon into complacence Kutusov consented to an armistice with the condition of 24 hours notice before it could be broken.

During Napoleon's march on Moscow and his sojourn in the capital, many important events occurred on the two wings of the Grande Armée that were intended to cover the army's communications with the Grand Duchy of Warsaw. At the beginning of the campaign and while the French right wing pursued Bagration with the goal of destroying his army, Tormassov, at the head of 40,000 men, crossed Volhynie and crossed the Bug. This movement threatened Napoleon's rear and even the Grand Duchy of Warsaw itself. The corps of General Reynier, reinforced by a division under General Kosinski, drawn from the army's reserves, was detached to face Tormassov, but this force was determined to be insufficient and Schwarzenberg's Austrian Hilfkorps, which was marching on the Dnieper, was ordered to reinforce it. Schwarenberg and Reynier, united, pushed Tormassov beyond the Styr. Having concluded a peace with the Turks, the Russians were able to move 46,000 veteran troops, under Admiral Tschitgov to support Tormassov and allow the two of them to reassume the offensive, advance on the Bug, and seriously threaten the lines of operations of the French army in Moscow.

While this passed in the center, to the north the troops under Macdonald, Oudinot, and Saint-Cyr maintained their positions on the Dvina. Wittgenstein, who commanded the Russian forces in Lithuania, received a continuous flow of new recruits. Reinforced by a division from the Army of Finland, Wittgenstein was able to assume the offensive. Napoleon, who had realized that the invasion of Russia would cost many soldiers, had established a strong reserve on the Vistula and Elbe to replace those casualties that were inevitable in such a war. These reserves advanced successively behind the army, but when they arrived in Lithuania they had to stop in order to bring support to both wings, which were seriously threatened.

During the armistice that was negotiated between Kustusov and Napoleon, the King of Naples camped near the village of Voronovo at the head of 35,000 men in the presence of Kustusov's army, which held a position at Taourtino, and received each day new recruits. The approach of winter increased the confidence of the Russians. Kutusov could no longer contain their impatience. Wishing to profit from the hazardous position of the forces under the King of Naples, who had supported his left on a woods that he had failed to occupy, Kutusov resolved to launch a surprise attack. Murat, on his side, wished to occupy the stronger and more secure position at Vinkovo. He ordered his troops to withdraw in the morning of October 17th, but the movement was foreseen by the Russians, who had prepared, during the night, an attack against the front and left flank of Murat's forces. Kutusov deployed his forces such that one corps marched thorough the woods of which we have already spoken. It was intended to turn that wing as other Russian forces attacked Murat frontally.

This movement was executed at daybreak and was immediately successful. The V Corps Cavalry force, under Sébastiani was totally surprised and its artillery captured. The Russians then moved against the position where the rest of the V Corps was encamped. It formed the extreme and fortunately found itself under arms as the Russians approached because its cavalry was intermixed with its infantry. This attack was so unexpected that Prince Józef barely had time to mount his horse. His presence amidst his troops gave them spirit and courage as did the valor of the King of Naples. Together they seemed to triumph over the danger. The Polish infantry formed themselves in square and slowly withdrew driving back the repeated attacks of the Russian cavalry. The Polish cavalry seconded the infantry and drove back a column of Russian infantry. Murat placed himself at the head of the French carabiniers that then launched a brilliant charge that threw back the Russian cavalry. Finally, the troops of the King of Naples reoccupied their position at Vinkovo without having suffered heavy losses, with the exception of Sébastiani's artillery, which had been captured at the beginning of the battle.

After several failed attempts to open negotiations with Alexander I, Napoleon realized his efforts were pointless and decided to abandon Moscow on October 19th. He then withdrew towards Smolensk. His line of operations ran through that city and, unfortunately, the countryside along them was completely devastated. He hoped to find sufficient supplies along the lateral routes. He intended to prepare magazines covered by strongly fortified posts and guarded by strong detachments. Napoleon, in his withdrawal to Smolensk, sought to strike a major blow against Kutusov's army near Kalouga, and then to gain a few marches on them. He moved first in that direction. As a result of those operations a bloody engagement occurred on October 23rd at Majo-Jaroslavetz where he again defeated the Russians. The Viceroy of Italy[28] and his corps earned all the honors on this brilliant day. At the same time the Polish corps was in Borovsk, covering the army's right. It pushed a reconnaissance force against Medyne. The troops charged with this task found themselves confronted with a powerful enemy force and suffered a check.

After Malo-Jaroslavetz the Grande Armée began its retreat, moving by Mojaisk on Smolensk. The V Corps, which moved on the left, rejoined it at Viazma, after being obliged to constantly struggle with a cloud of Cossacks that gave it no peace. Near this last city, Prince Poniatowski sought to observe the enemy and mounted a ridge some distance from the main road. However, his right arm was crushed when his horse fell under him. Because of this accident he was obliged to ride in a carriage for the rest of the campaign. The army was not only deprived of one of its most capable generals during the retreat, but also of a commander whose personality would have rendered immeasurable support during the retreat. The venerable General Zajączek assumed command of the V Corps during the remainder of the campaign.

Napoleon was deluded in his hopes of retiring in good order on Smolensk. The provisions, which he thought to find in abundance along his line of retreat barely sufficed for his guard. As the other troops had consumed the remainder before that had moved on Moscow all that remained to them was horseflesh. Forage could not be obtained except at a great distance from the main route of retreat. After a long march it was necessary to spend much of the night in foraging and both men and horses were fatigued and in need. Since Viazma, the cold had become more intense and descended to -12 degrees Réaumur. The army was badly clothed. Horses died by the hundreds each night, making it necessary to abandon the artillery. The cavalry mounts could barely be maintained and were no longer capable of launching a charge. Despite the admirable firmness of the corps commanders and the example of Napoleon himself, who marched on foot in the middle of his troops the troops were discouraged. Many soldiers abandoned their ranks and pushed ahead to reach Smolensk. However, nothing could shake the rearguard and it successfully sustained several engagements with the Russians and pushed them back constantly.

Once in Smolensk the army found sustenance and a few days repose, but it could not stop there. The news that reached Napoleon of Tschichagov's advance was alarming. The combined efforts of Victor and Oudinot were not sufficient to stop Wittgenstein's progress. It was feared that these Russian generals would link in the rear of the Grande Armée and cut off its retreat as Kutusov engaged them frontally.

---

[28]Editor: The Viceroy was Eugene Beauharnais, Napoleon's step-son.

Napoleon left Smolensk on November 14th and continued his retreat. In executing this movement his army marched by echelons at a day's interval. When these echelons arrived at Krasnoi they found themselves engaged by the Russians who had advanced to that point. The V Corps was the first to arrive and found the high road cut by Miloradovich's corps. However, the V Corps, ably directed by General Kniaziewicz[29] , succeeded in passing. Davout and the Viceroy were also stopped at this point. Reunited with the imperial column, on the 17th of October they engaged the Russian army under Kutusov. The engagement occurred in Napoleon's presence and victory resulted from his excellent dispositions. The Napoleon then withdrew in good order to Orsza and crossed the Dnieper. However, Marshal Ney, who commanded the rearguard, was unable to withdraw himself from the difficult position in which he found himself in crossing the river over the ice and returned to the right bank at the same point. Pressed, encircled on all sides by the Russians, he succeeded in triumphing over all obstacles and rejoined the imperial army at the head of the debris of his corps on the road to Borisov.

The Grande Armée was in tremendous peril. Tschichagov had gained several marches on Schwarzenberg, who followed him. He threw back the newly raised Lithuanian regiments and took Minsk, where he found and captured large magazines of equipment and food. The Russians lived in abundance and did not lack the clothing so indispensable for this season, while the French lacked everything. As the French withdrew on the Berezina Napoleon hoped to rally the corps that found themselves echeloned on the road and which were in good state, but they could not be reorganized. With the exception of the Guard, disorder had completely invaded all the army corps returning from Moscow. They communicated this disorder to the reserve troops and the number of fugitives grew until only a third of the army remained under arms. The rest had entirely disbanded itself and the large number of isolated individuals cramped the ability of the army to move.

At this critical moment Tchichagov's army advanced on the Berezina and took the bridge at Borisov where it cut the line of retreat on Wilna and Minsk. On the other side Wittgenstein was close to joining him. Despite this Napoleon did not despair for his fortune. He would contain Wittgenstein, cross the Berezina despite Tchichagov and Kutusov's army had been reduced by the hardships of the march. The V Corps, which had rallied on Dąbrowski's division, still had 8,000 men under arms. On the memorable day of November 28th and contributed strongly to the repulse of Tchichagov's army as it advanced to cut off Napoleon's retreat.

The Berezina crossed, Napoleon moved on Wilna. Food was more abundant in Lithuania but if the soldier suffered less from hunger, on the other the cold had reached minus 20 to 30 degrees and added greatly to his suffering. They froze to death along the length of the retreat and each bivouac was littered with cadavers. The army was no more than a mob as it withdrew in disorder. Baggage and artillery were abandoned. A weak rearguard, composed of the few troops that had suffered the least, stopped the advance of the Russian advanced guard only with the greatest difficulty. The horrors of the evils that faced it paralyzed courage and the moral of the troops began to fail.

We not turn our eyes from this horrible retreat and returning to Prince Poniatowski, who had been miraculously saved in the midst of this general disaster. He rode in his carriage during the retreat, reduced to impotence because of his health, he suffered of hunger as much as his emotions tore at him every day he heard the fire of the cannons without being able to join his brothers-in-arms. However, Napoleon had ordered his carriage to move with the treasury,

---

[29]Kniaziewicz had replaced Zajanczek, who was ill, as commander of the V Corps.

which was escorted, by an elite body of infantry. The prince arrived at the Berezina in the company of several officers. Once there it was necessary to cross the Berezina over the weak bridges over which a huge crowd of fugitives were also pressing. Thousands of vehicles clogged the approaches to the bridges and it was expressly forbidden for them to cross the bridges. Napoleon wished to profit from the obstacle, which this defile offered to destroy them in order to eliminate the baggage train that encumbered the movements of the army. Poniatowski's carriage found itself in the middle of this equipment. The officers accompanying him struggled in vain in order to allow him to pass, but failed until a detachment of the Imperial Guard Gendarmes d'élite came to his assistant. They cleared the road and opened a passage for him to the far bank and safety.

Napoleon was convinced of the futility of attempting to rally the army and decided to return to France to raise a new one, which would repair the disasters of the retreat, stop the discouragement of France, and the defection of his allies. He passed command of the Grande Armée to the King of Naples and ordered him to rally the debris of the army at Wilna before he left for Smorgonie on December 5th in a simple carriage, traveling under the name of the Grand Écuyer, the Duke of Vicence, who accompanied him.

Despite the resources which were to be found in the great city, and the immense provisions that were found in Wilna, the King of Naples would not support the army there for more than a few days and began a withdrawal on Kowno and Königsberg. From there he crossed the Vistula where the debris of the Grande Armée found refuge in the great fortresses that lined it, joining their garrisons. A small part of the army then moved on Posen where the King of Naples left the command, which had been confided in him to return to his states. He left the few troops that were under his orders to the Viceroy of Italy, who then withdrew on Berlin.

Poniatowski, after crossing the Berezina, moved to Warsaw where he arrived at the end of December. When his health returned he hastened to join the remains of the Polish army. Of the entire army only 5,000 men had returned to Warsaw, but they had brought with them all their artillery and their eagles. The General Council of the Confederation made preparations to resist an invasion. Within the Duchy levies were made of men and horses. The levee en masse (pospolite-ruszenie) was decreed, which had saved Poland in previous moments of danger. Poniatowski was named commander of the reorganizing army, but unfortunately it was too late.

The Russians, profiting from their success, quickly crossed the Vistula and paralyzed the tardy efforts of an impotent patriotism. Everything was enveloped with a fatalism that followed Napoleon in this sad and glorious campaign. How much he must have regretted not availing himself of the patriotic ardor of the Polish nation to organize a strong reserve of Polish troops at the opening of hostilities when the entire population of the duchy clamored to be armed. No one doubted that with this reserve joined to the corps of Schwarzenberg and Macdonald and to the remains of the Grande Armée it was thought would be able to hold the Russians on the Vistula. The Russians had been weakened by the battles and the weather would only be able to fill their ranks in the springtime with partisans that would be incapable of fighting Napoleon's soldiers. There appeared every chance of success.

THE 1813 CAMPAIGN

The Russian army crossed the Vistula at several points and Warsaw fell to them. The debris of the V Corps and Kosinski's division moved to Krakow after throwing garrisons into the fortresses of the duchy. Schwarzenberg's corps followed their movement. A single detach-ment of Polish troops withdrew on Kalisz, later forming the nucleus of a division to be formed by Dąbrowski. Prince Poniatowski profited from the resources available to him in Krakow and from two months of repose. He reorganized his corps and raised it to strength of 12,000 men. The Austrian corps, which was in the front line, covered it to the north.

Alexander presented himself as a liberator to the people and this representation made great progress in Germany. However, the spirit of the Poles remained unsettled. Alexander sought to neutralize the ill perception the Polish people had of him and while Poniatowski and the supreme Polish government found itself in Krakow, Alexander called Prince Antoine Radzi-will[30] , on the pretext of family affairs, to move to Krakow and attempt to subvert the fidelity of the Poles. He was to propose that the duchy assume a neutral stance for the duration of the war and that Poniatowski unite all the Polish troops at Zamosc to await events. Radziwill's mission was a thorny affair. He feared the surveillance of the Minister of France, Bignon, who watched his movements. Poniatowski's faithfulness was well known. Radziwill made no attempt to approach the prince directly. However he sounded the attitudes of several members of the Polish government, emboldened them bit by bit, communicated his propositions to people that he thought the least likely to be repelled by his proposals to abandon their alliance with France, and had decided to approach Poniatowski about accepting these proposals that would allow Poland an independent political existence. The prince was torn between his military duty and the apparent interests of his country, which seemed to exist in a new alliance. In the improbabil-ity of conciliating these two, he thought of an instance of suicide.[31]   However, he then realized that Poland could not await the regeneration of the same powers that had divided it and then become their tributary. He put his entire confidence in the fortunes of Napoleon and remained unshakable.

Radziwill's intrigues came to the attention of the French ambassador, Bignon, who for-mally demanded the cessation of negotiations. However, Poniatowski, obedient to the generosi-ty of his character, did not support this demand. He took under his protection this man who was proud of his loyalty and who, above all, he believed was acting only in the interests of Poland.[32] He had Radziwill escorted to the Russian lines.

The Russian and Prussian sovereigns met at Kalisz and concluded an alliance against Napoleon. After leaving a Russian army in Poland to blockade the fortress and observe Kra-kow, they moved their principal forces to the Elbe. The Viceroy evacuated Berlin and crossed the river, moving to Leipzig, where he drew together 40,000 men. The Allies crossed the Elbe and occupied Saxony. The Viceroy then withdrew to Magdeburg where he took up a position straddling the river and sought, by able maneuvers, to contain the Allies despite the superiority of their forces.

Meanwhile Napoleon had occupied himself with great activity in the reorganization of a new army, which he then led into Germany. This new army contained 140,000 men and con-sisted partly of veterans drawn from the Army of Spain and the Imperial Marine. However, the

---

[30]Radziwill was married to a Prussian princess.

[31]The prince personally recounted this to the author of this work at Kollyn, in Bohemia, where he had been sent on Napoleon's orders. He stated, 'You know, my dear Soltyk, that I do not have a romantic spirit, and except for the moment I thought to take my life at Krakow

[32]Before taking this prickly mission Radziwill had advised Alexander to recognize the independence of the Grand Duchy of Warsaw. However, he was unable to obtain from anything other than vague promises that he would offer some favorable opportunities to the Poles in these unfortunate circumstances.

most part of the army was formed of conscripts with little experience in the handling of their weapons. This brave army did marvels. United with the army under the Viceroy, this army moved to the victory at Lützen on May 2nd. Napoleon crossed the Elbe and marched on Lusace, defeating the Allies on May 21st at Bautzen. The chance of success was in Napoleon's favor. He had only to take one more step to arrive on the frontiers of the Grand Duchy of Warsaw, which certainly would have risen in revolt upon his approach. However, the hope of a negotiated, honorable peace seduced him. He signed, on June 4th, an armistice at Neumarck, during which he negotiated a peace under the mediation of Austria.

We now return to events in Poland.

Despite the occupation of the Grand Duchy of by Warsaw by the Russians, the hopes of the Polish people were not extinguished. The public spirit sustained it. An insurrection was prepared and they awaited the army of liberation. From the beginning of spring Prince Poniatowski sought to use the fortunate dispositions and to operate as a powerful diversion in favor of France by moving against Warsaw. He proposed to the Austrian general to second this offensive movement, but he refused, and interposed himself between the Poles and Russians, paralyzing the Prince's plan, which would have surely been crowned with success as it would have been supported by Napoleon's advance through Germany after his various victories.

As Napoleon had crossed the Rhine he had ordered Poniatowski to move into Saxony via Moravia and Bohemia and to concentrate his forces in the region of Podgorze, on the right bank of the Vistula. After reorganizing his regiments, he was to put himself in position to respond to Napoleon's orders. Prince Poniatowski had already made two marches, when he received, from General Sokolnicki, news of the French victory at Lützen. This general, full of confidence in Napoleon's fortune, and of an enterprising nature, consulted Poniatowski to move back up the road, recross the Vistula and attack, the Russian army corps standing before the Austrians by Krakow. However, the prince feared that this movement would not be supported by the Austrians and that it might immediately detach itself from the French alliance, so he continued his movement and took a position near Zittau in Saxony.

During this march he had the opportunity to flattering gesture from the Austrian Emperor for his army and for his person. After the convention concluded between the respective powers, the Poles were allowed to move, without their weapons, through the Austrian states with the intention impeding their movement, but the excellent discipline and order in the regiments in Poniatowski's corps as they passed convinced the Austrians to return their arms to them. At this time Poniatowski received word from Napoleon that he was to join the Marshals of France.

During the armistice Napoleon had organized 260000 men between Dresden and Breslau, and on the Elbe. The Polish troops under Poniatowski coming from Krakow were reinforced by an infantry regiment formed in Wittenberg from the debris of the Vistula Legion. This corps had a total of 13,000 men organized in six infantry regiments, eight cavalry regiments, and six artillery batteries. The infantry and artillery were organized into the VIII Corps and the cavalry became part of the IV Reserve Cavalry Corps under the orders of General Kellerman. To this force were joined two French horse artillery batteries. These forces were cantoned in the vicinity of Zittau. The cavalry was well mounted and very useful to the army, which was, overall, lacking in this arm. On the other side, a Polish division, formed of two infantry regiments, two cavalry regiments and an artillery battery, was organized in Wetzlaar by General Dąbrowski, who took command of it. This division was assigned to General Vandamme's I Corps and cantoned near Wittenberg.

The negotiations undertaken under the mediation of Austria stalled. This power wished to impose conditions on France that were too hard for Napoleon and stipulated the concession of vast territories. If these demands were refused it threatened to join France's enemies. Napoleon refused this offer, preferring to take his chances on the battlefield. He commanded an army inferior by one-third in numbers when compared to that of the Allies[33] and which was less battle hardened. The greater part of Napoleon's soldiers were 18 to 19-year olds, incapable of handling the fatigues of a military campaign. For two months there was a suspension of hostilities. When the war resumed, everywhere Napoleon appeared he was victorious, but his lieutenants soon suffered checks at Kulm, Gross-Beeren on the Katzbach and at Jutterbach. Driven back on all sides by the Allies, who following their successes, crossed the Elbe and simultaneously moved out of the mountains of Bohemia, forcing Napoleon back on Leipzig as he sought to reestablish his line of communications to the Rhine, leaving strong garrisons in the fortresses on the Elbe and two army corps that remained in Dresden. When the critical moment came these forces were all missing from his order of battle.

During the course of these operations Poniatowski's corps, which had about 8,000 men, was employed to guard the passes from Bohemia around Bagel. He did this successfully. He enjoyed several successes against the Austrians, principally at Friedland. He later joined the army under Marshal Macdonald and was engaged in hot battles at Bautzen, Leibau and Stolpe. Finally, he crossed the Elbe and recruited 3,600 Austrian prisoners of Polish origin into the ranks of his regiments. He was then placed under the orders of Murat, the King of Naples, moving to stop the Austrian army under Schwarzenberg. During this period he was in several engagements, notably Pennig, Froburg, and Wachau. The Polish corps joined the main army shortly before the battle of Leipzig and formed the extreme right in two memorable battles that occurred by this city. Its losses during the battles prior to Leipzig had reduced its ranks to 6,000 men. All the forces under Napoleon came to no more than 160,000 men, while those under the allies grew to 350,000 men during the course of the battle.

On October 16th victory appeared to be within Napoleon's grasp. The center the Army of Bohemia was driven back when a charge by the Russian Guard Cossacks stopped the French advance. During this day the VIII Corps held its position and finally its position by Dellitz, where it was posted. While there the Allies attacked it and the village was lost and retaken seven times. One Polish brigade, which was formed in square, was vigorously charged by a brigade of Austrian cuirassiers. It held firm and was not broken. The enemy cavalry then passed through two lines of French and penetrated as far as the reserves formed by the Old Guard. Assailed on all sides and seeking to rejoin the main body of the army, this cavalry force was French cannister fire. Poniatowski prevented the Austrian troops from moving into the right flank of the French army, and, towards the evening, supported by a division of Imperial Guard, the Polish troops achieved a major success by driving the Austrians back across the Pleiss and taking 1,000 prisoners, including General Merveldt. Napoleon rewarded Prince Poniatowski for his actions this day by elevating him to the rank of Marshal. This was the last favor he received from Napoleon.

The following day, October 17th, was employed by the two opposing armies to prepare for a renewed battle. Napoleon awaited the arrival of his grand park, which he had left in Ellenburg. However, every officer he had sent with orders for it to come forward had been captured.

---

[33] After Austria joined the coalition, the total of Napoleon's army was 400,000 men, while that of the Allies was 600,000.

This park was important because it would provide Napoleon with sufficient ammunition for two battles and a pontoon train that would permit him to establish several bridges over the Pleiss and Elster, which he would have to cross when he withdrew to Erfurth. Deprived of this resource that would have provided him with the necessary bridges he was forced to order the construction of a trestle bridge, which was to be constructed using materials taken from the city. However, not wishing to give any cause to doubt his eventual victory, which would break the moral of his troops and encourage his enemies, his orders were not executed. Meanwhile, on the 17th Napoleon resolved to evacuate his position and when engaging in combat on the 18th he sought only to gain time to save his sick and wounded, and to facilitate the retreat of his army. The day was, nonetheless, one of the most glorious of his army.

The French army sustained itself before Leipzig with great valor against forces twice its numbers. When the Saxons defected from his ranks he was forced to draw back towards the city to reform his line of battle. The Allies gained the terrain he abandoned but could not push the French out of their final positions before the suburbs of Leipzig. The honor of their arms was still safe. The Allies had once again demonstrated that their efforts were checked by the valor of our soldiers. Their loss was twice that of the French, but the defections of Napoleon's allies in his rear forced him to retreat without delay.

This retreat was executed during the night of the 18th and 19th, and during the morning of the following day. Only an rear guard remained in Leipzig that was formed by the debris of the corps of Macdonald, Lauriston, and Poniatowski. Napoleon confided command of this force in Prince Józef, certain that he would oppose the Allies with the greatest vigor.

The prince had 20,000 men, including 2,500 Poles; to defend the city from 300,000 allied soldiers at the city's gates. He could not hope to push back the Allies. All that would be possible was to slow their progress and to cover the retreat of the Emperor who withdrew on the Saale. The load passing over the bridges was extreme and having to cross two rivers increased the disorder of the retreat.

The resistance of the defenders of Leipzig continued until noon on the October 19th when a force of Baden troops defending a gate defected. This treason and the superiority of forces forced the French rearguard to withdraw slowly.

Prince Poniatowski had once again an opportunity to demonstrate his heroism. Seeking to stop the enemy's progress and having at his disposal the weak squadron of Polish cuirassiers that formed his escort, he put himself at their head, drew his saber, and threw himself and his escort against a column of Prussian infantry, overthrowing it, and routing it, personally sabering several enemy soldiers. At this point he was struck in the arm by a musket ball. He dressed his wound and remounted his horse with his arm in a sling and returned to the battle.

Allied skirmishers had turned the city and they advanced towards the masonry bridge. A sapper non-commissioned officer, believing the bridge was seriously threatened, fired the mine and destroyed the bridge. The retreat was now impossible. In order to cross the Elster it was necessary to swim because its waters were swollen because of the rains and had risen on their banks. The Pleiss, however, formed a considerable and fatal obstacle. The prince, at the head of his brave troop, found himself at the banks of the river. It was proposed that he pass to the far bank, but even though he had no hope of victory, he wished to continue the fight. He responded to the general[34] who recommended he cross the river saying, it was better "to die

---

[34]The officer was General Bronikowski, who had for a long time served under the Prince and held him in great affection.

bravely." He then ordered one further charge, which momentarily stopped the advance of the Allies. Thrown back on the Pleiss, surrounded by his enemies, Poniatowski and his staff were exposed to the fire of skirmishers. There was no time to lose. The prince, who awaited a glorious death, was going to fall into the hands of the Allies. In the extremity, Józef finally decided to cross the river. The water was high and the current carried his horse. However the devotion of an officer of his staff, Captain Bléchamp[35], saved his life. This brave young man, an excellent swimmer, threw himself into the river after the prince and aided him in gaining the far bank. However his dangers were not yet passed. The Elster still separated Poniatowski from the main army. He advanced on foot through the gardens between the Pleiss and the Elster where he was once again hit by a musket ball in the side and fell into the arms of the officers who encircled him. He returned to consciousness and was helped onto a horse that was brought forward for him. He held himself on the horse with difficulty. He was pressed on all sides to dress his wound, to pass command to another officer, and to save himself for his country. However his courage grew as did the peril and he responded vehemently, "No, no, God has confided in me the honor of Poland. I will not surrender it except to God." An engineering officer stated that he knew a place where they could cross the Elster by swimming. Prince Poniatowski moved towards the river's bank, but spotted an enemy force advancing to block his passage. He cried, "There they are!" turned his horse and threw himself into the Elster. However, weakened by his wounds, he was not able to direct his horse as it struggled against the current and reached the far bank. But it was too steep and he was unable to climb it. This all occurred under a hail of musket shot. At this fatal moment the Prince was struck by a third musket shot. He fell from his horse and the current carried him away. The brave Bléchamp dove into the Elster in one further effort to save him, reached him and raised him to the surface before both disappeared below the waters. Thus died two heroes who in this desperate battle, preferred death to captivity.

The body of the prince was recovered two days later by fishermen. His face bore an expression of celestial resignation. Prince Schwarzenberg, his old comrade in arms, then generalissimo of the Allied armies, rendered his funeral honors. The Polish officers held prisoner placed him in his grave. Later, his remains were exhumed and carried to Warsaw where they were placed in the Church of Sainte-Croix, where the people of the capital crowded to pay their respects. From there his body was transported to Krakow where it was placed in the same crypt as the mortal remains of Sobieski and Kosciuszko.

---

[35]Bléchamp was the brother-in-law to Lucien Bonaparte.

Prince Josef Poniatowski

RELATION
OF THE OPERATIONS OF THE ARMY
UNDER THE ORDERS OF
PRINCE PONIATOWSKI
DURING THE 1809 CAMPAIGN IN POLAND

CHAPTER I

Influence of the partition of Poland on the destiny of Europe – The partitioning powers intervene in the affairs of France – War – Rise of Napoleon to the throne – He fights Austria, Prussia and Russia – England is his most redoubtable enemy – Efforts England took to form coalitions against France – Napoleon is victorious – He attempts to bring Napoleon into his system – Erfurth Conference – The Emperor seeks to reconstitute Europe on a new basis – His influence on people – A new coalition forms against him in 1809 -- The arming of Austria, Spain and England – Secret agreements of the Allies – The coalition seeks an alliance with Prussia and Austria and is checked -- Forces of the two parties at the beginning of war – The state of Poland at this time – The Grand Duchy of Warsaw and the organization of its army in 1809 – Austria forms three armies, in Germany, in Italy and Poland – Ferdinand commands the latter – Force and composition of this army – Examination of the means of defense of both parties – The Polish government is informed of the war preparations of Austria – The army of the duchy is augmented with a levy of conscripts – Force of Poniatowski's army at the moment of the beginning of the campaign – Topographical description of the Grand Duchy of Warsaw and the two Galicias.

The European edifice, which sat on a solid base formed in 1648 by the Treaty of Westphalia, was, in 1772 shaken by the partitions to which Poland had to submit. In 1795 the Czarina Catherine II gave it the last blow, eradicating it from the map of Europe with a stroke of a pin. The destruction of Poland, which a celebrated publicist decried as the greatest political crime of modern times, was an audacious violation of the most solemn engagements. This act made all the treaties a dead letter, bringing to question the stability of all the thrones of Europe, breaking the equilibrium of powers, substituted force for law, and left it to the sword to resolve the difficulties that arose between the states of Europe.

All that remained to the partitioning powers was to involve themselves in the internal affairs of the people. The opportunity came quickly. A national revolution occurred that changed the political constitution of France. The partitioning powers aligned themselves against France in order to reestablish the old order of things, to reestablish the absolute power of the kings and perhaps even to divide up French territory as they had divided Poland. However the French ran to their arms. The Convention declared a dictatorship to deal with the interior forces that sought to reestablish the abolished regime and the exterior forces that threatened its frontiers. A terrible war ensued and the Republic triumphed over internal dissent and the coalition of the kings. The French looked, in their turn, subjugate their neighbors, bringing to them republican propaganda with the point of their swords. Germany, Italy, and Holland were put to the test and the rigors of conquest, while Russia, while its allies fought a war with the new Republic, profited from the chaos in Europe to extend its possessions in Sweden and the East.

These events brought Napoleon to power, who by his superior genius, stood at the head of the French nation. He reorganized the government, brought back the Church and the throne, and placed the crown on his own head. That done, he dominated the destiny of the universe. This audacious genius, full of the sense of his destiny, commanding a warlike nation, necessarily though of an extended domination and the circumstances past and present began to favor his projects, even giving them a perception of justification.

What powers stood to oppose this? They were Austria, Prussia, and Russia and could these nations complain about his ambition and claim for themselves the rights of law? Had they not recently made a sad spectacle of the first partitioning of Poland in a period of peace, and without any aggression on the part of this unfortunate republic, which succumbed to the blows of force and iniquity, for no other crime than that of defending itself. It was these same powers the aligned at Pilnitz against France and who attempted to destroy its liberties by the force of arms. Napoleon vanquished them, inflicting on them the humiliations and misery of defeat. It was, without a doubt, a great moral and political lesson, and no one looked to blame Napoleon, and no one could blame Napoleon if he invoked the right of the victor over the vanquished, yet he treated them with generosity, allowing the defeated states that had ravaged Poland a political existence.

These monarchs who were so humiliated by Napoleon drew neither regrets nor any sympathy from the European nations who had hated their despotism. However, the emperor still had a redoubtable enemy to fight – Great Britain. This power had at its disposal a formidable material force and a morale influence no less preponderant. Its fleet dominated the seas and it was unassailable on its island home, while it could carry the war anywhere on the continent. It was almost the complete mistress of the world's commerce and by its assumed right of navigation it had at its disposal an immense wealth and practically unlimited credit. The wise constitution that granted the inhabitants of the British Isles an individual and political liberty was unknown in the rest of Europe. This constitution was admired by authors and served as a reference point for reformers. England, raised by a powerful enmity in its people towards Napoleon, and speaking of their liberties, gave them a lesson. It did not fail to use this redoubtable weapon against its redoubtable enemy.

After the collapse of the Peace of Amiens, England had become the most intractable enemy of France. This dispute great steadily worse and soon changed into a war to the death. In Paris and in London stood the governments that decided the fate of Europe. The European continent was the battlefield where they would end this quarrel. Napoleon, who had threatened England with invasion, in reality, could not take the war to English soil. It found its security, as the Athenians had, in a fortress of wood.[1] Napoleon sought to close of the Continent to England and, thereby, destroy its power by destroying its commerce. He prohibited all English merchandise, but in order to achieve his goal, it was necessary to bring all the states of Europe into the Continental System. The European powers either submitted voluntarily or were conquered. It was the execution of this grand project as much as the personal ambition of Napoleon that drove him towards world domination. The north of Germany, Holland, nearly all of Italy, part of Poland, Spain and Portugal were successively occupied by his troops and the system implemented in them. However, in the execution of his plan immense difficulties were encountered. The interests of the various sovereigns often conflicted with this system. These states were humiliated

---

[1]Editor: The Athenians had erected a palisade behind which they fought in the Peloponnesian Wars. In the case of England, the "wall of wood" was an illusion to its fleet of wooden ships.

by a despotic military system.

On its side, England made prodigious efforts to augments its arms, to sustain Napoleon's enemies, and to support their struggle. However, all the wars undertake up to 1808 against France ended in France's advantage and only caused the power of the new empire to grow, increasing its dominance of the Continent. Only Russia, though weakened by its defeats, could not be broken, and remained independent. Too far from Napoleon's center of power, supported by the arctic to the north, it could once again draw its measure against Napoleon. A young, active prince, possessing good qualities and effecting a liberalism that as the effect of the situation of the moment as much as his character and principals, reigned in Russia. He was an antagonist that Napoleon sought to manage. Napoleon wished to gain his friendship and to found, on personal relations, a relationship between the two nations whose fundamental condition would be the participation of Russia in the Continental System.

The two sovereigns met at Erfurth in 1808. There they discussed points of great interest, including the destiny of Europe. Napoleon reserved the west for himself while Alexander hoped to dominate the east. The Czar, particularly fearing the re-establishment of Poland and the establishment of a powerful empire between the Oder and the Dnieper, which would never accept his ambitions in Europe, demanded that Napoleon formally promise not to re-establish Poland. Napoleon feigned his consent and Alexander did not oppose Napoleons plans of conquest in the Iberian Peninsula, wishing, no doubt, to see a continuation of a war that paralyzed a large portion of Napoleon's army. By this support he deprived the emperor of a powerful ally and gained for him a redoubtable enemy. By this both parties sought to gain time and to mutually deceive the other. However, it is necessary to acknowledge, that the diplomatic skill was totally on the side of autocracy.

A powerful genius like Napoleon could not allow to be knocked down what it had raised up. He sought to oversee the regeneration of a new organization of Europe, which would sit on a more solid base, that of nationality, which was so often misunderstood by his enemies. He desired to reunite the peoples of Europe in a body of nations and give then indigenous governments However, threatened on all sides by its powerful enemy, England, it was necessary to continue the dictatorship to oversee the execution of his plan and to continue to put in order the new political situation in Germany by the establishment of the Confederation of the Rhine. In Poland he did this by the organization of the Grand Duchy of Warsaw. In Italy he did this by the constitution of a kingdom, though he held its crown for himself. These great political measures doubtlessly gave hope to the inhabitants of these three countries for the realization of their political hopes, of which they were, in fact, a beginning. However, Napoleon could not reconcile himself completely with those national partisans.

The Poles, who had lost their independence and their liberty without losing the moral force, which had kept their nation free for so long, received Napoleons system enthusiastically when it promised the re-establishment of their country within its original boundaries. The Italians, who had for centuries been under different sovereigns, who had been subjugated by various foreign monarchs, saw the need to unite into a single nation. They could only hope for the arrival of true independence, but weakened by egotistical governments and narrow views, enervated by the delights of an indolent life, their patriotism could not revive them enough to throw off their abasement. The German states had been under the rule of their own princes for many years, but were born down by an old feudal system. Under these same princes, they had extended their domination over their neighboring states; to the east in Bohemia, Poland and

Hungary; to the middle, over northern Italy, to the west into ancient Gaul. Their amour-propre was flattered by this domination and they began to fear the loss of their many acquisitions. France had already taken the Rhine provinces and the Milanese. It was then farsighted men, those who were convinced like Napoleon of the necessity of forming into states people of the same origins, who could see what the long-term projects of Napoleon promised them.

At the beginning of 1809 a new coalition formed against the French Empire. England was its sole; Austria, however, would play the principal role; Spain and Portugal seconded their efforts. Since 1808 the Austrian government had worked assiduously to reorganize its army. It filled its ranks and organized its army, supporting it with a numerous landwehr or national militia. The Archduke Charles, who combined personal capacity with years of command experience, was placed at the head of the military affairs of the Austrian Empire. He worked with great ardor towards this goal. From the beginning of 1809 Austrian had 330,000 men in its line army and a further 100,000 landwehr. Resources were not lacking. Its rich provinces furnished it with everything that was necessary for the organization of an armed force and England assisted powerfully with a subsidy of £4,000,000.

Spain, which saw itself invaded and its royal house dispossessed without a declaration of war, ran to arms. Supported by English gold and supported by an army of 20,000 English soldiers, it was able, in 1808, to pull together an army of 140,000 men, who struggled bravely against Napoleon's armies. It was defeated, but its disbanded troops rallied in the mountains or found cover under the cannon of the English fleet. Despite the successes that crowned their efforts, the French were obliged to maintain a large army in Spain. On its side, Portugal was occupied by Napoleon's troops at the end of 1807, was abandoned by its royal family when they fled to Brazil. It was delivered in 1808 by an English army and became a base from which the British forces operated in the peninsula.

The armaments of England were in proportion to the grandeur of its designs and the patriotism of its inhabitants. More than 100 ships-of-the-line assured its domination of the seas, and 100,000 could debark at any moment to support its continental allies. In the interior it had 400,000 men under arms, ready to defend England against the aggression threatened by the French emperor. These immense preparations cost Great Britain £25,000,000.

Such were the military forces of the new coalition. However, its views did not stop there. It sought to raise new enemies against Napoleon in the name of liberty and of the independence of people in the countries occupied by his armies.

Germany had for a long time been worked by a secret society known as the Tugenbund, which had the goal of delivering it from the foreign yoke and establishing a liberal regime under German sovereigns. The chiefs of this association were the Duke of Brunswick, dispossessed of his states by France, and the Minister Stein, but their names were carefully hidden from the membership. Organized in the manner of the carbonari, it was wrapped in extreme mystery. The ramifications of this society penetrated into every element of German society. However these two principal arenas of action were, in the north of Germany, Hesse Cassel, and in the central part, Tyrol. A general insurrection was prepared in silence. These two countries were checked by the organization of the
Confederation of the Rhine, by the powers that were adverse to them, and they burned with the desire to return to the government of their former sovereigns. The Hanseatic Cities, whose prosperity was founded on maritime commerce, and which suffered greatly under the Continental System, were also disposed to join the coalition.

In Italy the allies had fewer chances of success. The majority of the nation had begun to attach itself to the French alliance and saw it as the path to a happy future. However, the material interests had been very hurt by the preceding wars and there were a god number of malcontents who murmured against the state, lamenting what they had lost. This one crack gave the Coalition some hope that it could rally the Italian public to its side.

The Polish saw with sorrow the designs of Napoleon directed to another front and, in consequence, the regeneration of the Polish state was delayed. They had, however, complete faith in the genius of Napoleon. They believed that his interests would sooner or later cause him to fulfill the hopes they had placed in him. No suggestion, no action on the part of the allies could sway the Poles from their support of Napoleon.

The Coalition sought an alliance with Prussia and Russia and established an intelligence system in Berlin and St. Petersburg. However, their intrigues were not crowned with successful. Prussia, its armies crushed in the field and its territories cut to a portion of its former size, now had only 40,000 men under arms. Its fortresses were occupied by Napoleon's troops. It groaned under the weight of the war reparations levied against it and which, allegedly at the request of Alexander, reduced its finances to a point where the state could not quickly re-establish itself.

Russian, recently entered into an alliance with Napoleon, could not disengage itself so quickly from its promises. It also wished to finish its wars with Turkey and Sweden before it engaged in a new fight with France.

A rupture with Austrian was inevitable. Napoleon returned from Spain after vanquishing the Anglo-Spanish forces there and reestablished his brother Józef on the Spanish throne. That done he turned his attention to Austria. Paying little attention to the protestations of friendship that Austrian directed towards him with the intention of lulling him into inattention, he observed all the movements and the assembling forces in preparation for a new campaign. The detachment of 200,000 men that he left in Spain permitted him to oppose Austrian with 300,000 French and allied troops. His forces were divided such that there were 190,000 men in Germany, 55,000 in Italy, and 20,000 in Poland, which were expected to be supported by an army of 35,000 Russians.[2] Napoleon wished to avoid any conflict, but made his own preparations and his forces could be drawn together at the moment where it was probable the Austria would begin its hostilities.

Poland was subject to, in 1809, a variety of rules. The sovereign authority was divided between three powers: that of the Grand Duke; who had no responsibilities; that of the Senate, formed of palatine castilians and bishops, and that of the chamber of representatives, elected by the nobility, the cities and the communes. Executive power was confined in the Grand Duke, and lived in Dresden or Warsaw. At this time the Stanislaw-Kostaka Potoçki served as the president of the council. Prince Józef Poniatowski, who was generalissimo, was at the same time minister of war. Dembrowski was minister of the treasury, Lubienski – minister of justice, Luszczewski – minister of the interior, and Alexandre Potoçki – minister of the police. The army of the duchy was known by the title "The Polish Army"; its flags were the national colors and surmounted by a white eagle. It was, so to say, the true representation of ancient Poland that the patriots hoped to re-establish and that it was necessary to conquer. This army was not very numerous and during this period did not exceed 32,000 men. However, called upon for such high goals it was the object of great care and the solicitude of the government. All the other branches of government, the judiciary and administrative branches were seen as secondary to the army.

---

[2]This figure includes only deployable forces and not of depots.

Of the 50,000,000 florins total annual revenue of the state, 60% was spent on the army. However, the country was ruined by past wars and political commotion, and tax collection was difficult. More than once the government had to turn to the Imperial Treasury for support for its military, which at that time had, since its formation, consisted of only a few thousand men.

The Polish army played a very important role in the wars of the Empire and particularly in the period of which we propose describing, and for that reason we will devote some time to discuss its formation.

The first troops of the duchy were organized at the end of 1806, as Napoleon delivered Prussian Poland from the yoke that bore it down. It was formed entirely with volunteers who had come under the flag from diverse points of the country as well as ancient Poland. These volunteers were the most ardent patriots, the elite of the nation, who were ready to spend their blood for the national cause. Various units were organized simultaneously by Polish officers who had served in the legions of Italy and of the Rhine, and who had rivaled the glory of the French troops. Among them one found the generals Zajączek and Dąbrowski. They were veterans of the Army of the Republic of Poland who had returned to their homes, coming to place themselves before the flag of independence. Prince Poniatowski was among the latter, and, since the arrival of Napoleon in Warsaw, he was charged with the portfolio of the ministry of war.

The Polish Army had, since its initial formation, three renown commanders: Zaioczek, Dąbrowski and Poniatowski. These three all had merit and years of experience. All three had had important commands. Zajączek had been at the head of the Polish Army towards the end of the 1794 campaign and was also a général de division in the French Army. Dąbrowski had commanded the Italian Legions and had also been promoted to the rank of général de division. Poniatowski had held the post of commander-in-chief of the Army of the Ukraine and had served under Kosciuszko as a divisional commander. Napoleon, wishing to conciliate the claims of these three to the command of the Polish Army, placed each at the head of a legion, each of which was under the direction of the Ministry of War. The first was under the orders of Poniatowski and formed in Warsaw. The second was commanded by Zajączek and was organized in Kalisz. The third was under Dąbrowski and formed in Posen. Each of these three legions was formed with four line infantry regiments, each regiment having two battalions. Each legion had two light cavalry regiments, one of chasseurs and the other of uhlans, were formed with three squadrons each. There were three companies of foot artillery, each with six guns, a proportionate number of sappers, and a force of train. Each legion was to be raised to a strength of 9,000 men.[3]

From the moment each took command, there was a competition as each zealously worked to perfect the organization of their respective legions. However, since Poniatowski was minister of war he held an advantage in the process. Despite this the prince had yet one more hurdle to overcome. This army was formed of volunteers from the different classes of society, most of them independent men, and from the beginning of the campaign it was marked with success, as its men had no difficulties adjusting to military discipline. This was surely the reason why the Prince, after returning from Dresden in 1807 from consulting with Napoleon that he issued the following proclamation.

---

[3]The uniforms of these legions were identical in cut and form, except for the turnbacks and lapels which different colors for each legion.

I regard it as my duty to repeat to you the words of the French emperor. He said, "I am very happy with the Polish Army. It has shown proofs of its courage and military virtue, though it has not yet acquired the spirit and the manner, the subordination and the cohesion, which forms the characteristics of a good soldier. This you will surely acquire under good commanders and in time of peace.

The prince continued:

Soldiers, you have acquired glory in battle and gained the esteem of those at whose side you have fought, but you have not yet done enough for your country, which awaits you, outside of military virtues, unity, order, subordination, and obedience. The most celebrated soldier of the century, the great Napoleon, has recognized your merit, but has stated that you need even more. Rejoice in his praise; but do not forget his reprimands. In realizing his views, we shall one day merit his approbation.

These truths, expressed frankly, produced the best effect and the Polish Army soon accomplished what was expected of it.

From the beginning of the war with Spain the army of the Grand Duchy of Warsaw was called upon to support Napoleon's efforts in Spain and sent France three infantry regiments, which were raised to a strength of three battalions and put on a war footing.[4] A company of foot artillery and a company of sappers accompanied them. Two other regiments of infantry were sent to Danzig with a company of foot artillery, another regiment was sent into Silesia and a cavalry regiment was sent to Westphalia. At the end of 1808 the Polish army was augmented by a company of horse artillery.[5] What follows is an exact state of the duchy's army on 1 January 1809 with the stations of each corps.

TWELVE REGIMENTS OF LINE INFANTRY

Regimental Numbers	Stations	Colonels	Effective Strength
1st	Praga	Malachowski	1,934
2nd	Warsaw	Stanislaw Potocki	1,962
3rd	Warsaw	Zoltowski	2,339
4th	In France	Felix Potocki	2,555
5th	Lissa and Częstochowa	Michel Radziwiłł	1,933
6th	Sierock	Sierawski	1,807
7th	In France	Sobolewski	2,855
8th	Modin	Godebski	1,888
9th	In France	Sulkowski	2,555
10th	Gdansk	Downarowicz	1,485
11th	Gdansk	Mielzynski	1,691
12th	Thorn	Weysenhoff	1,335
		Total Infantry	21,,039

[4]Editor: These were the 4th, 7th, and 9th Regiments.
[5]This battery was formed at the expense of Wladimir Potoçki.

SIX REGIMENTS OF CAVALRY

Regiment	Station	Colonel	Effective Strength
1st Chasseurs	Piaseczno	Przebendowski	
2nd Uhlans	Warsaw	Tyszkiewicz	
3rd Uhlans	Frontiers of Silesia	Lonczynski	5,500 men
4th Chasseurs	Frontiers of Silesia	Mencinski	5,000 horses
5th Chasseurs	Frontiers of Lithuania & Prussia	Turno	
6th Uhlans	Frontiers of Lithuania & Prussia	Dziewanowski	

THREE ARTILLERY BATTALIONS, ENGINEERS AND TRAIN
Commanded by Rebel, Gurski, and Hurtig

Cantonments	Companies of Artillery	Companies of Sappers	Companies of Train
Warsaw	3	½	1
Praga	1	¼	-
Sierock	1	½	½
Modlin	1	½	½
Czenstochowa	1	¼	½
Danzig	1	-	-
In France	1	1	1
Total	1,000 men	450 men	508 men 1,950 horses

Each of these three battalions had an effective strength of 860 horses.

IN ADDITION ONE COMPANY OF HORSE ARTILLERY

Stationed in Warsaw and commanded by
Captain Wlodimir Potocki –   75 horses   50 men.

ONE NEW COMPANY OF TRAIN

Stationed in Warsaw ....   100 horses   40 men

One Company of Artisans ....   50 men
One Company of Pontooneers ....   8 men
    Total of the specialized arms   1,035 horses 2,008 men

GENERAL STAFF

3	Généraux de division	Poniatowski
		Zajączek
		Dąbrowski
13	Généraux de brigade	Kaminski
		Bieganski
		Sokolnicki
		Rozniecki
		Kamieniecki
		Hauke
		Piotrowski
		Niemoiowski
		Hebdowski
		Fiszer
		Grabowski
		Woyczynski
		Isidor Kranski

Total 16

35	Aides de camp
1	Adjudant commandant
3	Inspectors of Reviews
6	Assistant inspectors of Reviews
3	War commissioners
3	Paymasters

MEDICAL SERVICE

1	Chief Physician
1	Chief Surgeon
1	Chief Pharmacist
3	Surgeons 1st Class
3	Surgeons 2nd Class

Total for the Army   31,713 men and 6,035 horses.

One can see, in the following table, that different corps were detached in foreign countries. There remained in the Grand Duchy of Warsaw only the following:

Infantry	11,265
Cavalry	4,584
Artillery	
Engineers	}1,548
Train	
Total	17,397

In addition, in the Grand Duchy was an auxiliary corps of Saxons that contained.

Infantry	2,864
Cavalry	194
Artillery	389
Total	3,447

The total Polish and Saxon troops in the Grand Duchy of Warsaw was 20,834 men.

The garrisons of the fortresses of Thorn, Modlin, Praga, Sierock, and Czenstochowa contained 18,100 men. One can see that the duchy was desperately short of the troops necessary to defend it in time of war. The National Guard of Warsaw contained only 2,000 men and those of the provincial cities were only partially organized. When one examines the war materials in the duchy there were only:

In Warsaw	39	cannon
In Praga	50	
In Sierock	37	
In Modlin	37	
In Czenstochowa	28	
In Thorn	52	
Total	243	Including 93 field guns

These troops were completely armed, but their muskets were of different calibers and, for the most part, in poor shape. One found in the Warsaw arsenal 21,000 reserve muskets. Coming to munitions, all the weapons were provided with 750 rounds and there were, in addition, 5,000,000 infantry cartridges in various magazines. The fortifications of Modlin, of Sierock, and of Thorn were not complete. They lacked 120 cannon for their armament. The armament of the fort at Czenstochowa and the bridgehead at Praga were the only works that were complete. The old lines at Warsaw, constructed in 1769, when the plague had desolated Poland, and then rebuilt by Kosciuszko in 1794, had never been more than a weak line and were entirely neglected. Several of the works were completely fallen down and others stripped of everything useful.

Such was the incomplete state of defense of the duchy on 1 January 1809. At the beginning of April the Austrians drew together three armies.

The first in Germany, under the orders of the Archduke Charles contained 185 battalions of infantry and 164 squadrons of cavalry, with a total of 230,000 men. It was destined for the invasion of Bavaria.

The second army, under the orders of the Archduke John, consisted of 53 battalions and 44 squadrons, or about 70,000 men. It was organized on the frontiers of Italy and was designated for the invasion of Italy.

The third army, under the command of the Archduke Ferdinand, was organized in the vicinity of Krakow. It contained 25 battalions and 44 squadrons, or 33,000 men, and it was assigned to invade Poland.

The Archduke Ferdinand d'Este was the brother of the Empress of Austria and had a great influence in the Aulic Council. His personal courage was well known; his affability, the softness of his character and the certainty of his principals, plus his military talents,[6] he was the choice of the Emperor of Austria for this important command. His mission was as much political as it was military. In addition to fighting the Polish Army, his mission was to gain the support of the nation. The choice of the regiments that were to be part of his corps was given to him. Nearly all of his force was formed of veteran regiments, formed in combat. They were, for the most part, formed of Hungarians, a warlike nation that was faithful to its flags. The remainder of it was formed of Germans, and Galicians, and though these latter were forced to march against their compatriots the Austrian government chose to ignore that fact.

Here is the exact composition of the army corps under the archduke at the beginning of the campaign:

VII AUSTRIAN ARMY CORPS
Formed in Galicia

Commander-in-chief: His Highness the Archduke Ferdinand
Corps Adjutant: Colonel Count Neyppert
Chief of Staff: Colonel Brusch
Artillery Commander: Colonel Gilet

Advance guard: Generalmajor Baron Mohr
        Emperor Hussar Regiment (6 squadrons)
        1st Siebenberger Wallachia Grenz Regiment (1 bn)
        2nd Siebenberger Wallachia Grenz Regiment (1 bn)
        Wukassovich Infantry Regiment (3 bns)
        1 Light Battery
        1 Brigade Battery

---

[6]The Archduke had several experienced generals under his command. His chief of staff, Colonel Bruch, was regarded as an officer of rare merit.

Main Body:
Division: von Mondet
    Brigade: Count de Civalard
        De Ligne Infantry Regiment (3 bns)
        Kolutinski Infantry Regiment (3 bns)
    Brigade: Baron von Trautenberg
        Baillot-Latour Infantry Regiment (3 bns)
        Strauch Infantry Regiment (3 bns)
    Brigade:von Piking
        Wessenfeld Infantry Regiment (3 bns)
        Davidovich Infantry Regiment (3 bns)

Division: von Schauroth
    Brigade: von Gringer
        Palatine Hussar Regiment (8 sqns)
        Szeckler Hussar Regiment (8 sqns)
    Brigade: Baron Speth
        Sommariva Cuirassier Regiment (6 sqns)
        Lorraine Cuirassier Regiment (6 sqns)

Detached Brigade: Generalmajor Bronowacki
        1st Siebenberger Wallachia Grenz Regiment (1 bn)
        2nd Siebenberger Wallachia Grenz Regiment (1 bn)
        3rd Emperor Chevauleger Regiment (8 sqns)

Artillery: 14 Batteries
        16 3pdr cannon
        48 6pdr cannon
        12 12pdr cannon
        18 howitzers
        94 cannon total

The manpower of the Austrian army, by combat arm was as follows:

Infantry	25,000 men
Cavalry	5,200
Artillery & Train	2,800
	33,000 Total[7]

The army of the archduke had, in addition, a reserve cantoned at two points in Galicia and it was commanded by Prince Hohenzollern-Indelfingen, who had under his orders Generals Merveldt, Egermann, Starzynski, Grosser and Biking. Its strength was as follows:

Infantry	7,200 men
Cavalry	200
Total	7,400 men

---

[7] The effective strength of the Austrian corps came to about 36,900 men, but it was diminished by desertion, detachments and sick in hospital. The estimate of its strength which we have adopted is that of the Austrian general Stutrchaim.

In the first quarter of March the Austrians had begun, in the two regions of Galicia they controlled, a levy of 20,000 recruits, which were intended to raise their army to strength of 60,000 men.

However, this levy advanced slowly and did not produce anything of use for the campaign. In addition, it did bring into the army a large of men who were ill intended towards the interests of Austria.

The diverse resources offered by these two regions of Galicia were considerable. They could provide excellent horses for the army, their soil was fertile, and they had mines for salt, iron and copper that were ready for exploitation. The capital city was Leopol, a city of 50,000 inhabitants. New Galicia was equally divided into fifteen circles and its capital, Krakow, had a population of 30,000 souls.

Austria held only two fortresses in this region: Zamosc and Sandomierz. Masonry walls surrounded both, but they were in a bad state. Parts of the walls of Sandomierz were tumbled down. Colonel Pulski commanded at Zamosc and General Egerman commanded at Sandomierz. Both fortresses were armed and well provisioned.

The magazines of the archduke, subsistence and equipment, were divided among the cities along the main roads to Krakow and Leopol. They were covered by the Vistula and the San, which formed a base of operations for the Austrian Army.

The Polish government was completely informed of the Austrian preparations by the inhabitants of the country as well as by deserters, who, being of Polish origin, abandoned the Austrian flag in great numbers. Prince Poniatowski, who found himself under the immediate orders of Marshal Davout, commander of the Army of Germany, sent him detailed reports on this subject. During January, February and March he informed Davout of the convergence in Galicia of ah Austrian army that he estimated to have strength of 40,000 men, and of the levy of 20,000 new recruits, which would bring the total force to a strength of 60,000 men.

At the beginning of March the King of Saxony came to Warsaw. The Diet convened on 10 March and voted a subsidy of 30,000,000 florins for the support of the army. A rupture with Austria appeared inevitable. It was resolved to augment the strength of the Polish Army. This began with the draft of 8,000 conscripts, but the treasury was almost empty and Poniatowski asked Davout to obtain from Napoleon a subsidy of 8,000,000 florins to begin the organization of these forces. These funds were used to form third battalions for the six regiments that were in still in the duchy and the three regiments than in Prussia. Each battalion was brought to a strength of 840 men[8] and the cavalry regiments were raised to a strength of 1,047. The artillery received a considerable augmentation, adding three new foot batteries and a horse battery.[9] General Pelletier was placed in command of the Polish artillery and engineers. This excellent officer, a colonel of artillery in the service of France, had been brought into the service of the duchy in the grade of général de brigade. In addition, Captain Bontemps was placed in charge of the artillery equipment of the Polish army. These two men left French service and entered the army of the duchy. Finally, Prince Poniatowski ordered the formation of an artillery park of 30 guns for the service of his army corps.

---

[8]Editor: The figure of 840 men indicates that the Polish battalions were organized in accordance with the structure used by the French at that time. This gave each battalion six companies of 140 men.
[9]The horse battery was formed by the financial contributions of Roman Soltyk, the author of this work.

On 21 March, the King of Saxony communicated to Poniatowski a letter that he had received from Napoleon. The emperor that written the king that he had confided the command of the army of the duchy in Prince Poniatowski, directing that he bring together his forces and advance his cavalry on Krakow in order to occupy the Austrians. He requested that the King of Saxony place withdraw his Saxon troops from the duchy (he had more than 2,155 Saxon troops in Warsaw) in order to form a corps of 30,000 men near Dresden.[10]

Poniatowski responded to the King of Saxony that he could not order any movement of his troops without the orders of Marshal Davout and that the withdrawal of the Saxons would greatly weaken his already weak forces, because had had under his orders only 12,000 men. Von Boze, the Minister of State to Saxony, who assisted in this undertaking, stated that the raising of 8,000 conscripts would easily permit the withdrawal of the Saxon troops. Poniatowski responded to him that he could not implement the levy for six weeks. The minister then responded that the promised Russian assistance would give the necessary assistance to which Poniatowski responded that the Russian assistance was far less certain than the cooperation of the Saxon troops and was nothing to be counted on.

On 25 March the king left Warsaw to return to Dresden and invested his powers in the Council of State. That same day the Diet was closed.

The necessary troops were withdrawn from the standing battalions to form the cadres for the organization of the third battalions and the new companies of artillery. The Polish army, at this time, contained the following:

INFANTRY

1st Regiment	Colonel Malachowski	1,612 men
2nd	Colonel Stanislaw Potocki	1,742
3rd	Colonel Zoltowski	1,927
6th	Colonel Sierawski	1,346
8th	Colonel Godebski	1,500
12th	Colonel Weissenhoff	1,102

Total 9,259 men

CAVALRY

1st Chasseurs	Colonel Przebendowski	730 horse
2nd Uhlans	Colonel Tyszkewicz	800
3rd Uhlans	Colonel Lonczynski	760
4th Chasseurs	Colonel Turno	505
5th Uhlans	Colonel Dziewanowski	709

Total 3,504 horse

---

[10]All of the Saxon troops were withdrawn from the duchy and sent into Saxony.

ARTILLERY

3 Foot companies, each with 6 guns	18 guns	600 men
2 Horse companies	9 guns	600
Train and ambulances	27 guns	100
		700 men

SAXON TROOPS

3 Infantry Battalions	1,619 men
2 Squadrons of Hussars	178
Artillery, 12 guns	358
Total	2,155 men

The active army consisted of 15,518 men and 39 cannons. The garrisons of the various fortresses were incomplete and was as follows:

Warsaw	1,509
Praga	979
Sierock	1,413
Czentoschowa	790
Modlin	1,265
Thorn	1,594 men

The garrisons formed of the 3rd battalions of the regiments stationed in the duchy and most of the depots of the regiments that were then in Spain, supported by eight companies of foot artillery and some engineering troops.

In addition, there were the cavalry depots, which were cantoned in the vicinity of Warsaw and contained 1,812 men and 1,141 horses.

After this account of the exact forces of the two armies we shall give a topographical description of the countrywide that would become the theater of war so that one might better understand the operations of the two warming armies.

The theater of war was bounded on the south by the Carpathian; to the east and north by the Prussian frontier, and to the east by the Russian border. This vast extent of territory was crossed by the Vistula, which ran first towards the east, then turned towards the north, finally swinging to the west as it moved towards the Prussian frontier. The river ran 144 miles. At its source, it was 125 toises (243.75 meters) above the level of the Baltic. Its median width was 250 toises (487.5 meters). It was navigable from its mouth as far as Przemsza. In this part of the river its depth averaged 10 to 20 feet (3.25 m to 6.5 m). The Vistula ran through a generally wooded country. At no point were there mountains on the banks of the Vistula, just low, rolling hills. From its source to Mniszew, the right bank of the river was higher than the left. The Vistula ran its entire length in a plain. From Plotsk to the Prussian frontier it was the right bank that dominated the left.

Many tributaries joined the Vistula, some 120 streams or rivers joined it. On the right were the Raba, Dunaiec, and the Wisloka, which flowed from the Carpathian and formed as torrents from the melting snow. They frequently flooded the surrounding territory. Further down the Vistula was joined by the San, the Wieprz, and the Narev. These three rivers are navigable. The latter is the most considerable of the three. From its entry into the duchy to its confluence with the Bug the Narev flowed through a flat and swampy country.

The rivers on the left bank of the Vistula were the Przemsza, the Nida, the Kamionna, and the Radomka. They were smaller rivers and navigable only near their mouths. The lowest, the Piliça, which was the greatest of the preceding, was navigable from Przedborz to the junction and ran through a heavily wooded, flat and sandy country. The Brzura, which was bordered by swamps, had inaccessible banks. It ran through a fertile country cut by rolling hills and fell into the Vistula at Wyszogrod. Further down we find the Skwa and the Braa, which were secondary rivers, and finally, the Notetz, which ran towards the west and was joined to the Vistula by the Bromberg canal, forming an important barrier on the Prussian side of the duchy. Its banks were marshy. It was navigable from Bromburg to its junction with the Warta.

Aside from the Vistula, which flows through the middle of Great and Little Poland, one finds yet another considerable river, the Dniester, which finds its source in the Carpathians, crosses Galicia, separates Podolia from Bessarabia, and enters the Black Sea at Akerman. Its course is 63 miles in length. It is navigable ten miles from its source and continues so to its junction with the Styr. Its banks are very steep. Its bed widens, as it flows through a rocky land, to a width of 50 to 60 toises (97.5 to 117 meters). As it leaves the frontiers of Galicia it widens yet again growing to a width at its mouth of 140 toises (273 meters).

In the west, the Warta runs. It is a considerable river having a length of 104 miles from the tiny village of the same name. It is navigable to its junction with the Oder and has a width of from 40 to 100 toises (78 to 195 meters). Its banks are generally sandy and wooded. Its major tributaries consist of the Obra and Notetz.

There is only one chain of mountains in Poland, the Carpathian, which separate it from Hungary. They are less high than the Alps or the Pyrenees. Their greatest elevation is 9,300 feet (3,022.5 meters) above sea level. However, they form an imposing barrier that can be crossed at only five passes, of which three, those of Jablonka, Dukla, and Jakubowo, are traversed by good roads. The other two are traversed with difficult back roads. All the passes are easy to defend, but they were not fortified. The slopes on the north of the Carpathian stretched through Old Galicia parallel to the Vistula and one of their ranches extends beyond the river and cuts the Palatinate of Sandomierz. This branch is known as Mount St. Croix and is not a major mountain. It is heavily wooded, especially on the northern slope. This country is well suited for partisan warfare. In the direction of Great and Little Poland two thirds of it is covered with woods. That side facing the Palatinate de Sandomierz and the right bank of the Narew are covered with the Prasnysz woods, which are very extensive and thickly wooded.

Ten grand routes converged on Warsaw from different directions, including three from the south. The first ran from Leopol to Warsaw following the right bank of the Vistula through a land that was filled with marshes and woods, which was regarded as a zigzag land because of the many streams that cut it. This route crossed the Wierprz at Kock and then passed under the cannon of the fortress of Zamosc, then through the Palatinate of Lublin to Leopold, a fertile land and less wooded than the preceding. The second road moved on Pulawy by the left bank of the Vistula, crossing a partially wooded country. It crossed the Piliça at Mniszew, passing from there through a heavily wooded country crossing the Vistula at Pulawy. There it forked, with a short road running to Lublin through a hilly country and the other moving to Sandomierz passing through forests, then through a fertile country. The third road goes to Krakow. It follows the Piliça through a rich, cultivated country, then into a lightly undulating country covered with woods. It crosses the Piliça at Nowemiasto, then moving through a wooded and sandy land until it reaches Radoszyce, and then passes to Krakow through a broken country crossed by high hills and deep ravines. The country is noted for its clay, but is fertile and dotted with occasional copses of woods.

Three other roads move from Warsaw to the frontiers of Russian Poland. The first moves through Lublin crossing a country that we will describe later, and then moves on Wlodawa, through a broken, hilly, yet fertile land that is partially forested. The second moves to Siedlce, passing through a heavily forested land, crossing the Kostzyn, whose banks are swamps, and from there moves on Brzesc, through a hilly land that is partially wooded before crossing the Bug near Brzesc. The third road moves to Sierock, crossing the forests, then crosses the Narew near Sierock, moves along its right bank to Ostrolenka. There it forks, with a short road passing to Lomza, through hills that are, for the most part, covered with thickets. From there it moves on Tykocin, moving along the Narew swamp, which it crosses at Tykocin, situated at the extreme frontier of the duchy. The other fork moves through Augustow on Kowno, crossing a flat country that is covered with immense forests. At Kowno it crosses the Niemen.

Finally there are the four roads that run from Warsaw to the Prussian frontier. The first is that from Breslau, the capital of Silesia. It crosses the plain that surrounds Warsaw and moves to Piotrkow, crossing a lightly undulating country that is mostly covered with forests. From there it passes through a country somewhat similar to what it just crossed, but more sandy until it reaches the Prussian frontier. The second road runs to Berlin, passing via Posen. It moves across flat country until it reaches Bzura, crossing the Suchedniow. It moves along the riverbank before moving on Lowicz, passing through a great forest and then to Kutno, Klodawa and Posen, which country is broken with low hills until it reaches the Prussian frontier. The third road runs to Thorn by the left bank of the Vistula. It passes through Sochaczew to the Bzura, crossing that river as it approaches the Vistula, moves through the great forests around Gombin, and finally across the fertile country of Kujavie, which is broken with light hills, and crosses the Vistula near Thorn. It moves through more forests, crosses the Narew at its confluence with the Vistula, at Modlin, and then moves on Plock through a country of fertile, bare hills. From Plock it moves along the river crossing a lightly wooded country until it reaches Thorn.

There were other major roads in the duchy. One major road crossed the length of the duchy, running from Brzesc and moving to Brelsau. It passed via Lublin and Pulawy, crossing a countryside that we will describe, then moving to Radom, Opoczno, and on to Piotrkoow, through a forested country. There it rejoins the main road that runs to Warsaw to the capital of Silesia. None of the eleven roads of which we are going to speak are paved or maintained with any care. Their state changed according to the march of seasons. They were easy to cross in dry periods, but difficult when it rained and almost impossible to use in terrain that was muddy or clayey, especially around Krakow. The many smaller roads that cut the countryside were generally in a better state than the main roads because the inhabitants of the neighboring villages had a vested interest in their maintenance so as to sustain their communications with the rest of the country. There was no difference between the highways and these back roads than their length. The various rivers were major obstacles. They were only rarely crossed by bridges erected on piles[11] and by pontoon bridges. Most crossings were effected by ferries or flying bridges. However, when there were major floods, communications were invariably interrupted.

Over the history of Old Poland, Old Galicia contained the only paved road, which ran its length from Bilitz to Brody. It passed through Leopol and crossed bridges erected on piles or pontoon bridges the various rivers that flowed from the Carpathian Mountains. Many side roads broke off it in the major cities and pierced into the interior of the country, but they were well developed. The terrain of Old Galicia was fertile and the greater part of the roads that crossed it was generally the worst in the duchy.

Such was the terrain on which the fate of the Grand Duchy of Warsaw would be decided.

———●———

---

[11]These bridges could resist the ice common on the rivers. Marshal Davout looked to establish a timber bridge at Warsaw. It cost 600,000 Polish florins and was immediately a debacle.

Gen. Jan Henryk Dąbrowski

CHAPTER II

The position of the army of the archduke at the moment the campaign began – It is 33,000 men strong – Observations on its organization – Instructions received by the archduke from his government – What it was supposed to do and what it did – Its presumption – Ferdinand's proclamation – Observations on the topography of the duchy under the strategic report – the Polish government, with great foresight, was able to maintain itself in Warsaw – Poniatowski must at least fortify Modlin and Thorn – He did not believe he would be attacked – The two opposing commanders commit errors because of overconfidence – Poniatowski's dispositions – He unites 14,000 men near Warsaw – The declaration of war – The beginning of hostilities – Diverse measures taken for the defense of the duchy by its government – Its manifesto – The Austrian Army advances on Warsaw -- Poniatowski waits it at Raszyn – Position of the Polish Army -- Engagement at Nadarzyn – The archduke's army advances – The Archduke attacks Falenty – Lively battle at Falenty – The Poles retire on Raszyn – The engagement extends over the entire line -- Poniatowski holds his position until nightfall – Losses on both sides – The Saxons retreat – Prince Poniatowski withdraws his army on Warsaw during the night – Ferdinand arrives before Warsaw – Interviews between the prince and the archduke – Armistice – A convention for the surrender of Warsaw is concluded – The Polish evacuate Warsaw and withdraw on the Narew – Events that occurred near Czenstochowa – Bronowacky raises the blockade and moves on Warsaw.

During the first days in April, the Army of the Archduke Ferdinand moved towards the frontiers of the duchy. On the 14th it occupied the following positions: the advanced guard, under the orders of general Mohr, was at Nowemiasto; the main body, consisting of the divisions under Mondet and Schauroth, were united near Odrzywol, as was the army's headquarters; Bronowacky's brigade occupied Olkusz moved against Czenstochowa; and finally a detachment of two squadrons of hussars, under the orders of Colonel Neipperg, was posted at Okuniew to observe Praga.

This army, 33,000 men strong, was formed of veteran troops and was able to render good service on the battlefield. Its organization, however, left much to be desired. Its light cavalry had only 3,800 horses, a number insufficient for the tasks that had been assigned to it. In effect it was to be used for advanced posts in a country that was in large part wooded, swampy and, in consequence, very favorable to ambushes and the army had to gather forage for its horses as it moved into a country whose entire population was hostile to it. Finally the light cavalry would be required to deal with the partisans that would surely appear everywhere, as this became a national war for the liberation of Poland.

The theater of war, which we will describe, was cut by many rivers and streams that the Austrian army had to cross during the course of its operations. The bridges, which were already rare in Poland, would be destroyed and it was necessary for the Austrians to use pontoon bridges to cross those rivers. Despite this, the archduke's army had no bridging train. The also had several fortresses which it would be necessary for the archduke to besiege, yet not only did he have no siege train, the largest cannon he had with him were twelve 12pdrs. The remainder of his artillery was of lighter field guns. The archduke's army also contained 25% ethnic Poles and this number would soon be augmented by a levy of 20,000 Galicians, which would be gathered in the depots. All of these men had no loyalty to the Austrian flag and it was feared that once they found themselves facing the Polish army, they would pass over to the ranks of their ethnic brothers. Prudence prescribed that those troops should be replaced by troops of other ethnic origins and to have sent the ethnic Polish troops to other armies or to garrisons of fortresses situated outside of the Polish territories.

The instructions given to the archduke directed that his corps should march directly on Warsaw and seek to take Czenstochowa, but that it should above all act with the greatest celerity to end the expedition promptly and to bring the Grand Duchy of Warsaw to where it unable to harm the interests of Austria. These instructions also stated that the Vienna Court was alarmed by the organization of a Russian army at Dubno and gave the archduke instructions as to how he was to act vis-à-vis it.

In order to complete the mission, with which he was charged, the Archduke had to defeat the Polish Army, takes its fortresses, occupy the countryside, and suppress the insurrection that would erupt, not only in the Grand Duchy but also in the two Galicias. It was an extremely difficult task for an army of 33,000 with a reserve of 7,400 men. It supposes a string of uninterrupted success on which Austria could not reasonably count.

Unaffected by reality, Ferdinand could see no situation where he might be obliged to move to the defense and did nothing to maintain himself, to anticipate the insurrections and to receive support that support that might be sent to him. However, be he on the offensive or defensive, he did have the prudence to make himself master of the course of the Vistula, which was the principal strategic geographical feature of the country. This river ran to the east until it joined the San. That part of its course, with that of the San, formed the archduke's base of operations and covered his magazines. Further along the Vistula turned sharply to the left and ran to the north and entered the duchy which lay on both of its banks. Ferdinand could not, as a result, view the Vistula as a defensive line. He could make himself master of its course by fortifying a number of points, which would permit him to straddle the river and allow him to operate on both banks.

To achieve this goal the most suitable points to hold were the junctions of the various tributaries with the Vistula and none of them were fortified. At this time the Austrians only held two fortified cities that could assist their operations along the Vistula. They were Krakow and Sandomierz. Krakow was encircled with an old wall flanked with tours that were not armed, but could be converted into a suitable post for the war. It also had a stone bridge over the Vistula. The wall around Sandomierz was originally very strong, but it had fallen into a state of great disrepair and was in ruins. The archduke ordered it rebuilt and added a few advanced works prepared. In addition, he had a bridge thrown over the Vistula and desired to cover it with a bridgehead.   These works could be useful, but Krakow and Sandomierz found themselves some distance from the line of operations and could only serve him as fortifications for his base. If Ferdinand wished to operate against Vistula, he was necessary that he assure a point closer that city, which could serve as an intermediary point between Sandomierz and Warsaw. The only suitable position was at the confluence of the Vistula and the Wierpz. This point, fortified by a triple bridgehead, at the same time made the archduke the master of that river and the Vistula and served as a pivot for his operations. However the archduke did not have the foresight to recognize this or to execute the works.

Ferdinand held the Polish army in low regard, seeing it only as it was organizing and believing he could defeat it easily.   He hoped that the inhabitants of the duchy would be infused with the spirit of opposition against Napoleon that had been seen in the other European countries and that in any case that he would paralyze their ill will with his first successes. He was unaware that Poniatowski had united his army before Warsaw and, conforming with his instructions, he intended to march directly against the Polish army and force a decisive battle immediately.

Before crossing the frontier the Austrian prince resolved to issue a proclamation. Dated from Odrzywol on April 12th this proclamation was not made public until the moment he crossed the Piliça. There Ferdinand declared to the inhabitants of the Grand Duchy of Warsaw that he was bringing an army into their territory, but that he was not coming as their enemy, as the Emperor of Austria was making his war against Napoleon and that he was the friend of all who did not defend the cause of France. He then gave them an explanation of the motives for the war, stating that it was to preserve the existence of the Austrian Empire and the prosperity of people that were threatened by the ambition of the French Emperor. He went on to say,

It is to you that I address myself particularly, the inhabitants of the Grand Duchy of Warsaw. I ask you, do you enjoy the happiness promised you by the emperor? Your blood, which was spilled below the walls of Madrid, was it spilled in your interests. What do the Tagus and the Vistula have in common? And has the valor of your soldiers brought you greater prosperity. The Emperor Napoleon has need of your troops for himself, not for you. You sacrifice your property and your soldiers to an interest that is far from yours, which is entirely opposed to them, and at this moment, you are, by your alliance, left without defense before my superior forces as the best of your troops are spilling their blood in the fields of Castille and Aragon.

Finally, he asked the inhabitants to not resist and said that if they oppose his army, he would exercise the rights of war. "If, faithful to your true interest, you receive me as a friend, His Majesty the Emperor of Austria will grant you special protection, and I will extend to you the necessary security with my arms and the substance of my army.

The Grand Duchy of Warsaw was covered, on the side of Galicia, on the right bank of the Vistula, by a defensive line that followed the course of the Bug from its junction with the Nurzeç to the Narew, then along the course of this river to its junction with the Vistula. This part of the line was not without importance, as much as it was protected by the fortresses of Sierock and Modlin. It would have been even better fortified if these two fortresses were equipped with bridgeheads which would have permitted the Poles to move at will to the left bank of the Bug and the Narew, and to take the offensive upon an opportune moment. The defensive line for the duchy them moved up the course of the Vistula from Modlin to Mniszew. In this space, covered by the river, was fortified by a bridgehead at Praga and the possession of it allowed the Poles to move to the right bank of the Vistula at will. However, from Mniszew, the line of the Piliça poorly covered Warsaw and the departments of the left bank as it was fordable at many points, particularly near its source, so it did not present a very serious obstacle to the advance of an enemy. Warsaw was, itself, not fortified and, once occupied by an enemy, Praga no longer offered any advantage to the Poles.

This review shows clearly that the weak side of the duchy's frontier was on the left bank of the Vistula and that it would be easy for the Austrians to invade on that side.

The same motives required the archduke to secure the course of the Vistula also applied to the Poles as they occupied their various fortifications. In fact, it was of even greater interest, since they would be on the defense because of their inferior forces. It was even more important for them to be able to pass from one bank to the other, so as to avoid any unequal battle as well as to seize more propitious occasions.

Three points were of particularly important in this regard: Warsaw, Modlin, and Thorn. Warsaw was fortified in 1794 by Kosciuszko. It had undergone a siege of six weeks against an army of 36,000 supported by a siege train. It was not impossible, in 1809, that it could be defended against the Austrian army of 33,000 men and had no heavy artillery. Kosciuszko had deployed an army of 18,000 men. Poniatowski had 17,000 men, including the depots in Warsaw, and this number could be augmented quickly by new levies. Poniatowski had withdrawn some cannons from fortified places on the Narew and from Praga to arm these lines, which were very extensive. They stretched 6,000 toises (11,700 meters). They were, however, in a very bad condition, though with the aid of many strong backs, six weeks would be sufficient to rebuild them. It remained, however, to be discovered if by acting two months before the invasion if the Polish government could prevent the Austrians Warsaw without striking a blow and if forced into a siege if it could be held while the Austrians awaited the arrival of a siege train, which could only be organized in Olmutz. During the long period that this would require, it was certain that the Polish government could have more than enough time to raise a force of partisans in the Austrian rear as well as to implement a mass levy. It is probable that the Austrian Army would soon find its lines of communications broken, interrupting the flow of food and munitions. Finally, pressed harder and harder, it is certain that the Poles would be forced to retreat as they had before Frederick Wilhelm in 1794.

However, the Polish government did not believe that war was coming and did absolutely nothing to prepare for it. Prince Poniatowski learned, in a letter from Napoleon, which was sent to him on March 21st, that war was imminent and this did not allow time to fortify Warsaw. It was necessary to immediately prepare the fortifications at Modlin and Thorn, which commanded the course of the Vistula between the Narew and the Prussian frontier.

The strategic importance of Modlin was recognized. The Swedish had had an entrenched camp there. Marshal de Saxe had sought to make it the center of the defense of Poland. Napoleon chose it in his 1807 campaign for the erection of a fortification. Modlin had received many improvements and had a triple bridgehead that commanded the Vistula and the Narew. If Poniatowski had had more foresight and had organized a bridgehead there on the left bank of the Vistula he would have been able, after the fall of Warsaw, to maneuver on the capital on the left bank of the river and either chased Ferdinand back or paralyzed his movements. The entrenchments at Modlin, at the time of which we speak, had only a six faced fortress on the right bank of the Vistula, but it had no advanced works. Its ramparts were 16 feet (5.2 meters) wide and reinforced with wood, making it open to a coup de main. However, the fortress lost the greatest part of its importance as a result of the negligence it had not extended its entrenchments to the left bank of the river.

The fortress of Thorn had seven faces. It was reveted and palisaded. It had a pontoon bridge over the Vistula, but it was covered on the left bank by only a weak entrenchment. Poniatowski had to make it ready for the defense quickly.

If the works at Modlin and Thorn had been completed before the war, as they could have been, Poniatowski could have used Modlin as the pivot of his operations and Thorn as his depot. They would have assured his communications with Great Poland and the line of the Oder. However, Poniatowski, three days before the opening of hostilities, still did not believe there would be an attack. He was not informed of the movements of the Austrians.

In a letter written to Marshal Davout on 12 April he expressed his opinion on the subject: "In comparing the circumstances contained in the various opinions with the positive opinion that the Archduke Charles was already in or would arrive shortly at Konski, it appeared evident that the Austrians would move their troops on the Piliça and that they would take the positions which I have had the honor of discussion to Your Excellency. I say one of these positions, because, despite their fanfares and threats, they certainly cannot occupy them all. It is generally said that the corps of the Archduke Ferdinand has about 30,000 men, but it is hardly likely that they can move to our side more than 15,000 to 18,000 men. From there the corps which will act against the Piliça will more likely be destined to observe our movements than to effect the invasion of the duchy that has been so long announced."

Thus the Prince, having neglected to take the necessary measures to permit him to undertake a vigorous defense, found himself obliged to defend Warsaw with only the bravery of his troops. It appears that the general opinion in the duchy was that the Austrians would not attack Napoleon had greatly contributed to Poniatowski's false sense of security.

By a singular coincidence the two opposing army commanders had mutually made errors that assisted the case of their enemy. These errors would have a great influence on the operations of the coming war.

Nonetheless, on 12 April Poniatowski deployed his troops as follows: the 6th Cavalry Regiment moved from Blonie and moved to Nadarzyn; the 3rd Infantry Regiment, commanded by General Bieganski, supported by four cannon, occupied Raszyn; the 3rd Cavalry Regiment moved to a position at Piaseczno; the 1st Cavalry Regiment moved between Gora and Mniszew; and the 5th Cavalry Regiment left Nieporent (left bank of the Vistula) and moved to Blonie. The 3rd Infantry Regiment was replaced in Warsaw by a battalion of the 6th Infantry Regiment, which was drawn from the fortress at Sierock, and by a battalion of the 8th Infantry Regiment, detached from Modlin. Two other battalions of the same regiments followed two days later. The garrison of Warsaw consisted of the 1st and 2nd battalions of the 1st, 2nd, 6th, and 8th Infantry Regiments, the 2nd Cavalry Regiment, and the Polish foot and horse artillery, plus a few depots and the Saxon division. The 12th Infantry Regiment was enroute to Thorn, but would not arrive in Warsaw until the morning of 20 April.

The total number of Polish troops ready to take to the field united under the orders of Poniatowski came to about 14,000 men supported by 39 cannon.

At 8:00 a.m., on April 15th Prince Poniatowski received an Austrian delegation, which presented the archduke's declaration. This declaration announced "the Austrian troops were entering the territory of the duchy at 7:00 a.m., on 17 April, and that they would treat as an enemy any forces that opposed them."[1]

Convinced that hostilities had commenced, Poniatowski directed his army towards the Piliça. He took up position, during the evening of 15 April at Raszyn, with the main body of his army, under the orders of General Bieganski. At the same time directed General Rozniecki to move at the head of the cavalry to scout out the movements of the Austrians. This general had five cavalry regiments and four horse guns under his orders. The 1st Cavalry Regiment took positions at Gora, the 2nd moved to Raszyn, and the 3rd, 5th and 6th Regiments advanced behind the 2nd.

During the morning of 16 April Poniatowski planned to leave Raszyn and move into contact with the Archduke. However, on one side reports from the cavalry general informed him that the Austrian army, 26,000 to 30,000 men; on the other, General Pelletier, who had Pon-

---

[1]This letter was carried to Poniatowski by Chef de bataillon Mallet, the Polish Director of Engineers, who had been sent to Nowemiasto to reconnoiter the course of the Piliça and the highway from Warsaw to Nowemiasto.

iatowski's confidence, expressed concern about advancing the Polish army too far forward and exposing it to the danger of being cut off from Warsaw. He went on to suggest to Poniatowski that a withdrawal to the Warta would permit him to maintain his communications with the line of the Oder. General Pelletier then observed that such a movement in the presence of a superior enemy army was highly dangerous. As a result, Poniatowski decided to hold his position in Raszyn in order to cover Warsaw.

The Polish government, seeing itself threatened by an invasion, adopted those measures for its defense, which it should have adopted long before the invasion.

It ordered that the defensive lines around Warsaw be restored, but there was not sufficient time to return them to a respectable state. The National Guard of Warsaw was reorganized and placed under the orders of Colonel Saulnier, commander of the fortress. There was no lack of muskets. In addition, a last call-up or *arrière ban* of the National Guard was formed from men aged 16 to 60 was organized and armed. This force was formed in tens, centuries, and battalions under elected commanders. A levy en masse was also ordered.

The government named in each department a fully empowered lieutenant and a military commander for the armed forces to be raised. Here are the names of the individuals invested with these functions:

Department	Empowered Lieutenants	Armed Forces Commanders
Warsaw	Prince Stanislaw Iabionowski	Colonel Siemianowski
Posen	Senator Wybiçki	General Kosinski
Kalisz	Prefect Garczynski	Colonel Biernaçki
Plock	Prefect Rembielinski	Colonel Zielinski
Lomza	Prefect Lasoçki	General Karowski
Bromberg	Prefect Gliszczynski	Colonel Lipzinski

All decrees were promulgated on 16 April. The Council of Ministers then issued an energetic proclamation dated the same day as the Archduke Ferdinand's proclamation. In this manifesto, addressed to the inhabitants to the Grand Duchy of Warsaw, the council recalled the restoration of the nation under the efforts of Napoleon. It went on to say that the political existence of the duchy was ratified by the Treaty of Tilsit by the two most powerful monarchs of the world; that from that time the duchy had taken a place among the independent states of Europe, and that its sovereignty was assured to the House of Saxony, called to the throne by the national voice and sealed by new oaths. It protested, in the following terms, the Austrian invasion.

A neighbor to whom we have offered no offense; a neighbor whose capital and empire were saved by the arms of our ancestors, has invaded our territory and treats us as a horde without a country and without a government, attempting to separate our cause from that of the man who restored our country and to keep us from making war in his support. Assured that we would summon the support of our powerful ally, should we not oppose force with force to defend our political existence? Such pusillanimity should enrage the Poles. We should sacrifice everything to defend our country and our honor. The government and the nation shall redouble their efforts to repulse the aggression of the enemy and they shall always regard the Galicians as their brothers. Inhab-

itants of the Duchy of Warsaw it is to the national defense that the government calls you by the ordnances that it shall issue......

The manifesto ended saying:

Hasten, Poles, who have never degenerated; you have given the world numerous explosive proofs of your patriotism, unite with your valiant army in the defense of your foyers! You, confident in your God and in the protection of the great Napoleon, shall battle in the name of the mother land and your virtuous sovereign; cover yourselves with what man finds most precious: your independence and your rights!

While the government took these different measures to vigorously support the war effort, the Polish cavalry, under the command of Rozniecky, had engaged the Austrians in numerous different engagements, all of which ended to the advantage of the Poles and they took 100 Austrian prisoners and killed or wounded another 100 men.

During the day of 18 April the garrison of the bridgehead at Praga directed a reconnaissance force on Grzybow, which encountered two squadrons of Austrian hussars. The Poles charged them vigorously, despite the Austrian superiority in numbers, drove them, routing them, and put 40 men hors de combat.

The army of the Archduke advanced on Warsaw. The Polish advanced guard evacuated Tarczyn and it fell back on Raszyn. This position was covered by the Rawka stream, which flowed into the Bzura and cut the road between Nadarzyn and Iaworowo and the road between Tarczyn to Raszyn. This stream was swampy around Raszyn, and during this campaign, it could be crossed by the Austrian Army at only three sites near Raszyn. All of these crossings were within a half-mile of one another: at Iaworowo, at Raszyn, and at Michaelowice, where there were dikes or bridges that were easy to defend. In front of the center of the Polish Army was the village of Falenty and further, towards the right, was a forest. On crossing the dike at Raszyn one encountered yet another considerable forest that was crossed by the roads to Falenty and Piaseczno. Overall the position was very strong. Before it stretched a plain bordered by vast forests. Prince Poniatowski placed his advanced guard in Falenty. It was formed of the 1/1st and 1/8th Infantry Regiments, supported by four cannon. Command was entrusted to General Sokolnicki. Poniatowski supported it with a battalion of the 6th Infantry Regiment and two further cannon, posted before the dike at Raszyn, which served the advanced guard as a reserve. The right of the village of Michalowice was occupied by the 1/2/3rd Infantry Regiment and four cannon, which would withdraw to Tarczyn and were under the orders of General Bieganski. In the center, behind Raszyn and straddling the road to Warsaw the 1/2/2nd Infantry Regiment, three Saxon infantry battalions, a squadron of Saxon hussars, and twelve Saxon cannon occupied a line of sand hills. They were commanded by General Polentz. To the left, Ioworowo was occupied by the 2/1st and 2/8th Infantry Regiments and six cannons under the orders of General Kaminski. Poniatowski had thrown detachments on his flanks. One company[2] of the 5th Cavalry Regiment occupied Blonie, a squadron of Saxon hussars was placed in echelons between there and Raszyn; a battalion of the 6th Infantry Regiment and two cannon

---

[2] Each squadron was composed of two companies, which had the equivalent strength of strong French squadrons. Editor: The footnote provi.ded by Soltyk is correct in that each squadron had two companies, but the authorized strengths of the squadrons for the Polish were 170 men and of the equivalent French squadrons at this time were 116 men

were positioned at Wola. The cavalry under the orders of General Rozniecki, consisting of the 2nd, 3rd, 5th, and 6th Regiments, supported by four horse guns, were facing Ferdinand's army and watching it as it fell back on the main body. The 1st Cavalry Regiment withdrew on Gora during the night of the 18th and took up a position about 1,000 toises (1,950 meters) behind the center of the army where five horse guns formed the army's artillery reserve.

Rozniecki's cavalry had, in the morning of the 19th, a serious engagement at Nadarzyn with the advanced guard of the archduke, in which the 2nd Cavalry Regiment launched a brilliant charge. It then fell back on the main body and placed itself in reserve to cover the flanks of the army, which could be threatened by the Austrians.

The Austrian Army advanced form Tarczyn via the woods of which we will speak later. General Mohr commanded its advanced guard. It consisted of three battalions of infantry (Vukassovich), two battalions of light infantry (Siebenburger-Wallachia Grenz), all of the light cavalry available to the archduke, and twelve cannons. The main body of the Austrian army marched simultaneously down the roads from Nadarzyn, Tarczyn, and Piaseczno. Mohr moved out in the afternoon. The Polish cavalry still masked Poniatowski's position from the sight of the Austrians. Towards 1:00 p.m., it followed the movement of the Austrian squadrons as they attempted to move towards the Polish right flank. When he observed this, Poniatowski withdrew Rosniecki's forces via Michalowice into the rear of his army.

The archduke was able to reconnoiter the Polish position and noticed that the Polish left was weak and could be turned because the Rawka stream is insignificant above Iaworowo, but he neglected to do it. In following the regulations prescribed by the art of war, the Austrian general moved his advanced guard towards Poniatowski while holding his main body at the edge of the woods. Ideally he would launch his attack the next day and to make his dispositions such that he could move part of his forces against the Polish extreme left, to turn the left while at the same time attacking the center. This would oblige Poniatowski to withdraw on Warsaw, a movement he could not execute without substantial danger in an open country, over clayey terrain broken by the thaw. He would be obliged, no doubt, to abandon his artillery in the quagmires. Under most circumstances such a turning movement would have been risky between the Polish troops and the Vistula, but in view of the numerical superiority of the Austrian army, the archduke ran little risk.

Ferdinand was impatient to engage the Poles. Without awaiting the arrival of the main body of his army, he ordered General Mohr to carry the position of Falenty and fed in the rest of his forces as they arrived on the battlefield. On his side, Prince Józef, who knew the slow pace of the Austrians, did not believe he would be attacked immediately. He expected to be attacked in the morning and did not withdraw his advanced guard, leaving it in harms way and where it had a single bridge over which to effect its retreat. However, Mohr's attack was so brisk that Poniatowski was forced to accept battle without being able to adjust his deployment.

Sokolnicki had only three battalions and six guns to oppose the five Austrian battalions and twelve guns in Civalard's brigade, which pursued them aggressively. The engagement began at 2:00 p.m. Prince Józef, who found himself at his headquarters in Raszyn, mounted his horse and rode to Falenty. He ordered three horse guns held in the reserve to take a position in front of the village. Sokolnicki now had nine cannons deployed to support his position. Thee guns redoubled their fire as the Austrians approached. Mohr responded with a brisk cannonade by his own artillery and his infantry advanced in columns.

The woods were carried by the Austrians at about 3:00 pm., and soon afterwards the village of Falenty was carried. The battalion of the 8th Infantry Regiment, which defended these two points, retreated in disorder. Poniatowski rallied it and placed himself at the head of the 1/1st Infantry Regiment, which he then led in a bayonet charge against the Austrians and recaptured the position. The Polish artillery contributed to this success with their well-directed fire. At this point Civalard's brigade arrived on the battlefield. Mohr now deployed three times the forces had had in the first attack and turned once again to the offensive. Twenty-four Austrian guns were now in battery and the greatly outnumbered Polish artillery could not long hope to resist them. A Polish howitzer was dismounted, several caissons were hit and exploded, and a large number of gunners were cut down. Austrian howitzers set Falenty afire. The Austrian infantry formed in attack columns, reoccupied the woods and occupied Falenty. At this point Colonel Godebski, a Polish officer of rare merit and commander of the 8th Infantry Regiment, was killed. At the same time a battalion of the 6th Infantry Regiment was heavily attacked and barely held its position against superior numbers.

Pressed on all sides, the Polish advanced guard was obliged to withdraw to Raszyn. This movement could not be executed without some disorder. The dismounted howitzer and one other cannon were abandoned on the battlefield. General Fiszer, chief of staff to the army, was wounded in the melee. General Sokolnicki led part of his troops across the dam while another part waded single file through the swamp and across the river. They completed their passage at 5:00 p.m.

The Austrians, emboldened by their initial success, sought to press forward and attacked Poniatowski in his position by Raszyn. They advanced across the dam despite the fire of the French infantry and seized part of the village, but were unable to totally clear it of Polish troops where the village was closest to the main Polish line. The Austrians also attacked the villages of Iaworowo and Michalowiec, but weakly and without success. Towards 7:00 p.m. they redoubled their efforts to move against the Polish center. One of their columns advanced through Raszyn while another force attempted to push through the swamp to the left of the village. Poniatowski moved a battery of sixteen guns (12 Saxon and 4 Polish)[3] to the right of the main road to Warsaw. These guns opened a heavy bombardment on the Austrian infantry. They fired cannister against them for more than an hour and eventually obliged them to retreat after inflicting heavy casualties on the Austrians. During the course of the struggle around Raszyn, Poniatowski exposed himself to enemy fire. Many officers of his staff officers were wounded or had horses killed under them.

The Polish howitzer shells set Raszyn afire and the Polish skirmishers fought with intrepidity and maintained their position in part of the village. All the Austrian's efforts to dislodge them proved in vain. The terrain did not permit them to deploy their cannon to support their attack. At 9:00 p.m. firing ceased, the Austrians recrossed the bridge at Raszyn and continued to occupy the damn and the woods that were behind the village. With the exception of Falenty, the Polish had lost no other part of the battlefield and maintained themselves on it.

---

[3]Schuster, O. & Francke, F.A., *Geschichte der Sächsischen Armee von deren Erreichtung bis auf die neueste Zeit.* (Leipzig: Dunker & Humbolt, 1885) p. 285 indicates that there were 14 Saxon guns in the center of the Polish line supported by the Saxon infantry, which consisted of 1 Battalion of the Oebschelwitz Infantry Regiment and the Einsiedel Grenadier Battalion.

The loss of the Polish army in the day was about 450 killed, 900 wounded, and 40 prisoners. The Austrians, who fought most of the day in the open, lost substantially more. Their losses were estimated at 2,500 men.[4]

In light of the inferior strength of the Polish forces present in the battle of Raszyn when compared to those of the Austrians, this battle must be viewed as one of the most glorious in the history of this campaign, and if one considers that the army of Archduke Ferdinand was formed of veteran and proven troops and that Poniatowski's army was composed of untried recruits who had never been under fire, one must admit the courage that they showed on this marvelous day.

The firing having stopped, the Saxon infantry, which had fought valiantly through the battle, began its withdrawal on Warsaw in order to return to Saxony, in compliance with orders it had received. This retreat has been strongly criticized in the Polish army. Abandoned by their allies in the greatest moment of danger the Poles were shocked.

Prince Poniatowski held a council of war at 10:00 p.m. on the battlefield. The losses suffered during the day, the great number of men who had abandoned their ranks to carry off the wounded, and finally the departure of the Saxons had reduced Poniatowski's army to about 9,000 men. Retreat was inevitable and it was executed during the night so as to escape pursuit during the next day. The retreat began at 11:00 p.m. and was executed with no other loss than the abandonment of two more cannons, which became stuck in the mud that rendered part of the road impassable.

Immediately after the action General Sokolnicki was charged by Poniatowski to move at the head of the 2nd Cavalry Regiment to the Vistula. He took a position near Wilanow and remained there through the night to observe the roads by which it was feared the Austrians might advance on Warsaw in order to cut off the Polish army from it.

However, the Austrians were too fatigued by the battle and the unexpected resistance offered by the Poles, so they made no effort to pursue them. General Sokolnicki withdrew during the morning of the 20th to the Warsaw lines where the Polish army had taken position. These earthworks were equipped with 45 cannon, including six 24pdrs. However, Poniatowski had no hope of maintaining himself there, even though he was reinforced during the day by the 12th Infantry Regiment, which arrived from Thorn, and 800 recruits that came from Kalisz under Captain Rybinski. Poniatowski's force rose to a strength of 12,000 to 13,000. The Warsaw National Guard had an effective strength of 5,000 men. These forces, however, were deployed in a defensive line that extended over 6,000 toises (11,700 meters) and was unable to stop the Austrians. In addition, the lines were in such bad condition that they could be broached almost everywhere, including by cavalry. All the generals declared that it was impossible to hold Warsaw. Dąbrowski, who had joined the army after the battle of Raszyn, and General Zajączek who arrived in Warsaw during the night, agreed with this opinion.

The Austrians advanced on Warsaw, but slowly. Their cavalry appeared before Warsaw around noon and was greeted by a few 24pdr cannon balls. This fire produced a strong effect on the archduke who had no idea the Poles had such heavy artillery and it caused him to suppose that the defenses of Warsaw were in a respectable consideration. This caused the archduke to

---

[4]Editor: D. Smith, *The Greenhill Napoleonic Wars Data Book*, London, Greenhill Books, 1998, pp.289-290, lists the Polish losses as above, but lists the Austrian losses at 450 dead and wounded. In addition, he identifies the following Saxon units: von Einsiedel Grenadier Battalion, Oebschelwitz Infantry Regiment (1 bn), von Rechten Infantry Regiment (2 bns), the Saxon Hussar Regiment (2 sqns), and 12 guns. Schuster, O. & Francke, F.A., gives the of the Saxons and Poles at 450 dead, 900 wounded, and 300 missing.

seek a negotiated arrangement.

Upon his arrival before Warsaw Ferdinand asked Poniatowski for an interview, which took place at 4:00 p.m. before the Jerusalem barricade. Ferdinand received Poniatowski with great courtesy, commended his conduct at Raszyn and the conduct of his brave troops. He suggested that they put an end to the effusion of blood, recommended that Poniatowski should abandon Napoleon, and that they not be a tool of Napoleon's ambition or part of an alliance that brought them no profit. He ended by protesting the good intentions of the Austrians towards the Poles. Poniatowski responded, "You have acknowledged at least, Sir, that we owe Napoleon much recognition, for having procured for us the honor of fighting you under the Polish flag." The interview concluded with the signing of a 24-hour armistice.

The following day, the 21st, the two commanders met again. They arrived on the basis of a convention by which Warsaw would be evacuated by the Polish troops. The archduke did not readily agree to Poniatowski's conditions, but after seeing Poniatowski's escort, formed of cavalry troopers drawn by the levy en mass, dressed in civilian cloths and armed with lances, he displayed an emotion he could not hide. He judged by this that the war would become a national war and he wished to avoid this at all costs. He hastened, as a result, to conclude the convention, which gave the Polish army 48-hours to evacuate Warsaw, that hostilities would cease until two days later at 5:00 p.m. The Austrians could then occupy Warsaw, but they could not levy any war contribution against the city. The Polish and Saxon civil employees, the French officers and soldiers were also free to withdraw over a period of five days. The Polish army had the right to take with it all the arms and munitions that were in Warsaw. The sick and convalescents were to be left to the care of the Austrian Army and those that could, were permitted to rejoin their regiments. The people, property, and religion of the city were to be respected. The convention was signed at 5:00 p.m., on the 21st.

The convention greatly saddened the entire army and the inhabitants of Warsaw. Poniatowski reproached himself for having consented to it. However, he said to General Pelletier, who was under his command, "General, I am afraid I have signed my dishonor." Pelletier responded, "You can be calm, as the cause of Poland can not but gain from the convention that you have concluded. Fall back on the right bank of the Vistula. The army shall be free in its movements and the Austrians shall see a great part of their forces paralyzed by the occupation of Warsaw."

The munitions and weapons found in the Warsaw arsenal were loaded on the boats that formed the pontoon bridge over the Vistula and moved to Modlin. The army crossed the river and moved on Modlin and Sierock. On the 23rd, at 4:00 p.m. the Polish movement was complete. The Council of Ministers withdrew to Tykocin and took with it the Polish archives.

As these events occurred in the principal theater of war, General Bronowacky advanced at the head of his brigade, some 3,000 infantry and ten cannon, on the fort at Czenstochowa. He crossed the frontier on the 15th and arrived before Czenstochowa on the 17th, forcing back its advanced posts and summoning it on the 18th to capitulate. The fort was commanded by Major Stuart, who had under his orders the 3rd Battalion of the 5th Infantry Regiment, a detachment of the 3rd Uhlans, and a company of foot artillery that manned 28 cannons on the fort's ramparts.[5] The garrison had about 800 men and was sufficient to defend the fortress. The Czenstochowa

---

[5]Editor: The 5th Regiment was the 1st Garrison Regiment, but in 1807 it was broken into the 1st and 2nd Garrison Battalions. In addition, there were only two uhlan regiments in the Austrian army at this time. This may actually be a chevaulegers squadron.

Fort was a square bastion that was 100 toises (195 meters) on each face. Its armament was complete and its garrison was well supplied with ammunition and supplies. In order to take this fortress it was necessary to dig entrenchments and batter a breach in its walls. It is not surprising in light of this that the fortress's commander refused the summons. Bronowacky blockaded the fort, but was forced to lift it shortly and moved on the 21st via Radomsk and Piotrkow on Warsaw.

The Battle of Razyn

CHAPTER III

Entrance of Ferdinand into Warsaw – His administrative measures – The Polish authorities are retained – Services that they render in the national cause – Negotiation and additional convention for Praga – Its influence on the war – Ferdinand's proclamation – The Polish Army on the Narew – Poniatowski, Dąbrowski, Zajączek, Pelletier, Sokolnicki, and Fiszer – Project Ferdinand to cross to the right bank of the Vistula – He detaches Mohr to Praga, who summons it to surrender – Poniatowski attacks – Battles of Radzymin and Grochow – The Austrians withdraw in disorder to Karezew – Poniatowski returns to the Narew – He organizes the active army and the defense of the duchy – He divides the army among his generals – The Austrians construct a bridgehead at Ostrowek on the Vistula which is not completed – Sokolnicki advances to the attack – Hesitation of Poniatowski – Sokolnicki attacks and takes the entrenchments at Ostrowek – The Austrians lift their bridge – Proclamation of Poniatowski to the troops and Galicians.

Upon the expiration of the delay fixed by the armistice, Ferdinand made his entry into Warsaw at the head of his troops.[1] His army found nothing but a profound sadness and absolute silence. The streets were deserted, the houses closed. The inhabitants, plunged into sadness, did not wish to assist in the triumph of their enemy. This reception did not flatter the Austrians and increased their ill will. They announced themselves as the liberators, hoping to find sympathy in Poland and found nothing but rejection. The inhabitants of Warsaw proved, in this sad circumstance, that they were animated by the purest of patriotism. Previously they had risen against the Muscovites and they had defeated them. Today, obliged to submit momentarily to force, they prepared in silence to draw satisfaction from the unjust aggression of their enemy and to smash the yoke that they sought to put on them.

The Archduke established himself in the royal palace in the evening of the 23rd and, without losing any time, established a government for the capital and for the invaded territories. He named the Count de Saint-Julien as military governor of the duchy, assigning him the counselors Bresani and Baum, to handle the different branches of the administration and confided in Baron Trauttenberg the command of the fortress of Warsaw. The city was given a garrison of 10,000 men and the remainder of the Austrian Army was cantoned around the city. Despite some repugnance at the thought, some Poles in the public administration remained at their jobs, judging it more useful to the Polish cause to work under the direction of the Austrian governor. The prefect Nakwaski remained at his post. Zaluski was maintained at the head of the administration of the hospitals. Wengrzecki remained in his post as president of the city. Finally, Prince Stanislaw Iablonowski, who, from the beginning of the war, had been named lieutenant of the Polish government in the Department of Warsaw, was charged by Poniatowski to serve as an intermediary between the military authority of the Austrians and the Polish Army. These devoted citizens contributed to maintenance of the public spirit. They ran great risks by maintaining secret relations with the commander of the national army. They escaped all surveillance and passed to him exact information on the movements of the Austrian army.[2] The Warsaw

---

[1]The Austrian soldiers had decorated their hats with green sprigs, a particular symbol that they had adopted in the Austrian Army during the course of this war and which was intended to simulate the branches of the laurel.

[2]The previous marshal of the Constitutional Diet, Stanislaw Malachowski, and that of the diet before that, Thomas Ostrowski, also remained in Warsaw. They contributed, by their influence and their council, to support the zeal of the inhabitants of Warsaw and to moderate their boiling enthusiasm, would could have compromised them with the Austrians.

National Guard, commanded by Pierre Lubienski, remained armed and coordinated with the military authorities to maintain order and to suppress any abuse. This was easy, as the Austrian troops were well disciplined. Archduke Ferdinand gave constant proofs of his humanity and sought to temper as much as possible the hardships of war.

When the convention for the evacuation of Warsaw concluded, Praga was not included in the arrangement. This suburb was separated from the city by the Vistula, which, at this point, was 390 toises (760.5 meters) wide. The bridge was broken and the communications with the right bank were broken. The position of Warsaw completely dominated the opposite bank. The Austrians could, from their position, bombard not only the interior of the bridgehead, which was open on the side facing the Vistula, with their artillery. They could also, under the protection of their artillery, force a passage over the river. The Polish garrison of Praga, under the command of Major Hornowski, could not hope to maintain itself under these conditions. And, if the Austrians crossed the river, the entrenchments of this work would work against the Polish as the Austrians worked on repairing the bridge. This situation convinced Poniatowski of the necessity to evacuate Praga, to destroy the works or to make it open to an attack.

To this end Poniatowski designated Colonel Paszkowski, an aide-de-camp to the King of Saxony, to negotiate with the Austrians. The archduke named Colonel Neipperg to represent the Austrians in the subsequent negotiations. Poniatowski proposed a 48-hour suspension of arms during which the Poles would be able to evacuate the bridgehead. The archduke initially seemed to agree with this, but he revised his position and raised difficulties. The negotiations paused and the Austrians lined the Vistula with their artillery, directing it on Praga. Hornowski, in the bridgehead, brought a few howitzers into battery and prepared to respond.

These military preparations scared the inhabitants of the capital. During the morning of the 24th a crowd gathered on the banks of the Vistula. The Austrians could not get them to clear the banks. Paszkowski profited from the crowd of civilians, broke off the negotiations, and, at the moment he left for the Praga the Austrians declared that if arrangements were not concluded in one hour between the Austrian authorities and Hornowski, the Austrian artillery would receive the order to fire on Warsaw and burn it. The news of this declaration spread through the city. The people gathered and threatened the Austrians with a general insurrection if they began firing. The archduke was alarmed by these threats and renewed the negotiations with Hornowski. During the evening a convention was concluded which stipulated that the garrison of Praga would not fire on the capital and the Austrian garrison would not fire on Praga.

This important convention would have a great influence in the upcoming events of the campaign, not only for reasons to be discussed, but because the presence of Polish troops in the suburb so close to Warsaw exercised a great power with the inhabitants of the city while it was occupied by the Austrians. The archduke had published an account of the successes of the Austrian emperor's armies and fired cannons. The commander of Praga, on his side, responded with salvoes of his own artillery and loud noises to celebrate the victories of Napoleon's armies over the Austrians. At the same time he erected large signs to post French and Polish bulletins that, in the obscurity of night, were illuminated and spread the joy of hope. In addition, Hornowski retained clandestine relations with the authorities and the inhabitants of Warsaw and knew exactly what happened in the city.[3]

---

[3]These communications were made by fishers who, in the night, crossed the Vistula in light boats and by Polish soldiers who had convalesced and who rejoined their troops in conformance with the convention of April 21st, and at the same time by divers who swam the Vistula in front of the Austrian authorities.

The efforts of the commandant of Praga did not fail to produce the best effect. The public spirit of Warsaw was constantly sustained and the inhabitants constantly displayed their aversion for the Austrians. The theaters and the gardens were deserted and the women dressed in mourning cloths. As things improved so too did the public spirit. The Polish authorities could only barely restrain the enthusiasm of the public from a premature open insurrection. The disposition of the citizens of Warsaw filled the Austrians with apprehension. The least movement caused them to fear that the insurrection was beginning and brought to their minds memories of the fate of the Russians who were victims of the last uprising. They were finally obliged to remain constantly under arms and they camped in the streets of Warsaw.

At the beginning of his occupation of Warsaw, the Archduke Ferdinand sought to rally the Poles to the cause of Austria. He frequently showed himself in public, holding brilliant reviews and parading his troops in the street. He visited the most notable ladies of the city, showing good will and indulgence to everyone, giving justice to all claimants. After the conclusion of the convention concerning Praga he published a proclamation in which he stated his goodwill to the citizens of Warsaw, saying he knew the strength of his position, but that he wished only to listen to the voice of humanity. On 25 April he addressed a proclamation to the Saxon troops to draw them to his ranks. He stated, "The Royal Saxon Army, having take up arms in opposition to the true interests of their country, and solely to support the ambition of a foreign conqueror…… as a result of the events of the war, I order the formation of a Saxon battalion in Warsaw. He extended his hopes further and sought to engage the Poles under his flags, ordering the formation of a Polish Cossack Regiment. It is hardly surprising that these ordnances and proclamations had no effect.

The Polish Army was withdrawing on the Narew. It occupied Sierock, Zegrze and Modlin. Poniatowski's headquarters were established in Nowydwor, which was near Modlin. The occupation of Warsaw, the retreat of the army to the left bank of the Vistula, the apparent abandonment of the duchy by Napoleon had broken the spirits of the defenders of Polish independence. It was feared that the archduke would not cross the river and would not follow the retrograde movement of the Polish Army. What would the Polish Army do? It could withdraw to the Lithuanian frontier or it could march on Thorn in order to assure its passage over the Oder, abandon the entire duchy, which would them become the possession of the Austrians. The Saxons had already hastened down this road to return to their country. It was wondered if the Poles might not have to soon follow their example. However, their discouragement was not long lived. The confidence of the Polish troops in the genius of Napoleon and his fortune was without bounds and supported their hops. The presence of Prince Józef in the Polish camp contributed strongly to the resurrection of their courage. Józef was held in high regard in the army. He was loved and respected by his soldiers. His chivalrous character, his bravery, his loyalty and his zeal were well known. In addition, several experienced generals served under him.

These generals included Dąbrowski, who at the beginning of his career, had served in the Saxon Army and had acquired considerable military experience. He passed into Polish service and fought in the 1792 campaign and then distinguished himself in the 1794 campaign. He had chased the Prussians from Great Poland and had acquired a powerful reputation among the Prussians. After the third partitioning he showed no pubic despair, left for France in 1796, and was sent by the Republican government to Italy where he formed a Polish legion. He fought with distinction in the 1797, 1799 and 1801 campaigns. When Napoleon went to Posen, Dąbrowski accompanied. He formed another legion there, which then took its place in the ranks of the French Army and took part in both the siege of Danzig and the battle of Friedland. From that point on he remained constantly at the head of his legion and occupied himself in completing its organization and training. At the time of the 1809 campaign he was 54 years old, but he was still capable of the hardest work. Though he had never commanded an army he was one of the most capable divisional generals in the French Army. The citizens and soldiers held him with affection and esteem. His name alone could raise entire provinces. One found in him a citizen who had never despaired of the national cause and a spirit strongly mixed with the courage to resist an enemy's blows.

Zajączek was new to the service. As an aide-de-camp to General Branecky, he was quickly raised to the rank of colonel. He served in two diets, that of 1786 and 1788, and served zealously in his functions. When the republic was invaded by the Russians, Zajączek returned to the army. He fought under the orders of Kosciuszko and distinguished himself with his bravery. He subsequently emigrated, but returned to serve under the dictatorship and the patriots, exposing himself, in order to serve his country, to the vengeance of the Russians. He was arrested by order of the Russian ambassador, who when confronted by Zajączek, was so impressed by the firmness of his responses, that he was put at liberty and expelled from the capital. He served under Kosciuszko in 1794, in the insurrectional army. He commanded a separate corps and rendered good service to the national cause on several occasions. He was among the most ardent of patriots and joined the Jacobin Club. He had the misfortune of being the commander of the Polish forces in Praga during the capture and sack of the fortress. He was wounded and only barely escaped to Warsaw. Because he arrived after the great defeats, he was held responsible. History will say if these accusations are justified. Whatever may be the case, Zajączek paid with his person and should be regarded as the bravest of the brave. He retired to France and entered service under the Republic in 1797, where he was charged with an important command during the Italian campaign that year. Zajączek left the following year for the Egyptian campaign; he was promoted to the rank of général de division and returned to Europe with the French army.[4] He commanded divisions in the Boulogne Camp and was employed actively in the 1805 campaign. In 1806 he organized a legion of Poles at Kalisz, which then operated along the Vistula towards Thorn and Graudenz, then later in old Prussia. If the vicissitudes of his career did not permit him to enjoy in Poland a reputation equal to that of Dąbrowski, he was no less a capable a general because he was personally honored by Napoleon. He should always be regarded as the ideal divisional commander. In his political career he can be reproached for certain instability of principals. It is said that he varied, according to circumstances, from the extremes of a supple courtier, devoted to power, to a rabid Jacobin. However, one cannot dispute his zeal for the cause of his country. In 1809 he was 57 years old. He was tall and had a robust constitution. He was at the height of his physical prowess and capable of great service to his country.

Sokolnicki was, at this time, a général de brigade. He was an engineering officer and served in that capacity in 1792. He left that arm and became a colonel of light infantry. He was taken prisoner in 1794 at the battle of Maciowice and was imprisoned with his companions in the casemates of St. Petersburg. In 1797 he left Russia and went to France where he took service in Dąbrowski's Italian Legion. He then passed to the Legion of the Danube under Kniaziewicz,

---

[4]Editor: Napoleon only took the absolute best of the officers that had served with him in Italy. Many of the senior officers would become marshals. That Zajączek was selected to go to Egypt clearly states that Napoleon held his military skills in the very highest regard.

becoming adjudant-commandant and rose to the rank of chef de brigade in 1800. He returned to Paris where he undertook a study in science. He returned to the military in 1806 as a général de brigade in the new Polish Army.

Sokolnicki was trained and capable. He was extraordinarily active, brave beyond words, had a remarkable spirit when in the presence of danger, and he seemed called to a higher destiny. His character was cold and reserved, generally winning the esteem of those who surrounded him causing some envy. At this time 49 years old. He had developed an ambition to rise to greater things and aspired to a general command.

Fiszer was a général de brigade and chief of staff to the army. He had served in the Polish army since his youth and began his career as an aide-de-camp under Kosciuszko during the 1792 and 1794 campaigns. He was captured and imprisoned with Kosciuszko. He was set free in 1797 and went to France where he found service in the Danube Legion under Knasiewicz, and had the misfortune of being captured by the
Austrians. During the 1800 campaign he returned to his family after a long captivity and in 1806, after the French victory at Jena, accompanied Napoleon into Berlin. He was one of the Polish patriots who encouraged Napoleon to march on Posen and to support an insurrection in Greater Poland. He returned to service in 1808 and was made a général de brigade dating from the time of the definitive organization of the Polish Army. In 1809 he was around 40 years old. He was equally adept working an office as in the field. His character was cold and his spirit was methodical. He was a friend of order and believed in strict subordination. He was best qualified to serve as chief of staff who was responsible for the details of the service.

Pelletier had continual service in France and did not pass into Polish service until early 1 809. He entered into the artillery service at age 16 and served in the Republican campaigns of 1792, 1793, 1800, and 1801, and under the Empire he fought in the 1805, 1806 and 1807 campaigns. Filled with merit and highly trained, he had risen to the rank of colonel by the age of 30. He had the particular confidence of Napoleon and in 1808 was sent into the duchy to serve as its commander of artillery. Pelletier was 32 at the time of the 1809 campaign. He had a calm courage in the middle of the greatest perils, a hard worker in the office, his council was farsighted, he was destined to play a major role in this campaign, and his being French increased his influence. This was because, on one side he could act as an intermediary between Napoleon and the commander of the Polish Army, and on the other, he could act as an honest conciliator between the Polish generals, whose rivalries could produce a dangerous division.

Such were the influential men who were principally called to second Poniatowski in the difficult struggle he was to undertake. After these men cane a second line of generals and many superior officers who commanded the various corps, who had acquired in previous wars the practical and theoretical knowledge that allowed them capable of directing their commands.

Poniatowski occupied himself with reorganizing his army. The ranks of the battalions and squadrons were filled out with new recruits from the depots. One company of foot artillery, detached from the garrison of a fortress, also joined the army. The army was organized as follows:

INFANTRY

1st Regiment	2 battalions
2nd Regiment	2 battalions
3rd Regiment	2 battalions
6th Regiment	3 battalions[5]
8th Regiment	2 battalions
12th Regiment	2 battalions
Total	13 Battalions

CAVALRY

1st Regiment (chasseurs)	3 squadrons
2nd Regiment (uhlans)	3 squadrons
3rd Regiment (uhlans)	3 squadrons
5th Regiment (chasseurs)	3 squadrons
6th Regiment (uhlans)	3 squadrons
Total	15 Squadrons

ARTILLERY

4 Foot companies, each with 6 guns	8 guns
2 Horse companies, each with 4 guns	32 guns
Total	24 guns

Including the engineering train and ambulances, each battalion had an average strength of 800 men and each squadron 200 men.

The total infantry came to 10,400 men and the total cavalry came to 3,750, which adding a further 1,000 specialized troops and train, brought the total of the reorganized Polish army to 15,150 men. If one reduces this by 1,150 non-combatants, that leaves an effective force under arms of 14,000 men.[6]

Poniatowski and the government occupied themselves with the new levy. The Departments of Plock and Lomza each furnished 300 horses and the District of Ostrolenka was to provide a battalion of light infantry drawn from the population of the region known as Kurpie, which were employed as huntsmen. Poniatowski sent General Niemoiewski to Lomza and General Hauck to Plock to organize these new conscripts.

Ferdinand continued to look to making himself master of the Praga bridgehead, which would facilitate his passage over the Vistula. Since the convention regarding Praga had been signed, this operation had become far more difficult. The Austrian artillery could not support an attack from the Warsaw side. Ferdinand developed a plan to take Praga by sending his advanced guard, under General Mohr, to the far bank. On the 24th the advanced crossed the Vistula on a bridge of boats near Karczew and moved towards Praga. Mohr was joined by the two squadrons of hussars that were in Okuniew and joined them to the rest of his command – 5 battalions of infantry and 8 squadrons of cavalry - a total of about 6,000 men. With this small

---

[5]The 6th Infantry Regiment had suffered little in the battle of Raszyn and had received 800 new recruits.
[6]Poniatowski's troops passed under the command of Marshal Bernadotte, commander of the IX Corps of the Grande Armée, but it submitted its reports directly to the Prince of Neufchâtel (Berthier).

force Mohr had two tasks: to observe Poniatowski's army and to take Praga. He detached on his right, towards Radzymin, two battalions (Wallachian Grenz) and two squadrons of hussars, which occupied that village, while he advanced with the rest of his troops on Praga. He arrived on the 25th before the bridgehead and summoned Hornowski to capitulate. The Polish commander rejected his summons and Mohr began his blockade of the bridgehead. Seeking to take the bridgehead the following day, he occupied the Szmulowszczyzna heights with one battalion and six guns, while at the head of two battalions and six cannons he encamped near Grochow. His cavalry formed a chain around the entrenchments and invested the entire position. In this position the Austrian general was separated from the main body of the archduke's army and did not have a bridge over which to assure his retreat.

Poniatowski, informed of Mohr's offensive movement, resolved to attack him. Nonetheless, not knowing the size of the force that Mohr commanded, he advanced with circumspect.

Poniatowski made issued his orders. During the night of the 25th the troops destined to attack Mohr were ordered forward in three columns; the first under General Sokolnicki, consisted of the 12th Infantry Regiment, the 2nd Cavalry Regiment, and two horse guns. It moved from Modlin via Iablonna on Grochow. The second column, under General Kaminski, consisted of the 1st Chasseur Regiment and two squadrons of the 3rd Uhlan Regiment. It was ordered to move from Zegrze, via Nieporent, directly against Okuniew. The third column, under Colonel Sierawski, consisted of a battalion of the 6th Infantry Regiment and a squadron of the 3rd Uhlans, supported by two horse guns. It was to move from Sierock on Radzymin. General Dąbrowski, who marched at the head of the 5th Chasseur Regiment and the 6th Uhlans, followed this column. These three columns advanced in silence, seeking to avoid the Austrian patrols, so they could surprise the Austrians, while Prince Poniatowski, at the head of his army, occupied Nieporent and Iablona. At the same time, Major Krukowiecki, profiting from the night, was to cross the Vistula near Modlin, at the head of a company of the 3rd Infantry Regiment, to distract the attention of the Austrian forces on that bank.

These dispositions were successful. Sierawski's column arrived before Radzymin around midnight. Situated in a glade, this village was surrounded on three sides by forests at a distance of around 1,000 toises (1,950 meters). Sierawski took a position on the edge of the woods, on the road to Sierock, directing a company of grenadiers on Radzymin in order to observe the Austrian position. After having executed its mission and exchanging a few shots with the Austrian pickets, the captain who led this company, rejoined Sierawski. The instructions he had been given were to leave the road from Radzymin to Grochow open so that if the Austrians withdrew in this direction they would fall into an ambush by General Sokolnicki, who would attack them at the same moment from Grochow. However, Sierawski found himself having to cover about 4 miles before he would arrive in the presence of Mohr. He could not attack before daybreak. Sierawski judged it appropriate not to begin his operations until the morning of the 26th. Around 6:00 a.m., Sokolnicki's cannons began firing. The engagement started Sierawski directed Captain Rybinski, at the head of his company, to penetrate into the Radzymin while Captain Woiakowski lead two other companies forward on the right, penetrating it from the east. He then led forward the remainder of his forces and took a position on the road to Grochow in order support the attack of the two detachments.

Rybinski and Woiakowski executed their instructions with precision, forcing entry in to Radzymin and penetrated into it. The Austrians, seeing themselves threatened on two sides, hastened to evacuate from the village via the road to Okuniew. Some detachments of their infantry could not follow the main columns and threw themselves into the houses and farms of Radzymin. Rybinski's company overwhelmed them and forced them to surrender. The squadron of the 3rd Cavalry Regiment launched its pursuit of the retreating Austrians. The Austrians had been stopped by a copse of woods. Their infantry stood in two columns covered by two squadrons of hussars. The Polish cavalry deployed, charged them, and drove some of them in disorder into Radzymin, and penetrated into the village behind them. Captain Rybinski, who had pulled his company back together, received the Austrians with a steady fire and drove back their leading elements on the main body. Sierawski then moved at the head of his reserve and took up a position on the road to Okuniew. He placed his two horse guns into battery and directed their fire on the Austrian infantry that was withdrawing on Okuniew. The Austrians lost 200 men hors de combat and 130 prisoners. The Poles lost around 50 men killed and wounded. Dąbrowski rejoined Sierawski at 11:00 p.m., after the engagement was over.

On his side, General Sokolnicki had marched all night. After a stop of an hour at Iablonna, he detached Lieutenant Colonel Fredro, of the 2nd Cavalry, with his squadron and a company of voltigeurs from the 12th Infantry Regiment through the woods to cut the road to Grochow to Milosna, the road down which they believed Mohr would withdraw. The goal of this movement was to threaten their rear while they attacked him frontally. At daybreak on the 26th Sokolnicki presented himself before Praga, leading his troops who were fatigued by a night march, and launched his attack without hesitation on the Austrian battalion positioned at Szmulowszczyzna. He threw them back and forced them to withdraw on Mohr's position. Mohr had deployed his troops behind Grochow on a series of sandy hills, supporting his right on a woods and his left on a swamp that extended to the Vistula. Grochow was occupied by a detachment of infantry, four cannon stood before the village, and four more stood further to the right. Sokolnicki had broken the blockade of Praga and established communications with Hornowski, who sent him a company of voltigeurs. His forces, around 2,000 men supported by two cannon, faced Mohr who commanded around 4,000 men and twelve cannon. However, Sokolnicki anticipated the arrival of Fredro and resolved to march on the Austrians. After having allowed his troops a short respite, he lead them on Grochow and deployed them to the right of the main road, his artillery forward, and his two squadrons of cavalry echeloned to the left. From the first cannon shot, the entire population Warsaw was extremely agitated. They moved in great crowds to the banks of the Vistula, praying for the efforts of the national army. The Austrian garrison was under arms and the Archduke Ferdinand, watching the engagement from the windows of the palace, anxiously watched the battle that would decide the fate of Mohr's detachment that he had so imprudently sent across the Vistula. He could send Mohr no support. Sokolnicki's forces, watching the movements on the far bank, redoubled their efforts. The Polish infantry advanced with fixed bayonets while their cavalry charged Mohr's cavalry, taking the cannon placed before Grochow. However, before they could carry their prizes away, the Austrian infantry counterattacked and recaptured the guns.

This attack was so impetuous that the Austrians were forced to withdraw from the village of Grzybow and fall back on Grochow. Sokolnicki followed them. The two cavalry forces charged repeatedly with no conclusive result. If Fredro arrived in time, the destruction of the Austrians would have been complete, but Fredro, obliged to move over bad roads, cross a terrible swamp, was unable to arrive before nightfall. His appearance, however, still obliged the Austrians to hasten their retreat. Their infantry dispersed into the woods and if Sokolnicki had forces capable of pursuing them he should have taken a great number of prisoners. The Austrian losses were 100 dead and several hundred wounded. They left 116 prisoners in the hands of the Poles. Sokolnicki's losses were substantially less.

General Kaminski, who had marched from Nieporent on Okuniew, collected about 100 prisoners. On his side, Major Krukowiecki had crossed the Vistula and pushed as far as Lomazy during the night of the 26th. He had spread alarm in the city of Warsaw. During the following night he withdrew to Modlin without suffering any losses.

Prince Poniatowski should have profited from this success to throw Mohr into the Vistula and crush those troops that resisted him. However, Poniatowski was unaware of the true state of things. He had no reason to believe that Mohr had crossed the Vistula without any support and that he had not assured his passage back over the Vistula. As a result, he did not advance, but instead stopped his pursuit and withdrew on Narew, where he united his forces before Sierock, leaving only an advanced guard, under Sokolnicki, at Radzymin and Nieporent. The headquarters were established Zegrze. This retrograde movement was inopportune. Poniatowski should have focused his efforts on preventing the Austrians from establishing themselves on the right bank of the Vistula. Since he had determined not to advance his force, he should have at least, established himself with his entire force before Praga in order to observe the course of the Vistula from Modlin to its confluence with the Zwider, where one could suppose the Austrians might attempt to cross the Vistula, and then held himself to follow Mohr if he should undertake some enterprise, or to move back on the Narew if circumstances required it. Poniatowski should have been less concerned about-facing the enemy now that he found himself at the head of 14,000 men and Ferdinand's army was reduced by its obligation to garrison Warsaw if it should advance into the field.

Mohr, when he found he was not being pursued, rallied his forces at Karczew where he gathered a number of boats. From this position he found himself able to cross the Vistula if it became necessary as well as to cover the works at the Gora bridgehead, which the Austrians were beginning to construct in order to cover the construction of a bridge over the Vistula.

If the operations about to be discussed give rise to some criticism of Poniatowski's actions, the actions of Ferdinand are infinitely more flawed. The first may have been too prudent in his moves, while the second was positively timid. The archduke commanded, at this time, around 30,000 troops, including Brenowasky's corps. Ten thousand formed the garrison of Warsaw and were sufficient to assure its control. This left him 20,000 to act against Poniatowski on the right bank of the Vistula. It is true that the Vistula was a serious obstacle, but between the confluence of the Piliça to Bielany, the right bank, which the archduke occupied, dominated the left. However, even with his artillery superiority, he could not cross in the face of Poniatowski's army, unless he deployed his entire army. To push a single division across the river without the rest of his army behind it to support it and without communications via a bridge would have been incredibly dangerous and culpable.

Upon his arrival at Zegrze, Prince Poniatowski occupied himself with taking those measures necessary for the defense of the country, and divided his command among the generals under his command. Despite the merits of Dąbrowski and Zajączek, their presence in the same army was more disadvantageous than advantageous. An old rivalry existed not only between these two, but also between them and the Prince. The division of the army of the duchy into legions had communicated these sentiments to the soldiers and it was feared that disorders would result. Already, in the bivouacs and camps the vestiges of the various legions had begun disorders and the exchange of insults. In the council, Zajączek and Dąbrowski tended to announce diametrically opposed opinions. After the evacuation of Warsaw the former advocated a withdrawal on Thorn and the second advocated a march into Galicia. The two rivals, it is true, gave to the Prince all exterior marks of difference required by the obligations of military service, but each secretly believed he was superior in his capacity and his experience. Each of them chaffed under authority or another's advice, and thought it better exercised by themselves. The prince resolved to give each of these generals an independent command with only généraux de brigade[7] Dąbrowski was charged with moving on Posen and there organizing the levies of Great Poland[8], taking with him only 200 cavaliers drawn from the depots and a detachment of infantry from the garrison of Thorn, supported by a few gunners who were to serve as cadres for the newly forming units. Beyond the personal influence that the general had in a province where he had long commanded, he hoped to find some propitious elements for his enterprise. He counted on the military talents of General Konsinski, on the zeal of his own son, Michel Dąbrowski, and on the patriotism of the well known Generals Wybicki and Biernacki, founded on the power of the government in the departments of Posen and Kalisz. Greater Poland was stripped of line troops, but if they could reach the depots of the legions of Dąbrowski and Zajączek, and the National Guards of the cities of the country were partly organized, they could organize a respectable force.

Poniatowski gave General Zajączek command of the reserves on the right bank of the Vistula, including the garrisons of Modlin, Sierock, and Praga to form the cadre of his new army. The 3rd Battalions of the 1st, 2nd, 3rd, and 8th Regiments were assigned to him, as were the cadres of the cavalry depots that were cantoned in the region. The patriotism of the departments of Plock and Lomza, activated by the presence of the government of the duchy, assured Zajączek of a prompt expansion of his forces. Zajączek had under his command several généraux de brigade. His principal commanders were Général de brigade Hauck, who was charged with command of the right bank of the Vistula from Wyszogrod to Wroclawek, and who established his headquarters at Plock; Général de brigade Piotrowski was governor of Modlin and commanded from Wyszogrod to Praga; Général de brigade Isidore Krasinski was governor of Sierock; and Major Hornowski who commanded at Praga. Later Général de brigade Niemoiowski, who was at that time employed in the Department of Lomza, assumed command from Praga to Mnissow. These dispositions being made, Prince Poniatowski found himself at the head of an active army of around 14,000 men, conducted by capable officers and talented généraux de brigade that he could trust. General Fiszer, Poniatowski's chief of staff, had been wounded at Raszyn and was provisionally replaced by Colonel Rautenstrauch, who had directed the work of the chancellery while General of Artillery Pelletier replaced Fiszer in the prince's councils. Colonel Paszkowski, aide-de-camp to the King of Saxony, who we saw charged with a mission to Archduke Ferdinand for the Praga Convention, and who had served well, was also assigned to the staff.

The archduke, despite the check that Mohr had sustained, was impatient to cross to the right bank and pursue operations. He hastened the construction of the bridgehead at Gora (near Ostrowek) and pressed the construction of the bridge. The Baillet-Latour Regiment was placed in the entrenchments with three cannons. Lacking boats, Ferdinand moved up the Vistula and gathered them. He had the necessary wood cut in the Wilanow Forest, but the Poles charged with the work delayed it as much as possible, transmitting to Poniatowski that they

---

[7]Editor: *Généraux de brigade* is the plural form of général de brigade and was the individual who commanded a brigade.

[8]It was General Pelletier who was charged by the prince with making this proposal

were obliged to do the work.[9]

The 28th passed quietly. On the 29th General Sokolnicki, who commanded the advanced guard of the prince, consisting of the 12th Infantry Regiment and two horse guns, moved forward and occupied Okuniew. General Rozniecki, commanding the 2nd and 4th Infantry Regiments and four horse guns, supported it in its movement. The Austrians withdrew on Karszew and broke the bridges at Swider. They placed their advanced posts along the swampy stream that ran there. On May 1st General Sokolnicki crossed the Zwider, chased the Austrians before him, and moved on Karczew. Mohr evacuated that city and withdrew, part to the right bank of the Vistula and part on the bridgehead at Gora. Poniatowski's headquarters and the main body of his corps then moved on Okuniew. Zajączek and Dąbrowski accompanied the prince, wishing to take part in the operations of the active army before taking their respective posts. On May 2nd Dąbrowski offered his services and was ordered to move on Karczew at the head of the 6th Infantry Regiment and the 6th Cavalry Regiment. General Sokolnicki marched on Dziecinow, a village that stood before the bridgehead at Gora. He arrived there at 7:30 p.m. General Roaniecki established himself in Osick on May 1st. He had with him the 5th Cavalry Regiment and four cannon. The 2nd Cavalry Regiment, which was part of his brigade, was in Wionzowna. During the morning of the same day, the 5th Cavalry Regiment observed the bridgehead from Ostrowek. One of its detachments captured a convoy of boats coming down the Vistula. Colonel Turno, who commanded the regiment, observed the entrenchments with care. He convinced himself that they lacked the boats necessary to construct a bridge that would stretch across the Vistula and that only a single Austrian regiment, supported by three cannon occupied the bridgehead, which was no longer protected with a palisade. He sent a detailed message to General Sokolnicki during his march on Dziecinow. The general then forwarded it to Poniatowski, adding that he was determined to take by force the Austrian entrenchments. However, Poniatowski was deceived by false information which was sent to him via Warsaw and responded to Sokolnicki that he had received positive word that 12,000 Austrian troops were already on the right bank of the Vistula and that he was not to engage them. However, fearing the disunity that existed between Sokolnicki and Rozniecki,[10] he sent General Pelletier to Dziecinow with authority to act as the circumstances merited. He ordered the 6th Infantry Regiment and two howitzers manned by horse gunners to join Sokolnicki, sending them from Okuniew where he had established his headquarters during the evening of the 2nd. However, the two guns did not arrive at their destination until daybreak on the 3rd.

General Sokolnicki also had at Dziecinow the 6th Infantry Regiment (3 battalions), the 12th Infantry Regiment, the 5th Cavalry Regiment, and six cannons. Upon his arrival he reviewed the Austrian position and realized that Turno's report was correct. The Austrians, however, were working diligently to complete the bridge, which further augmented his impatience to seize the bridgehead. General Pelletier joined him that evening and the two decided that they should attack immediately. As their troops prepared for the assault, they wished to summon the commander. Pelletier prepared a letter, which said, "General Sokolnicki has received orders to occupy all positions on the right bank of the Vistula. The Austrian garrison has one hour to evacuate the bridgehead. If the commander fails to do so, the results shall be on his head."

[9]The Prefect of Warsaw, Nakwaski, furnished the archduke with a civil engineer, who had secret orders to retard the work.

[10]Poniatowski frequently stated that he had to stop Sokolnicki and to push Rozniecki.

The letter was carried by Captain Siemiontkowski, of the 5th Cavalry Regiment, to the bridgehead and he was also charged with verifying the conditions of the entrenchments. The Austrian commander, Czerwinka, commander of the Latour-Baillet Regiment, retained the parliamentary for a long time. After eleven hours when he had not returned, Sokolnicki was at the point of sending a second, when he finally arrived carrying the Austrian rejection. He responded saying, that "he knew well to defend the post which was confided in him." Siemiontkowski gave Sokolnicki positive assurances that the bridge was not yet complete. He had been closely watched by the Austrians, so he had been unable to verify this himself, but he had heard Czerwinka request a boat to carry an officer to the far bank get orders from General Schauroth who was at Gora. Siemiontkowski had only spoken French and pretended not to understand German. The Austrians were taken in and had openly given the aforementioned order in his presence.

Generals Sokolnicki and Pelletier, after ordering their troops to prepare, mounted their horses and put themselves at their head. Sokolnicki made the following dispositions: The 6th Infantry Regiment, with three battalions, charged with attacking and carrying the bridgehead. The regiment was divided into three columns, each of a battalion. The first was commanded by Chef de Bataillon Boguslawski, and advanced down the Vistula, moving up the river. The second column had Lieutenant Colonel Suchodolski at its head and moved down the Vistula. The third column, under the orders of Chef de Bataillon Blumer and had with him all the regiment's drummers. Blumer had deployed his battalion in skirmish formation and sent them forward in a charge with battle cries in order to draw the attention of the Austrians to them. As soon as the lateral columns began their attach he was to rally his forces and push over the front of the entrenchments. The 12th Infantry Regiment and the artillery were held in reserve. The 5th Chasseur a Cheval Regiment was broken into detachments and spread in a great semi-circle around the bridgehead in order to cut down any escapees.

At 1:00 a.m., the silence of the night was broken by the sound of carpenters working on the bridge. The attack columns closed on the entrenchments to within the distance of a musket shot without being discovered.[11] When the first shots were fired by the garrison the columns of Boguslawski and Suchodolski charged forward and broke into the entrenchments with bayonets fixed before the Austrians could present any serious resistance. Blumer's column, directed by Sierawski, commander of the 6th Infantry Regiment, engaged in a lively fusillade and had attracted the entire attention of the Austrian musketry and artillery fire. They rallied promptly, as ordered, and in their turn drove over the parapets of the entrenchments. Boguslawski's battalion was the first into the interior of the entrenchments, which was soon invaded on all sides. A company of the 12th Infantry Regiment also participated in the attack. The Austrian garrison had been unable to retreat and rallied around the barracks of their encampment and prepared a vigorous resistance. The garrison consisted of Belgians and French émigrés who had served for many years in the Austrian army. They defended themselves bravely during a man-to-man struggle that lasted a half hour. However, finally the Latour-Baillet Regiment surrendered and threw down its arms. All the survivors were taken prisoner: 38 officers, including the regimental colonel, and 1,800 non-commissioned officers and soldiers. Three cannons were also taken. One detachment of Austrians, which sought to escape, was surrounded by a platoon of the 5th Chasseurs. The regimental standard bearer threw himself into the Vistula while a non-commissioned officer followed him with the regimental flag. Another detachment attempted to escape

---

[11]Editor: A musket was considered to have an effective range of 300 feet.

in a boat, but when it was exposed to the fire of the Polish infantry it surrendered. The battle ended at daybreak. The prisoners were brought together and sent under escort to Karczew. A large number of wounded covered the ground. In the light of day the Austrians were able to see from the far bank and opened fire with 14 cannon. The position at Gora dominated the bridgehead and the shot and cannister swept the bridgehead. The Polish infantry moved into the ditches and only a few men were hurt in the cannonade, which lasted all day. The Polish medical officers distinguished themselves during the day by their intrepidity under enemy fire. The Austrians had 500 men hors de combat in this engagement and the Polish losses came to about a 300 killed or wounded. Chef de Bataillon Suchodolski was wounded. These losses were considerable. The first two battalions of the 6th Regiment were rebuilt using men from the third, which was then sent to Sierock as a cadre to receive new replacements.

Prince Poniatowski moved the Dziecinow on the morning of the 3rd. During his trip he encountered Austrian prisoners escorted by a detachment of the 6th Infantry Regiment, which was taking them to the headquarters. He spoke with some of the Austrian officers and gave them a sum of money, asking to accept it from an old comrade.[12] These prisoners were then evacuated to Praga.

The bridge over the Vistula lacked only a few boats to be completed and Poniatowski greatly feared that during the 3rd they would attempt an attack over the river, supported by their numerous artillery. General Sokolnicki gave an order to Captain Soltyk, who had brought with him two howitzers, to select a position in the faces of one of the bastions of the bridgehead where he could fire on the bridge unobserved by the Austrians and burn it. However, the Austrians removed the bridge during the night of the 3rd/4th, as Soltyk prepared to obey his orders.

The brilliant victory caused Poniatowski to issue the following proclamation:

Soldiers!

The 3rd of May, dear to the hearts of the Poles as a solemn memory, has not ceased to be propitious for us. In the two years that have passed since the consecration of your eagles you have already prove you deserve this distinction. Today, at 2:00 a.m., the advanced guard commanded by General Sokolnicki carried with bayonets, and without firing a single shot, the Gora bridgehead, forcing it to surrender. Eighteen hundred soldiers, 38 officers, among whom was a colonel, were taken prisoner. We are masters of the all the left bank of the Vistula. Soldiers! I have not made a practice of flattering you, but your have shown that you are the equal of the greatest armies. You merit the recognition of your country and the most glorious recompense – the satisfaction of the great Napoleon!

The capture of the bridgehead at Ostrowek made Poniatowski master of the entire left bank of the Vistula. His cavalry detachments pushed as far as Wieprz. The regions of Stanislawow, Biala, and Siedlce were occupied by his troops. He established his headquarters at Wionnzowa on April 4th and addressed the inhabitants of the countryside with the following proclamation:

---

[12]Poniatowski had served in the Austrian army early in his military career.

Poles!

*Your compatriots find themselves on your territory. It is as the defenders of their national exis-
tence that they have opened the road. You will receive them, without doubt, as brothers; and our
hearts, animated more than ever by the same sentiments, bring them nearer and understand them.
Long separated by the disasters suffered by our common country, the glory and honor the Polish
name shall bring us together. It would be painful for us to treat you as enemies, because destiny
has been less favorable to you than to us.*

This proclamation, which was written in light of the existing circumstances, produced
an excellent effect among the Galicians. They provided Poniatowski's army with everything it
needed and flocked to it, to enter the ranks of their liberators.

The same day Poniatowski sent a report to Berthier telling Napoleon of his military successes and asking for instructions vis-à-vis the Galicians. "Their sentiments are known, he wrote,
but it is not possible to use them without giving them positive assurances of a reunion to their
homeland as the price of their efforts.[13]

---

[13]See appendices.

The Battle of Razyn

CHAPTER IV

The Polish Army learns of Napoleon's victory at Rattisbonne – Events in Germany and Italy – Colonel Stoffet brings Poniatowski orders to enter Galicia – Letter from Poniatowski to the Prince de Neufchâtel; he reports on the operations of the army and his plans – Ferdinand's plans. He decides to send a division against Thorn and Greater Poland – Poniatowski arrives at Thorn and the garrison sends a detachment into Greater Poland – Battle of Sissy (11 May) – The archduke arrives with Mohr's division at the Thorn bridgehead, which he takes on 15 May - He summons the fortress to surrender – Woyczynski's response – Ferdinand's bombardment of Thorn produces no effect – He learns of Poniatowski's progress in Galicia and returns to Warsaw – Mohr marches on Radziewo – Poniatowski crosses the Wieprz – Poniatowski arrives at Lubartow on 11 May and receives a deputation of the Galician nobility – A letter from Gotschakov to Ferdinand is intercepted – Poniatowski sends Bronikowski to the emperor – Poniatowski enters Lublin on 14 May and establishes a government for Galicia – Proclamation to the army – Capture of Sandomierz and its bridgehead.

On the eve of the attack on the entrenchments at Ostrowek, the Polish army learned of Napoleon's victories near Rattisbonne; word of which Colonel Stofflet had carried from Napoleon's headquarters on 24 April to Poniatowski. These singular successes were greeted with great enthusiasm by the Polish soldiers and inspired them to imitate the great acts of their brothers-in-arms.

We are uniquely imposed to attempt to describe in a detailed manner the operations of the Polish troops during this campaign, which includes those of the Poles serving with the Grande Armée. As a result we will give a summery, which we believe indispensable to give our readers a general history of the war.

On April 8th the Austrians had begun hostilities simultaneously in Bavaria, the Tyrol, and in Italy. Everywhere they obtained marked advantages. The Archduke Charles, who commanded the Army of Germany, advanced to the Isar, pushing before him the French Army, then under the command of Marshal Berthier. However, the arrival of Napoleon at Donauworth (17 April) changed the face of affairs. Napoleon immediately assumed the offensive, sending his forces against the decisive points and from 19th to 23rd April successively defeated, on different battlefields, the corps with which the archduke opposed him. He carried Ratisbonne, which had been occupied by the Austrians. He forced the Archduke Charles to withdraw into Bohemia and abandoned the road to Vienna, on which Napoleon did not fail to advance.

In the Tyrol the entire population rose in revolt and massacred the occupying troops. The Austrian General Chasteler moved to support the operations of the insurgents, who soon rendered themselves masters of the entire country. However, Marshal Lefebvre hastily arrived and returned the Tyrol to Bavarian domination.

In Italy the Archduke John had defeated Prince Eugène de Beauharnais at Sassile, and had advanced as far as the Adige. Eugène, reinforced by two divisions, and stimulated by the news of Napoleon's victories, resumed the offensive and drove the archduke's army back into the Alps.

Some limited revolts had occurred elsewhere during the course of April, in Westphalia. Kat and Dornberg lead them, but King Jérôme soon crushed these troubles. At the end of the same month, the Prussian Major Schill left Berlin at the head of 500 hussars. He set out (without the authorization of his government) and advanced into Saxony, calling on the people of northern Germany to arise, but they responded only weakly to his call. Schill did succeed in organizing a force of 5,000 men under his orders, but he was contained by Westphalian and Dutch troops which marched against him and did not cease to harass him.

Stofflet arrived on 5 May at Wionzowa, where he found Poniatowski's headquarters. He carried with him an order from Napoleon, which concluded, "In view of the distance that separated the emperor from the Polish Army, His Majesty has learned of the zeal of the Prince and what he has done for the common interest; but the emperor's army marches on Vienna and the prince should march on Galicia." This order had been foreseen. All the country between the Bug and Wiepbrz was already occupied by Polish troops, which, as we have seen, had gained several advantages. The prince sent a report to the Berthier and informed him that the Austrians had already lost 6,000 men, including 2,800 prisoners, that the army of the Archduke had taken a position between Warsaw and the junction of the Piliça, and pushed its advanced posts as far as Kalisz and Pock. He went on to say that when he had formed the new levies and the garrisons of the fortresses of Praga, Sierock, Modlin, and Thorn, he intended to move his forces on Wieprz, cross that river, and advance as far as San. Poniatowski added that he thought that Archduke Ferdinand, weakened by the occupation of Warsaw, would not undertake anything decisive, and indeed, that he would seek to move to Sandomierz. Poniatowski said he would move to either the San or Wieprz where he would Ferdinand as he attempted to cross one of these two rivers, or that he might cross the Vistula at Modlin and attempt to reach Teschen in Silesia where he could operate in conjunction with the Grande Armée. If, in contrast, the Austrians sought to abandon the duchy, moving into either Bohemia or Moravia, Poniatowski would advance down the right bank of the Vistula, using the high road from Leopol to Krakow, in order to follow their movement. Poniatowski asked Berthier's advice regarding what he should do in this event and ended by expressing his concern over the ill-will of the Russians, who, if they might declare war on France and attack the Poles, he would have no option other than to withdraw to Danzig, after having thrown garrisons into the various fortresses in the duchy.

Upon seeing the fruitlessness of his efforts to cross the Vistula, Ferdinand, still finding himself at the head of 27,000 troops, looked to extend his conquests in the departments of the right bank of the Vistula, which were now entirely stripped of troops. Separated from Poniatowski's army by the Vistula he calculated that the Poles, who had no fortified position on the left bank between Wieprz to Thorn, they were incapable of attacking that bank or of retaking Warsaw. Judging that his forces were sufficient to occupy the capital and observing that Poniatowski had invaded Greater Poland, he decided to march on Thorn with a force of 6,000 men. He looked to take the fortress or at least to capture its bridgehead, and thus cut the sole passage that Poniatowski had with the fortresses on the Oder. This operation was not only militarily important, but also politically. It could, if successful cause Prussia and northern Germany to embrace the cause of Austria. Ferdinand knew that there were secret negotiations between his government and King Frederick Wilhelm of Prussia, who was at that time in Königsberg and that preparations were underway at many points in Germany for an insurrection that von Schill's actions were to be the signal. He believed that these events would decide the outcome of the war and appeared to believe that Poniatowski's actions would have no influence on the course of the war. He left Galicia without a defense and abandoned it to the Poles. The garrisons of Zamosc and Sandomierz, as well as those of Leopol and Iaroslaw were not certain of stopping the Polish advance into the province. The Austrian magazines and the depots were undefended. The many small detachments of recruits enroute to join the Austrian army could be easily captured. Finally, as the Galicians were disposed to joining their brothers in the Grand

Duchy of Warsaw in the struggle against their common enemy, a general insurrection was probable. However, Ferdinand closed his eyes to these dangers and only saw the opportunity of conquests in the west.

A force of Austrian cavalry took Piotrkow on 26 April and pushed detachments as far as Kalisz. Some Prussian volunteers, disguised as Austrian soldiers, had come from Silesia to join them.[1] Another Austrian detachment pushed to Klodawa on the 28th, gaining the highroad to Posen. Mohr followed these detachments at the beginning of May and advanced down the left bank of the Vistula on Thorn, sending a few troops along the river and down the highroad to Posen.

General Dąbrowski left Poniatowski's army the day after the capture of the bridgehead at Ostrowek and had gone to Thorn. When he arrived at that place he set about concerting with General Woyczynski the upcoming operations. The garrison of Thorn was to furnish him with a detachment of infantry and artillery, which when joined with the cavalry given him by Poniatowski, would serve as the cadre for his formations. However, impatient to begin his mission, he had not waited for his troops and moved to Posen, evading the Austrian forces that had spread across the country. He arrived at Posen on May 10th and without losing time, immediately occupied himself with drawing together the new levies and organizing his new corps. The Wybicki, the lieutenant of the government in the Department of Posen, powerfully seconded him. As a result of the arrangements made by Dąbrowski and Woyczinski, the first detachment of troops, under the command of Colonel Cedrowski, departed for Posen on May 10th. It consisted of 160 line infantry, 40 light infantry, and 70 cavalry troopers. On 11 May, Cedrowski and his force encountered, near Szlesin, Austrian Major Gartenburg at the head of four squadrons of hussars and found his route blocked. Colonel Cedrowski, seeing only their advanced guard, ordered Captain Suminski to charge and he and his 70 troopers threw back the leading Austrians. However, the three other Austrian squadrons arrived to the support of the first and drove back Suminski's cavalry at sword point. Fearing he would be enveloped, Suminski fell back on the infantry, which was advantageously posted and received the Austrians with a well-maintained fire that stopped them. The Austrians vainly renewed their attacks several times, but were always driven back with heavy losses, falling back on Wilatowo, leaving 80 dead on the battlefield. They were as many wounded, including Major Gartenberg and two of his officers. The Polish had four dead and 16 wounded. The brave Captain Suminski was among the wounded. After this engagement, Colonel Cetrowski continued his march on Posen and joined Dąbrowski safely.

Meanwhile General Mohr advanced on Thorn Klodawa and Kutnon were already occupied by the Austrians. Kowel, Bombin and Brzesc in Kujavie were occupied shortly later. The Austrian advanced posts appeared before the bridgehead at Thorn during the evening of 14 May. The archduke departed Warsaw on the 12th and joined Mohr's division, personally directing the operation.

The garrison of Thorn had been reinforced by two battalions coming from Danzig and was composed as follows:

---

[1]See appendices.

3/10th Infantry Regiment	1,130 men
3/11th Infantry Regiment	949
3/12th Infantry Regiment	1,455
1 foot artillery company	114
Total	3,621

In addition, there was a small detachment of cavalry.

The Thorn fortifications were, as we had said earlier, open to a coup de main and the archduke could not hope to take it without beginning a formal siege. However, the entrenchments at the bridgehead were not in a condition to resist a sudden attack. Colonel Mielzinski, who occupied it with a battalion of his regiment and six canon, about 1,000 men, was ordered to withdraw from the bridgehead and to withdraw into the fortress if he was seriously attacked. He had communications with the left bank by boats, formed in two groups. The first was on the left bank via an island defended by an entrenchment armed with several guns. The second was on an island by the fortress.

During the night of the 14th/15th the Archduke Ferdinand prepared his assault without the Poles being aware he was present. At 4:00 a.m., on the 15th, Colonel Mielczinski spotted the Austrian infantry advancing in columns and thought they were troops coming from Bromberg. The Austrians deployed their skirmishers and their columns stopped some distance away. A lively fusillade began that lasted until 6:00 a.m. The observed the Polish response and ordered an assault. His infantry advanced in columns, by battalions, against the entrenchments. The movement was executed rapidly with artillery firing in support. The Poles were only able to weakly respond to the Austrian artillery because they had few guns. The bridgehead was taken at bayonet point, despite the strong Polish resistance, and Mielczinski was forced to withdraw to the island mentioned earlier. He took all his artillery, except for two canons, which became stuck in the sands on the banks of the Vistula and were captured by the Austrians.

The Austrians pursued the Poles as far as the bridge, which separated the island from the right bank. But the artillery located at that point, which was ably directed by Chef de Bataillon Hurting, showered them with cannister and forced them to renounce their enterprise. Shortly later an Austrian parliamentary presented himself with a letter, from the chief of staff to the archduke, who demanded the governor of Thorn to surrender in 24 hours or the city would be burned. Woczynski responded in these terms: "Only when the city is reduced to ashes, when a practicable breach is made, when the last wall is broken down, and when the garrison is driven from its last redoubt, will I enter into an agreement. In the interim, it is the Polish artillery that shall respond to your summons."

The Austrians, who had deployed their forces on the left bank of the Vistula, opened fire. A violent cannonade showered the city with projectiles. Fires broke out at several points, but were quickly extinguished. A small magazine was the only victim of the flames. The Polish artillery, which was on the small island and on the right bank of the Vistula, responded vigorously to the Austrian fire and reduced the Austrian artillery to silence. During the evening the Archduke established his camp behind the heights that dominated the bridgehead and only occupied the entrenchments with a detachment of infantry. The Poles burned the part of the bridge that touched the left bank. The Thorn garrison lost only 45 men hors de combat and 60 prisoners during the day's action. Colonel Brusch, chief of staff to the archduke, and an officer of great merit, was killed. During the following days there were exchanges of artillery fire. On the 20th the assailants evacuated the bridgehead and withdrew to Radzeicwo. The archduke returned to Warsaw.

While these events occurred in the north of the duchy, Polish cavalry penetrated into the interior of Galicia. Two squadrons of the 5th Cavalry Regiment presented themselves before Kock on April 6th and chased out 300 Hungarian hussars after a violent engagement in which the brave Chef d'Escadron Berko was killed. The Hungarians were aggressively pursued that they did not have time to destroy the bridge over the Wieprz. On 7 May three horse guns arrived at Kock. They were put into battery before the entrance to the bridge.[2] They were followed on the 8th by two companies of voltigeurs from the 2nd Infantry Regiment. The 6th Cavalry Regiment crossed the bridge that same day. One of its squadrons pushed as far as Lublin, which it occupied on the 9th. A second squadron moved on Biala and a third moved to Woldawa, where it encountered an Austrian clothing convoy escorted by a strong column of infantry. The squadron moved quickly and surprised the Austrians, capturing the convoy and 700 prisoners. The capture was valued as being worth more than one million florins. During these various movements, the Polish cavalry delivered 3,000 recruits, which joined their depots.

Prince Poniatowski's corps began marching in the following order on 6 May: The advanced guard consisted of the 6th and 12th Infantry Regiment, the 2nd and a squadron of the 5th Cavalry Regiment, with four horse guns under the commands of Generals Sokolnicki and Fozniecki. It moved to the Wieprz, which it crossed at Bobrowniki. From there it moved back up the Vistula and was joined at Opole by two squadrons of the 5th Cavalry Regiment, which had crossed the Wieprz at Kock. The two generals then advanced to the confluence of the San into the Vistula.

Poniatowski, at the head of the main body of his army, moved via Kock on Lublin. The headquarters arrived at Parizow on the 7th, at Kock on the 10th, and at Lubartow on the 11th. Poniatowski stopped for three days at Lubartow and while there learned of the archduke's movement with part of his forces into Greater Poland, which reaffirmed his resolution to march into Galicia.

The rapid movement of the Polish cavalry resulted in the capture of a letter from the Russian general Prince Gorchakov, which congratulated Ferdinand on his successes, and expressed the hope of seeing the Russians joining their efforts with those of the Austrians. The presence of Russian officers in the Austrian camp had already been reported to the prince. He could not doubt any further the connivance of the two courts or at least of their general staffs. He immediately directed General Bronikowski to go take the intercepted letter to Napoleon and with it a dispatch from Poniatowski saying, "The rapidity of the cavalry advanced guard under my orders has resulted in the attached letter from the Russian general, Prince Gorchakov to Archduke Ferdinand, falling into my hands. It appears to me to be quite important that you are aware of the attitude of the Russians, or at least of their troops and commanders, which I have hastened to send to you. General Bronikowski, a great landowner in Galicia, has served with us since the

---

[2]Captain Soltyk, who commanded these guns, received at Wionzowna the order of General Pelletier to move to Kock. He asked the general what would escort him; the general responded that he was a man of energy and that if he encountered the Austrian fugitives he should have his gunners saber them. Soltyk captured 125 prisoners during his march, without firing a shot. We have thought to relate this incident, which had little overall significance, because it indicates the manner in which the Poles fought this war.

beginning of hostilities and is charged with carrying this dispatch to Your Majesty. He has advised me of the desire of his people to participate in and to come under the protection accorded to the national existence of Poland. I am pleased, sir, that you receive the good will, the homage of my most profound respect and recognition."

Napoleon was indignant about Gorchakov's letter. He transmitted it to the Minister of Exterior Relations, who then sent it to the Russian ambassador with a note complaining of the general's conduct. The ambassador, directed by his government, responded that Austria and Russia were not at war and that the general had a right to express his personal opinions in a confidential letter. This explanation was not judged to be sufficient and Gorchakov was recalled.

Upon his arrival in Lubartow, Prince Poniatowski found himself surrounded by the notables of Galicia, who expressed to him the sympathy of the inhabitants. A deputation from many of the circles came to him the request of their fellows for unification with the Grand Duchy. Prince Constantin Czartoryski took service in the Polish Army. A large number of inhabitants of all classes followed his example. If it were not for a lack of arms, the army would have risen to a strength of 20,000 men.

The inhabitants of the duchy did not lag behind in their demonstrations of devotion. The new levies gathered in haste and began to line the right bank of the Vistula, which they were to defend. The volunteers quickly filled the ranks of the old and new units.

On 14 May Poniatowski left Lubartow and moved to Lublin, where he found the same enthusiasm and patriotism. Lublin contained a population of 12,000 souls and was one of the largest cities in the province. Poniatowski chose it for the seat of the provisional government of the two Galicias. Stanislaw Zamoyski, who owned immense properties in the province, was named president of the government. This government included Mssrs. Maruszewic, Mionczynski, and Lewinski. Rembielinski, prefect of Plock, was charged with the functions of intendant of the army. Lublin presented itself as a warrior city. The elite of the youth of the province flooded there, presenting themselves on their horses and bearing their weapons. Poniatowski organized a company of guides from them, placing it under the command of Colonel Mionczynski. He ordered the formation of three new corps. Czartoryski and both offered to raise an infantry regiment at their personal expense and the Circle of Lublin undertook to raise a third regiment.

The army corps, which had stopped at Lublin on the 13th, left on the 14th for the San. General Kaminski was detached to Zamosc at the head of a squadron of the 3rd Cavalry Regiment and two squadrons of the 6th Cavalry Regiment.

The occupation of Lublin was the subject of the issuance of a new proclamation, which said:

SOLDIERS!

You have arrived in this city, where your only presence is a claim to fame; I like to recall to you your last actions and to make known to you the goal to which you still strive. A foreign government has dwelled too long on us, and everywhere the name Pole was almost regarded as a crime, when the victorious arms of the heroes of France, awaking in our hearts the ancient value, made you desirer to prove that no consideration would know to you stop when the happiness of your fatherland is price of your efforts. Heaven has recompensed so pure feelings; those feelings that that crushed your enemies, enabled you to convince heaven that you deserve that your fatherland be returned to you. Many battalions, whose meeting alone was wondrous, bought with their blood the honor due still the name of their ancestors. The raising of your national existence was the price of your warlike virtues, and the defense of your fatherland entrusted to your efforts, has just shown what your great liberator can await from your courage. But already, soldiers, you have justified such beautiful hopes; already a stronger enemy has shown that numbers are not enough to gain the victory. You proved it on the land of your brothers, and the exploits by which you opened the road, will undoubtedly convince them that it was formerly your common fatherland.

We have left the Polish advanced guard at the mouth of the San. On 16 May Generals Sokolnicki and Rozniecki concentrated their forces to capture Sandomierz and its bridgehead. This city was commanded by Generalleutnant Egermann, and contained a garrison of 4,000 men, most of whom were recruits. The fortress was covered by an old wall flanked with towers, but the wall was in ruins at many points and by the Krakow Gate it was, over a considerable distance, three to four feet high. The Austrians had accommodated for this by starting, but not completing a trench on the interior. They had also constructed several advanced works on the side of the Opatow gate, which though fort, were not completed and were open to the rear. Sandomierz was armed with 27 cannon, of which 15 were siege guns and 12 were field guns. The Austrians worked on the right bank of the Vistula in erecting a bridgehead, which was composed a bastioned work with two fronts, and three lunettes. It was armed with 15 guns.

One can see by this description that Sandomierz and its bridgehead could be taken by a coup de main. The Polish generals resolved to attempt it. Sokolnicki, taking the most dangerous role, chose to act against the fortress and directed Rozniecki to attack the bridgehead. During the night of the 16th/17th Rozniecki crossed the San in boats with the 2nd and 5th Cavalry Regiment, a battalion of the 6th Infantry Regiment, two companies of voltigeurs from the 8th Infantry Regiment, and two cannon. Sokolnicki, on his part, ordered Colonel Surawski to put himself at the head of the battalions of his regiment (the 6th Infantry) and to cross the Vistula a mile below the Sandomierz, while he crossed with the 12th Infantry Regiment, a squadron of the 6th Cavalry Regiment, which had arrived from Lublin, and two horse guns, crossed the Vistula at Zwichost and joined Sierawski.

The attack was to occur simultaneously on both banks during the night of the 17th/18th.

Sierawski completed the instructions of his commander exactly. He crossed the Vistula during the night of the 16th/17th and took position on the banks of the river, in a fold of the terrain that was covered by a woods on the side of Sandomierz. Having the Vistula at his back with no bridge to effect a retreat, he waited anxiously until the hour arrived. Fortunately for him, no Austrian patrols came in his direction. Sokolnicki encountered some delays in his march. He was obliged to pull together the necessary boats near Zawichost, then crossed the river, and moved towards the point occupied by Sierawski. The two columns united at 5:00 p.m., and moved on Sandomierz. A patrol of Austrian hussars spotted them and withdrew in great haste back to Sandomierz, spreading the alarm. Sokolnicki, seeing his advance was discovered, sought to convince the garrison that he was advancing at the head of a considerable force, so he waited until nightfall and when Egermann could not accurately observe his forces. His two cannon were positioned within range of the works that covered the Opatow Gate. When there had been an exchange of a few shots, he deployed his troops on the heights facing the Austrian redoubts and sent a parliamentary to the city to summon Egermann to evacuate the city. Egermann refused.

As night began to fall, Sokolnicki addressed the 12th Infantry Regiment, telling them that the 6th Regiment had covered itself with glory when it captured the Gora bridgehead. He went on to say that the same honor had been reserved for the 12th with the opportunity to capture the Sandomierz bridgehead and to renew the great deeds of Grochow. The officers and men responded to him with cries of acclamation and then marched forward. There was a long defile before them, which they resolutely crossed. The head of the column, formed by the grenadiers of the 1/12th Infantry Regiment under the orders of Prince Marcelin Lubomirski, passed through this defile and was received by violent musketry from the infantry holding the bridgehead. It continued forward, nonetheless, followed by the rest of the 12th Infantry Regiment, and charged the Opatow Gate. The gate was barricaded and the walls had been raised, crenelated, and flanked with towers. In an instance the ground was covered with dead. The intrepid Lubomirski lost his life as well. He was only 24 years old, in his first campaign, and his loss was greatly regretted by the army.

Such was the strength of the defense, that the attackers were forced to fall back and re-cross the defile in great haste. They had, on this occasion, lost 100 men hors de combat.

This check did not discourage Sokolnicki. He ordered the 12th Infantry Regiment to re-form behind the reserve formed by the battalion of the 6th Infantry Regiment and the squadron of the 6th Cavalry Regiment. He resolved to find another, more favorable point, that evening, against which to launch another attack. He ordered Colonel Sierawski to place himself at the head of a squadron of cavalry and a company of voltigeurs of his regiment, then to move along the right of the Vistula to examine the wall on that side. The night was dark, but the garrison continued to illuminate it as best they could. The Polish colonel, however, completed his inspection. He found that it was in good condition, but when he arrived at the Krakow suburb, he found a section of the wall, some 30 to 40 toises long, where the wall was only 3-4 feet tall and where the ditch was filled with rubble. Sierawski, an intelligent and resolute officer, did not hesitate to advance his company of voltigeurs. He crossed the ditch and climbed the wall without the Austrians discovering him. Further in he encountered a trench that was not palisaded, but where the Austrian infantry was placed in ambush. Sierawski could not prudently attack it nor penetrate into the interior of the fortress without support. He held his position between the wall and the trench and sent an officer to Sokolnicki to inform him that he had found a weak point in the fortress and to ask him to immediately send the rest of the battalion.

It was midnight and the attack against the bridgehead by Rozniecki's troops had begun. A lively fire by the infantry and artillery extended along the right bank of the Vistula and stopped after about 30 minutes. It was unclear if Rozniecki had won or lost. The fate of Sandomierz depended on this. This uncertainty did not last long and ended when Egermann requested to capitulate. Hostilities ceased. A detachment of the 6th Infantry Regiment, lead by Sierawski, occupied the Opatow Gate, where the brave soldiers of the 12th Infantry had suffered their check.

Rozniecki, who, as we have said, was to cross the San during the night of the 16th/17th with the troops that were assigned to attack the bridgehead. He had executed this movement and taken up positions near Trzesnia. The day of the 17th passed without any action and the troops of the Polish general prepared to launch their attack the following night. Rozniecki had Captain Strzelecki, of the 6th Infantry Regiment, observe the bridgehead. Strzelecki had been trained in the Vienna engineering school and was known for his bravery. He advanced dressed as a peasant to within a musket shot of the entrenchments.[3] He completed his reconnaissance of the bridgehead as well as the footpaths that passed through the adjacent swamps. Strzelecki informed Rozniecki that the advanced lunettes were in a respectable state of defense, that they were palisaded and closed in the gorge, but that the bridgehead was far from complete and had no palisade and the ditch was not very deep. This information confirmed his resolution to carry the bridgehead that night. The battalion of the 6th Infantry Regiment, under the orders of Bouslawski, was charged with attacking Lunettes Nos. 2 and 3, and Captain Strzelecki was to serve him as a guide. Chef d'escadron Wlodimir Potocki, on his side, marched at the head of two companies of voltigeurs of the 8th Infantry Regiment, and was to carry Lunette No. 1. When the lunettes were taken the two columns were to advance against the wall of the bridgehead and carry it. The 2nd and 5th Cavalry Regiments, which formed the reserve, were at the same time to spread in a semi-circle around these works ready to support the attacking columns if they were checked, and block, in the case of success, the flight of the fugitives attempting to escape into the countryside. When night arrived Rozniecki's troops advanced forward. At midnight they launched their attack, with Boguslawski and Potocki at their head. They marched in silence and approached the lunettes to within a musket shot without being detected. When they were discovered a well-sustained fire greeted them, supported by the nine cannons that were in the lunettes. The Polish infantry paid no attention to this fire. The Austrian troops that defended the lunettes were bayoneted or forced to surrender. The two intrepid Polish chiefs marched, without losing an instant, against the bridgehead, which was only weakly defended. The parapets were promptly overrun. Boguslawski and Potocki led the assault.[4] The élan of the assailants was such that only part of the Austrian garrison escaped over the bridge to Sandomierz. They were pursued with such vigor that the Polish were able to enter pell-mell into the fortress before orders from their commanders stopped them.

Six canons were in battery on the ramparts and fell into the hands of the victories. The garrison of the bridgehead, which had contained 1,500 men, only 500 were able to escape, the remainder being captured or killed. The loss to the Poles was only 50 men, but among the dead were a captain of the 8th Infantry Regiment and two officers of the 6th Infantry Regiment.

Egermann, chased from the bridgehead and threatened from the left bank, requested to capitulate, as mentioned earlier. Sokolnicki, on his side, desired to bring about a quick end of the expedition. An arrangement was concluded that day. The Austrian garrison had twelve hours to evacuate the city. It could take with its baggage and field artillery. It marched out of the city that evening, parading past its conquerors, and retired to the Nida. It was partially composed of Galicians, many of whom, when they saw the national uniform and the flags surmounted with white eagles, left the ranks of the Austrians and joined their compatriots, loudly demanding to serve their country.

The Austrians officers were humiliated; left with their heads lowered and made no comment. Eight hundred men abandoned their ranks and joined the Poles. Egermann had retained only about 2,000 men in his column as he marched on the Nida. Sokolnicki took possession of Sandomierz in the evening of the 18th, finding 15 siege guns, and considerable military stores and provisions left as a result of the capitulation. [5]

[3]With a spade in his hands, he pretended to be a ditch digger and fooled the Austrian sentinels.

[4]Boguslawski had served in the legions and was one of the most capable infantry officers of the Army. Potocki was only 20 years old and was not only an excellent artillery officer, but one day would hold the most important commands. He was regarded by all the army as a hero who would have an immortal voice.

[5]See appendicies.

When Rozniecki's troops occupied the bridgehead they immediately set about destroying the entrenchments and in three days they were completely razed. This was strange and can only be explained by the conviction that the Poles had towards next capture of the city by the Austrians. Poniatowski, who had a better military perspective, and which assigned a great importance to holding Sandomierz, was greatly upset by this demolition, but did not learn about the demolition in time to stop it.

———•———

Gen. Jozef Zajączek

CHAPTER V

Poniatowski leaves Lublin on 15 May – He marches on Ulanow – Pelletier is detached to Zamosc – Proc-
lamation of Poniatowski to the Galicians – Blockade and capture of Zamosc on 20 May – Poniatowski re-
views Pelletier's troops, leaves a garrison in Zamosc, pushes on Leopol part of the cavalry under Kaminski,
and reunites his army corps at Sandomierz – Examination of the position of the Polish Army after the cap-
ture of Sandomierz – Sokolnicki councils the prince to march on Radom – Poniatowski takes a position near
Sandomierz – What was about to happen – Observations of the works of the fortress of Sandomierz – The
wall is reinforced, the bridgehead is not reestablished – Inconveniences of the failure to do so – Rozniecki
takes Jaroslaw – The troops employed in this expedition return to the San – Kaminski occupies Leopol on
23 May – Rozniecki rejoins him on the 28th – He recognizes the sovereignty of Napoleon – He organizes
the government – Blockade and siege of Czenstochowa by Grammont – The Austrians are pushed back by
Stuart – They withdraw on Krakow – Diverse engagements on the Vistula – Poniatowski sends Pelletier to
Galitzin in Bialystok – Position of the Russian Army – Duplicity of Galitzin – Bad attitude of the Russian
generals towards Napoleon.

Poniatowski only spent the day of the 14th in Lublin. The following day he moved to Belzyce. The army had preceded him to that point and he put himself at its head, and then moved to Janow where he received news of the investment of Zamosc by the cavalry under Kaminski. Domanski, Commissaire General of the ground of the Majorat of Zamosc, proprietor of Zamoyski, who was named president of the Galician government, brought with him interesting details of the fortress. He informed Poniatowski that the walls were not in a state suitable for defense, that the inundations that constituted the principal defense were not complete. Finally, he informed Poniatowski that Zamosc was open to capture by a *coup de main*.

Poniatowski was only one hard march from Zamosc. He directed General Pelletier to observe and to capture it if the opportunity arose. He then moved on Ulanow, a small city located on the San, where he thought to await the results of the movements that had been directed on Sandomierz and Zamosc. From Ulanow he issued the following proclamation to the Galicians.

Poles, Citizens of Galicia!

When the troops under my orders entered on the our common ancestral territory, I sought to
ensure myself that you had not ceased seeing us as brothers The reception that you made us met
my expectations; the enthusiasm which is excited in you by the mere sight of the Polish soldiers
and your eagerness to prove to us combines in your hearts to understand and to share our feelings,
shows the desire which you have to join us and to share work that the love of the fatherland makes
easy to achieve. From the proclamations of the archduke Ferdinand we learn how he endeavored to
shake the fidelity of Saxons towards our king, and attempted, though in vain, to form Polish irreg-
ular forces: these processes give me an opportunity to call you to our ranks, where for two years, so
many of your brothers have asked for the honor to fight for the fatherland and our common cause.
I will not say to you to follow their example, this does not make you wrong, to believe that you can
resister what pushes you to do it; it is enough for me to you recall what your brothers did to re-
cover their national existence. Do not only forget, guided only by the confidence which they put in
their great liberator, they ran to arms and fought with perseverance, in spite of the disasters which
dwelled too long on their country. Think that the effects are the continuation of the actions, and
that its merit must precede the recompense. The cold souls and egoists can only ignore this truth;

let us recognize their indifference with the shame, which is its due.

Poles are the same everywhere; tested, but not cut down, by a long succession of misfortunes, we merit, all the more with the sense of obligation, the laurels of glory, the crowns of good citizenship.

Poniatowski had still not received instructions from Napoleon on the manner with which he should treat the Galicians. He could not, in this proclamation, as in the previous ones, give them assurances of the future of their country. He drifted between the desire to see them fight with the troops of the duchy and feared being obliged to abandon them to the vengeance of the Austrian government. This was well understood by the inhabitants, who had the most ardent love of the sacred cause of their fatherland, and who did their duty, without anxiety for the results of the audacious events. On his side Poniatowski, informing Napoleon of the general enthusiasm of the Galicians, insisted in all the dispatches that he addressed to Napoleon of the necessity of giving them positive assurances of what was to come.

Meanwhile Pelletier had begun his march to Janow on the 17th, with the 1/2/2nd Infantry Regiment, two companies of voltigeurs of the 3rd, a company of voltigeurs of the 6th,[1] forming a total of 2,000 men, supported by two 6pdrs and four 6-inch howitzers.[2] After a forced march he arrived before Zamosc on the morning of 18 May. Here he was joined by Kaminski's detachment, which consisted of a squadron of the 3rd and two squadrons of the 6th Cavalry Regiments. Kaminski, who had arrived there on the 15th, had blockaded the fortress and seized the floodgates that controlled the inundations. Pelletier took up position with his troops a quarter mile from the ramparts and sent forward his voltigeurs. They threw back the Austrian advanced posts and occupied the floodgates that controlled the great inundations on the road to Szczebrzeszyn.

The two generals mounted their horses, and accompanied by Domanski, observed Zamosc; He gave them precise information regarding the state of the area, the strength of the entrenchments, and the interior of the city.

The fortress of Zamosc was constructed towards the end of the 16th century to serve as a refuge against the incursions of the Tartars and Cossacks. It was situated on the edge of a vast swamp, cut by several streams. It was in this swamp that the River Wieprz found its source. The wall of the fortress had seven bastioned fronts, faced with masonry and of an irregular trace. The swamp covered part of it. Another part ran between the road to Lublin and Leopol, and was a plain that rose from the covered road and could be covered to a great distance by the artillery on the ramparts.

The scarpes on the part of the wall that was not covered by the inundations were 28 to 30 feet high (9.1 to 9.75 meters) and faced with masonry. The ditch was 30 feet wide (9.75 meters) and 20 feet (6.5 meters) deep. The counterscarp was not faced; the covered road was not indicated. The part of the fortress that was situated on the side of the swamps and the inundations had a similar revetment that was equally high, with the exception of Bastion No. 4, whose scarpe was only 14 feet (4.55 meters) high and Bastion No. 3, whose scarpe was 16 feet (5.20 meters) high. Before the inundations, the swamp could only be crossed on foot and by a few footpaths. Positive reports informed Pelletier that the Austrians had occupied the last several days in repairing the parapets, had armed the ramparts with several cannons, and had constructed

---

[1]This company was part of the 3rd Battalion, which was at Sierock.
[2]Four of these guns were served by foot artillerists and two by horse gunners.

a redan by the Szczebrzeszyn Gate. He also learned that the garrison, commanded by Colonel Pulski, had 3,000 men formed in two battalions of Wallachian Grenz, the depots of several infantry regiments, a detachment of cavalry and a few hussars.

Pelletier's perception of the fortress suggested to him that he could take it by a coup de main on the side of Szczebrzeszyun and that any delay would only render this more difficult in that it would permit the Austrians more time to repair the faults in the defenses. As a result, he immediately made preparations for the attack.

In order to keep the garrison distracted and to begin the cannonade of the fortress, Pelletier ordered Captain Soltyk to move forward in the afternoon of the 18th with two howitzers served by his horse gunners, to put them in battery a short distance from the Szczebrzeszyn Gate and to throw bombs into Zamosc. Soltyk, favored by the houses and walls of the suburb, approached without being discovered to a range of 300 toises (585 meters) from the fortress and opened fire. However, he was too close to the ramparts to maintain his position too long. The Austrian artillery responded with vigorously and dismounted one of his howitzers. He was obliged to withdraw to the floodgates by Szczebrzeszyn and to change his position frequently, covering himself with gardens and houses, he continued to fire with the howitzer that remained, throwing shells into Zamosc. His fire eventually started fires in a number of places within the fortress.

When night fell General Pelletier constructed an epaulement near the Szczebrzeszyn floodgate and relieved Soltyk's howitzer with two other howitzers manned by foot gunners and commanded by Captain Rudnicki.

The preparations for the assault were completed during the 19th. Domanski, by his zeal and his indefatigable activity, contributed substantially to the effort. Fifty Cossacks, employed by the central territorial administration of Zamosc, who were well mounted and equipped militarily, were armed with lances, and were sent out into the countryside in order to bring together the material necessary for the fabrication of fascines and gabions, as well as the ladders necessary to climb the walls. Several volunteers, armed with hunting rifles, joined the assault teams. These Cossacks knew the region perfectly as well as the swamps around the fortress. In addition, they served as guides for the assault parties.

Skirmishers invested Zamosc and established themselves in the houses closest to the Szczebrzeszyn Gate. The Austrians sought in vain to dislodge them and pushed them back several times. They fired on each other for a long time. The Polish volunteers shot a good number of Wallacian grenzers.[3] Pulski made several defensive preparations while he awaited the attack. He lined the redan by the Szczebrzeszyn Gate with palisades and burnt the Leopol suburb in order to clear the rampart of obstructions to his fire.

It was 8:00 p.m. as the assault preparations were completed and Pelletier received the order to delay the attack no longer. He formed his attack columns.

The first, led by Chef de Bataillon Hilaire Krasinski, consisted of the grenadier company of the 2/2nd Infantry Regiment, the voltigeurs companies of the 1/2/2nd Infantry Regiment, the 1st center company of the 1/2nd, and a voltigeur company of the 3rd Infantry Regiment. This force was charged with climbing Bastion No. 4.

---

[3] I regret that I cannot give the name of one of these volunteers. He was 70 years old and had served under the republic. He had left his humble habitation, so he said, to kill a few Austrians. He succeeded in striking down 18 and returned the following day to his work in the fields.

The second column, commanded by Chef de Bataillon Czyzewski, was formed by the 4th center company of the 2/2nd Regiment, and a voltigeurs company of the 3rd Regiment. It was assigned the mission to take Bastion No. 3.

The commanders of these two columns were ordered to designate in advance the grenadiers who were to carry the ladders and to have them preceded by several sappers equipped with axes and fascines. They were to advance in the greatest silence, to avoid any fires, to not respond to any musket shots, to push rapidly to the foot of the parapets and to climb them as quickly as possible. They were then to form up on the ramparts and advance in good order into the interior of the fortress. The first column was charged especially with opening the Lublin Gate and the second the Szczebrzeszyn Gate.

The third column marched under the orders of Chef de Bataillon Suchodolski. It was composed of the 2nd and 3rd center companies of the 1/2nd Regiment, and a voltigeurs company of the 6th Regiment. It was ordered to support the first two columns. If necessary, it was to deploy in skirmish order and respond to the fire directed on the attacking columns, but only in the case that the fire from the ramparts became general.

The fourth column, under the orders of Colonel Stanislaw Potoçki, which was formed of the grenadiers of the 1/2nd Regiment, the 1st, 2nd, and 3rd center companies of the 2/2nd Regiment, and two cannons was assigned to move against the Lublin Gate as soon as the assault began. Once there it was to break the gate with cannon shots, occupy the gate, and to establish a bridge.

Finally, one squadron of the 3rd and 6th Cavalry Regiments were held in reserve on the Lublin road in case of special need.

The columns were to attack at 1:00 a.m. The two howitzers placed behind the epaulement at the Szczebrzeszyn floodgate continue to fire howitzer shells into the place. At 11:00 p.m., they joined the forth column under the command of Chef d'Escadron Brzechwa.

At 12:30 a.m., the fourth column was in position on the rod to Leopol. The first, second and third columns were united in a fold of the ground about 700 meters from the fortress. General Pelletier ordered them to join the fifth column, which was on the road to Lublin.

A half hour later passed without hearing anything but the cries of the Austrian sentinels. Finally, a few musket shots were fired. The general, with the fifth column, moved against the fortress. He fired a few rounds of canister and a lively fusillade erupted. Almost immediately a Polish coronet appeared on the ramparts.

The two columns charged with the escalade had arrived at the foot of the walls and had mounted their ladders unobserved. Captain Daine[4] , who commanded the grenadier company, marched at the head of the first column. After erecting the ladders he ordered one of his grenadiers to climb it. He refused and Daine ran him through with his saber with hesitating and ordered two more to take the place of the man he had punished, following them up the ladder. His energy and intrepidity held the company in order and he led them to the rampart and up the ladders.

The Austrians were taken by surprise and abandoned the rampart, falling back into the interior of the city.

The 2nd column carried Bastion No. 3. Both columns opened the gates they were assigned to take. They turned the cannons against their former owners and disarmed the Austrians defending the ramparts. The brave Daine, with his company of grenadiers, penetrated into the

---

[4]This excellent officer was Belgian by birth. After 1793 he took service in the French army and had passed into Polish service in the grade of captain.

interior of the city and pushed on the *place d'arms* where he found Colonel Pulski at the head of a battalion of Wallachians. As soon Pulski saw the Poles he threw himself at them. He personally attacked Daine and was disarmed and wounded. Surrounded by the Polish grenadiers, he was taken prisoner. The Poles then advanced at the *pas de course*[5] against the Austrian battalion and forced it to surrender.

When General Pelletier arrived at the Lublin gate he ordered a squadron of the 3rd Cavalry Regiment to move into the city by pelotons and to break up any groups of Austrians they might encounter.

The third column had deployed in skirmishers and had responded to the Austrians fire with a lively fusillade. It succeeded in making itself master of the redan covering the Szczebrzeszyn Gate and penetrated into the fortress.

The fourth column did not rest inactive. It had opened fire with its cannon on the fortress, later advancing with cries and hurrahs to distract the attention of the Austrian garrison during the escalade of Redans No. 3 and 4. The Austrian artillery responded with a heavy cannonade that lasted a half hour before it stopped suddenly. Chef d'Escadron Brzechwa advanced against the Leopol Gate. The infantry lead, followed by the lancers who had dismounted and marched with their lances in their hands. They lowered the drawbridge and pushed into the city. The horse artillery gunners, about 20 in number left their cannon with the foot gunners, mounted their horses and charged into Zamosc at the gallop with their captain at their head, sabering the Austrians that they encountered.

The Austrian treasury chest, containing more than 1,000,000 florins, was captured and the Wallachians, who still continued to fight at that point, surrendered. At 4:00 a.m. all fighting ceased. Pelletier sounded the recall and all the Polish troops returned to the *place d'armes*. The Austrian garrison was brought together and dispatched down the road to Lublin. Of the 3,000 Austrians who had formed the garrison, 2,500 were not prisoners. The remainder were either killed or wounded. Forty-six cannon were found on the ramparts. Large quantities of ammunition and provisions were found and also came under the power of the Poles.

The bold assault had cost the Poles only 30 men hors de combat. One cannot praise too much the resolution and the bravery shown by the Poles in this occasion, or the precision with which their commanders had executed the attack, or Pelletier's excellent dispositions.

Poniatowski learned of the happy outcome of the assault on Zamosc during the day of the 20th. The following day he traveled to Zamosc, reviewed the troops, and praised them for their efforts. A battalion of the 2nd Regiment and an artillery detachment formed the garrison of Zamosc. Domanski, who had previously served in the Polish Army, was promoted to the rank of chef de bataillon and made commandant of the fortress in return for the services that he had rendered. General Kaminski was ordered to move at the head of two squadrons of the 6th and of the 3rd Cavalry Regiments were sent on Leopol. The remainder of the troops set out on the 21st and rejoined the main body of the army on the San.

Thus, Poniatowski had executed with rapidity a bold movement that would have the greatest influence on the campaign. The generals who served under him had perfectly seconded him. Kaminski had stopped the inundation around Zamosc; Rozniecki had take the bridgehead and Sandomierz; Pelletier had boldly planned and launched the escalade of Zamosc; and Sokolnicki had boldly executed one of the boldest enterprises of the war when he attacked Sandomierz and forced the Austrian garrison to capitulate.

---

[5]Editor: The pas de course was a cadenced run of 250 paces per minute.

Poniatowski's army now occupied an excellent position on the San. The occupation of Zamosc offered him the ability to extend his conquests in Old Galicia. There was nothing to prevent him from moving to the Dniester River and the Carpathian Mountains.

Sokolnicki advised Poniatowski to advance from Sandomierz to Random with his main force. He stated that the Austrian Army, which was spread across Greater Poland as far as Warsaw, would be unable to prevent this move. The archduke had only a few weak garrisons between the Piliça and the upper Vistula. Poniatowski could snap them up with ease and spread the insurrection beyond Sandomierz into a country covered with immense forests and inhabited by a population of hunters who could provide the army with 2,000 or 3,000 crack shots, all of whom would be armed. Once cut off from Krakow and Vienna, the archduke would be obliged to evacuate the Grand Duchy of Warsaw. If he moved in force into the Palatinate of Sandomierz and chased Poniatowski's army from it, he would have great difficulties suppressing the insurgents who would take refuge in the Sainte-Croix Mountains. These mountains were difficult to access and covered with forests, were impracticable for conventional soldiers. The partisans, once established in this broken terrain, could launch continual incursions into the neighboring countryside and constantly interrupt the main roads with little risk of being engaged.

Sokolnicki added that, if as a result of the events of war, the Polish Army could no longer maintain itself between the Piliça and the Vistula; it could always retreat safely on Sandomierz.

In truth, Poniatowski had only 8,000 to 9,000 men to execute this movement, as he was obliged to leave garrisons in the many fortresses he had recently captured. Despite this, the enthusiasm that animated the Polish soldiers at this time and their justified confidence in their commanders, were a sure guarantee that, despite their inferiority of numbers, that they could obtain further successes in this expedition.

Sokolnicki's plan was seductive and presented favorable chances. However, the views of Poniatowski had turned to Old Galicia where he could defeat the few troops there under the command of Hohenzollern, to carry the archduke's magazines, to capture the detachments showing up at the depots, and to recruit new drafts into his army. He could push the insurrection to the borders of Hungary and Bukovine into the middle of a population ready to arm itself and throw off the yoke of Austria, and finally to profit from the capture of the immense resources of this province and its capital. This operation would last 15 days and require the use of most of Poniatowski's forces. The other forces would be sufficient to take an offensive to the north of Sandomierz at the same time. Finally, if Poniatowski adopted Sokolnicki's plan, he feared that Hohenzollern would evacuate his magazines beyond the Dniester, that he would unite his forces, call to himself part of the troops that were in the neighboring provinces, and present a large force before Sandomierz while the Polish Army was engaged on the left bank of the Vistula. Poniatowski also feared that Hohenzollern would cut off his line of retreat and leave him between two fires. These considerations decided Poniatowski to reject Sokolnicki's plan. Executing his plan to move into Old Galicia, he sent detachments forward and held a reserve near Sandomierz to support them in case of need, and to defend the fortress if the archduke should attack, or to cross the Vistula, should the opportunity arise. The execution of this plan required, above all, that Poniatowski had a secure fortified position to serve as a pivot for his operations. Poniatowski could chose either Sandomierz or Zawichost. Sandomierz had two problems. It required a garrison of 6,000 men, which would greatly reduce his forces for the other operations, and it was located above the junction of the San with the Vistula, which, if the Austrian Army moved against Poniatowski along the right bank, it would force him to withdraw under the cannons of the bridgehead and deprive him of the use of the line of the San or to force him to withdraw across that river to dispute its course and find himself cut off from Sandomierz.

Prince Poniatowski could use Zawichost, destroying Sandomierz, but this required that he quickly built there a bridgehead. This new position, it is true, had the advantage of requiring no more than 3,000 troops for its defense. It was covered by the San on the right bank of the Vistula and if Poniatowski was threatened from that side he could take a position on the river ant defend its passage without losing his communications with Zawichost and still be able to maneuver on both sides of the Vistula. However, the construction of these entrenchments required significant effort and even though it required only the construction of a bridgehead on the left bank, there was no guarantee that it would be completed before the Austrians attacked it.

These were the advantages of the Zawichost position over that of Sandomierzz and Poniatowski had to choose, assuming that the walls of Zawichost could be put into a state of defense and that the bridgehead could be constructed before the archduke had time to attack.[6] But in view of the difficulties resulting from the destruction of the bridgehead, he did not wish to reconstruct it. Rebuilding the walls of Sandomierz without rebuilding the bridgehead was half measure and deprived Sandomierz of its importance. Poniatowski could not maintain himself straddling the Vistula or assume an offensive on either bank without a protected crossing.

On the 22nd General Pelletier and Colonel Mallet reviewed Sandomierz. They undertook the most urgent steps to place it in a state of defense, ordering the erection of a new entrenchment in front of the Opatow Gate, raised palisades on all the advanced works, and completed the armament of the fortress by adding six guns brought from Zamosc. The Prince's army moved to a position above this position, its right on the Vistula and communicating with Sandomierz by a floating bridge. However, because of the lack of entrenchments, this bridge remained unprotected on the right bank. The headquarters were established at Trzesnia.

After the capture of the Sandomierz bridgehead Poniatowski detached Rozniecki on Iaroslaw at the head of four companies of the 8th Infantry Regiment, the 2nd and 5th Cavalry Regiments and four cannons. Rozniecki presented himself before the open city of Iaroslaw on the 25th. The 1,000-man garrison took up a position before the convent of Ste. Marie, on the road to Przeworsk. Summoned to surrender, they sought to take their chances in battle, but as the bulk of these men were recruits, a few cannon shots put them to flight. A colonel, 20 officers and 900 non-commissioned officers and men were taken prisoner. Iaroslaw contained large quantities of provisions, forage, and immense stores of clothing. The capture of this city was also important because it sat on the intersection of the roads from Leopol to Krakow and from Sandomierz to Sambor.

The 26th Rozniecki was ordered to quickly return to the San with the troops under his command and to leave just a company of infantry in the city to defend the magazines until they could be evacuated to Lublin and Zamosc. Rozniecki set out on the road to Leopol at the head of the elite companies of the 2nd and 5th Cavalry Regiments.

Prince von Hohenzollern evacuated the capital of Old Galicia on May 22nd. Taking with him 2,000 newly raised troops he fell back to Stanislawow upon the approach of Kaminski's mounted scouts. These scouts occupied the city without any resistance on the 23rd and Rozniec-

---

[6]The bridgehead at Sandomierzz, which had been occupied by the Austrians, consisted of two fronts and three lunettes, and a height of 10 to 12 feet (3.25 meters to 3.90 meters) and required only 2,500 workers and 15 days of work to perfect.

ki made his entry into Leopol on the 28th to cries of joy from the population. The proprietors of the region, happy to be delivered from foreign domination and full of zeal for the national cause, flocked to him. Among them were Ignace Potocki, Marshal of the Grand Duchy of Lithuania, Prince Mathieu Iablonowski, Francois Mlocki, Castellian of Wolhynie, Stanislaw Tarnowski, Ignac Cetner, Jean Uruski, Ignace Krosnowski, Józef Dzierzkowski, Bonaventure Fredo, Theodore Potocki, Palatin of Belz, and his son Adam Potocki[7], who raised a cavalry regiment at his personal expense. Adam Potoçki was extremely popular. His character and his talents earned him great general esteem. The most distinguished youths of the country struggled to join his corps. The city of Leopol also sought to raise forces. The richest landowners of the provinces presented great sums of money to the public treasury to cover their organization. All the country was in movement and the insurrection extended to the Dniester and to Zbrucz (frontier of Podolie). Everywhere where the detachments of Polish cavalry appeared, the population ran to arms.

Rozniecki addressed a proclamation to the Galicians from Leopol and in this he announced that he was occupying the land in the name of the French emperor and that the Austrian coat of arms would be replaced everywhere by the French eagles.[8] In order to avoid the disorders, which could result from a change of government, the Austrian authorities were left in place. However a certain number of notable citizens of the country were attached to those offices and they were to assure the loyalty of those officials to Napoleon. Colonel Bleszynski, aide-de-camp to the King of Saxony, was made commander of the Leopol fortress, and the garrison was formed of a new levy and a detachment of Polish cavalry. The squadron of the 3rd Lancers that accompanied General Kaminski received orders to move to the Dniester. It was ordered by Chef d'Escadron Strzyski, an officer of rare capacity, to organize the insurrection in central Leopol. Rozniecki, as well as General Kamienski, returned to the San, with all the other cavalry squadrons that had accompanied them.

Prince Poniatowski announced to Berthier the successes he had achieved, and transmitted to him a copy of the proclamation that he had issued to the Galicians. He went on to tell Berthier that he expected to be attacked shortly and that the demonstrations of the archduke to force a passage over the lower Vistula had no other goal but to confuse him.

During the course of May the Austrians had attempted several times to cross the Vistula. The forces combined under the orders of General Zajączek had delayed them constantly. Zajączek commanded 9,000 new conscripts, including 2,000 who were excellent shots armed with hunting rifles and 800 cavalry, supported by several line battalions, which formed the garrisons of the various fortresses. Several engagements of varying intensity occurred. General Piotrowski pushed back the Austrians at Wyszogrod; Hauke beat them at Dobrzyn, at Nieszawa, at Tokary, and Wloclawek; and the most important engagement occurred on 15 May on the Island of Tokarowka near Plock.

The Vistula, which at this point was quite broad, contained several islands among which that of Tokarowka was the largest. Between this island and the right bank was a small island covered with brush known as Plock Island. The Austrians, who looked to cross the Vistula, surprised the Poles on Tokarowka Island on 13 May and threw back the detachment of 320 men,

---

[7]He had served since the age of 16 as an aide-de-camp to Kosciuszko and had received the honorary distinction of the commander of the insurrection for his conduct at the battle of Szczekociny in 1794.

[8]This measure had been ordered to reassure the Russian government that Galicia would not be incorporated into the Grand Duchy of Warsaw, which it feared above all. Galitzin would later enter Galicia and it was feared that there was a possibility of conflict between the Russian and Polish troops if the Russians saw the Polish eagles replacing the Austrian coats of arms.

which occupied it. They then established themselves on the island and placed 500 men and two cannon there. Plock was separated from Tokarowka by an arm of the Vistula spanned by a foot-bridge, which could easily be crossed by infantry. It was feared that the Austrians would take the second island and then cross the last arm of the river, reaching the right bank. On Plock the Poles had a company of a newly formed infantry regiment and a force of National Guard. The total garrison was around 400 men.

The prefect of the department, Rembielinski, engaged the captain of the 2nd Cavalry, La-gowski, who was recovering from his wounds suffered at Plock, to put himself at the head of the National Guard and to attempt to retake Tokarowka. Lagowski did not want to take on this task with such inexperienced troops. He went to the military hospital where he found several hundred wounded soldiers and informed them of the plans. Seventy-five convalescents requested to follow him and these volunteers brought his force to about 200 men ready for the assault on the island. The brush that covered the island concealed his troops and prevented the Austrians from observing his dispositions. He embarked Lieutenant Rokicki with 25 soldiers on a boat employed on the Vistula. These men were concealed under a load of straw, which gave the boat the appearance of a boat of merchandise destined for Warsaw. It moved along the left bank without exciting any attention, but as soon as it touched ground, the troop threw itself ashore and pushed into the island with great cries. Lagowski, with a hundred men, presented himself on the bank of Plock and began a lively musketry fire to support the 25 men ashore. The Austrians jumped up and were completely disordered as they rushed to their boats, which, encumbered with soldiers and overloaded with the weight of the artillery, foundered and sank. Those who did not reach the boats were killed and a small number were taken prisoner.

Lagowski left a detachment a detachment on the island and returned to Plock at the head of his brave soldiers. The population received them with open arms and prepared a solemn banquet for them. However, the greatest part of the soldiers was unable to take part. Their wounds had reopened and they were forced to return to the hospital.

At the same time an Austrian corps, under the command of Grammont and containing 1,500 infantry, 200 cavalry, and seven cannon, presented itself on 2 May before Fort Czensto-chowa. On the 3rd this force established its camp near the city of Kamien and attacked the Church of St. Jacques, situated between the city and the fort. There was a Polish detachment in the church, which defended itself and drove back the Austrians with some losses. On the 4th, in the afternoon, the Austrians renewed their attack, attacking the rear of the church, throwing its skirmishers into the houses of the new city, which at that point, extended towards the fort. The Polish detachment, which had so bravely defended itself the previous day, was forced to evacuate its post and withdrew into the fort, firing at the Austrian infantry which followed them and closed to within 200 toises (390 meters) of the ramparts. During the night of the 15th/16th the Austrians established their first parallel at the distance of a musket shot from the covered way. They then pushed their approach from this point and occupied it in force with their infantry. Colonel Stuart saw himself being seriously menaced and decided to recapture Sainte-Barbe. The convent, the cemetery walls, and the garden had been crenelated. Stuart launched a sortie at daybreak with three companies of the 5th Infantry Regiment, and supported it with a heavy cannonade. Perhaps it could have taken the convent if it had marched straight at the Austrians, but they deployed into skirmish order and engaged in a firefight, which resulted in nothing. The attack was renewed several times and it was repulsed every time. At 1:00 p.m., Stuart, not at all disheartened, rallied his troops and led the column into the cemetery after forcing its gate. The Poles reformed inside the cemetery, charged with bayonet, clearing it and moved into the garden. The Austrians sought refuge in the church and maintained themselves there until evening, when they abandoned the church and returned to their trenches. They lost, during the day, 250 men hors de combat and 14 prisoners.

This vigorous blow convinced Grammont that his efforts were useless; that a fort defended by such a firm and well-commanded garrison could not be forced. He raised his siege and withdrew in the night of the 16th/17th moving via Kozieglowy and Slawkow on Krakow. He had lost in his operations nearly 500 men. He left a rearguard of 200 infantry and 60 cavalry, supported by two cannons, which then withdrew after it had gathered in the various detachments that had been spread about the city.[9]

Despite his progress in Galicia, Poniatowski was unsettled. The Russian Army had delayed its entry into the campaign and made few dispositions to support it. Poniatowski sent General Pelletier to Prince Galitzin who commanded the Russian Army.

Galitzin appeared well disposed and announced his intention to march on Warsaw with all his forces and drive them from it. He commented energetically on the necessity to come to the support of Poniatowski's Army, which at that time occupied the important position at Sandomierz, with forces far inferior to those of the Austrians. Galitzin acceded to Poniatowski's requests and promised to march one of his divisions on the San. He designated Souvarov's division, which was in the vicinity of Wlodawa and was the closest to Sandomierz. He gave Pelletier a letter for this general in which he ordered him to move on the San. Pelletier promptly went to Souvarov in order to hasten his movement. However, an aide-de-camp to Galitzin had gone along with an counter order. Souvarov, who was a loyal individual, did not conceal this, saying to Pelletier that he did not wish play a deceitful role. He added that the bulk of the Russian divisional generals regarded Austrians war as highly impolitic and he shared that opinion. Pelletier was obliged to return to the Polish headquarters without having determined if the Russians would immediately support the Polish Army. However, he did bring Poniatowski a sense of the ill will of the allied generals and the duplicity of their commander.

---

[9]See Appendix.

The Battle of Razyn

Return of Ferdinand to Warsaw – Mohr falls back on Bzura – Schauroth moves on Sandomierz
– Combat of 27 May before Sandomierz – Dąbrowski arrives in Posen – New levies – Dąbrowski
assumes the offensive on 22 May – He advances on Bzura – Mohr retires on Lowicz and devas-
tating the countryside. Dąbrowski is joined at Kutno by a detachment sent him by Woyczynski
– Dąbrowski occupies Lowicz – Forces of his division – Hauck receives reinforcements from
Thorn – He crosses the Vistula on 25 May – The Archduke decides to evacuate the duchy and
unites his forces between the Piliça and the upper Vistula – He takes command of his troops before
Sandomierz – Mondet commands in the duchy – Warsaw is evacuated by the Austrians on 2 June
and retire on the Piliça – Engagements at Zuranie and Obory – Zajączek enters Warsaw on June
2nd and publishes a proclamation to the public – Kosinski enters on the 3rd – The Council of Min-
isters return to the capital on the 8th – Poniatowski receives at Trzesnia, a letter from the Prince
de Neuchâtel on 18 May – Operations of the belligerent armies in Italy and Germany – Official
communications between Galitzin and the prince –Poniatowski accelerates the new formation of
new Galician forces – Ferdinand arrives before Sandomierz – The engagements of June 5th and
6th – Movement of the archduke on Polaniec – He crosses the Vistula and moves on Wisloka –
Egermann joins him – Geringer covers the movement on the left bank – Poniatowski is unable
to profit from his advantages – He detaches Rozniecki to the Wisloka; quo encounters the enemy
and retires on the main army which takes a position by Wrzawy, Poniatowski raises the bridge at
Sandomierz. Zajączek advances on the Piliça and joins Haucke – Engagement at Warka – Zaion-
owskiczek crosses the Piliça and occupies Iedlinsko – Dąbrowski maneuvers on Piotrkow instead
of following Mondet – Mondet unites his forces at Pszytyk, attacks Zajączek on the 11th and in-
flicts a check on him – Zajączek withdraws via Kozenice on Gora vis-à-vis Pulaw – Critique of this
movement – At the same time Dąbrowski remounts the Piliça, occupies Piotrkow and his advance
guard Soleiow, which, after violent engagement, moves on Kouski – Motives for Dąbrowski's con-
duct – Politics of Czar Alexander and disposition of the Russians – Position of the Russian Army
– Galitzin publishes a manifesto and enters into the Duchy on 2 June – The slow Russian march,
complaints of Poniatowski – Souvarov's division arrives on the San – Combat of Wrzawy – Poni-
atowski recrosses the San with his forces on the 14th and raises the bridge at Czekay.

Ferdinand learned of the fall of Sandomierz when he returned from his expedition to Thorn. He realized the importance of Sandomierz and resolved to retake it. His army was eche-loned between Rdzieiewo and Warsaw. He was unable to begin his march on Sandomierz until he reunited his forces. However, according to his method of operations he detached Schauroth, around noon, at the head of a division of 8,000 men and ordered Mohr to return to the Bzura. His columns spread about in this manner, he was unlikely to be able to strike a decisive blow. Despite this, Schauroth marched on Sandomierz and presented himself before Sokolnicki's advanced posts on 26 May.

On the other side, when Poniatowski learned of the march of the Austrian general he dispatched the 3rd Infantry Regiment and a squadron of the 1st Cavalry Regiment to Sandomierz. The garrison now consisted of the 3rd, 6th and 12th Infantry Regiments, one squadron of the 6th, one squadron of the 1st Cavalry Regiments, and three artillery companies.

The Austrian troops arrived before Sandomierz during the morning of the 27th and pushed the Polish advanced posts out of the suburbs, pressing them back towards the fortress. The

Poles launched a sortie after noon with the 3rd Infantry Regiment, the squadron of the 1st Cavalry Regiment, and a battery of artillery. Schauroth's troops were driven a half-mile back from the fortress, losing around 100 men hors de combat and 200 prisoners. Sokolnicki deployed his troops so as to cover the fortress and to observe the enemy closely.

On his side, General Dąbrowski, who, as we had noted earlier, had been in Posen since 10 May. He set about raising new levies with great vigor from the three departments assigned to him. In a few days he brought 4,000 volunteers under the flag, the most part the national guards of the cities of Greater Poland and had exercised them in the management of the arms and other military evolutions. He was seconded in this operation by the indefatigable zeal of the most notable patriots of the region and those generals who served under his orders. The cadres of many new units were formed. Dąbrowski had more than 1,951 men available to him, including 1,140 infantry, 792 cavalry and 29 artillerists serving two guns.

Dąbrowski's advanced posts occupied Sleszyn, Kolo and Unieow. The Czenstochowa Fort, which was part of his command, supported his right while the left extended as far as Bromberg, on the Netze. On 22 May, he assumed the offensive along his entire front and threw back the Austrian advanced posts. From Czenstochowa, Colonel Stuart pushed parties on Kozieglowy, Piliça, and there surprised an Austrian detachment. General Michel Dąbrowski carried Lenczyca. General Dąbrowski, in person, advanced on Klodawa, and General Kosinski marched on Kruszwica. The Austrians retired everywhere, abandoning to the Poles a large number of prisoners.

General Mohr, who we had left on 20 May in Radzielewo, moved on 22 May to Klodawa and drew to him the various detachments facing Dąbrowski. That same day, conforming to the orders issued by the archduke, he began his retreat on Bzura. For the first time since the beginning of the war the Austrians were retreating into a devastated land. Their conduct exasperated the inhabitants, who ran to arms and ambushed individual men and small detachments.

General Dąbrowski, who had several new formations join him, continued his offensive movement. Kosinski advanced from Kruszwica in two columns, the first moving via Radzieiewo on Klodawa, the second via Piotrkow (on Lake Goplo) to Kutno, while in the center Dąbrowski followed the main road with the main body of his division. On the right General Michel Dąbrowski marched on Kutno, on which all Dąbrowski's forces were converging. Once he arrived, on the 27th, Dąbrowski established his headquarters there. That same day Kosinski, who commanded Dąbrowski's advanced guard, occupied Zyczlin.

Mohr withdrew promptly, reaching Lowicz, on the Bzura, on the 27th. He remained there until May 30th, at which time he fell back on Rokitno, where he received some reinforcements that joined him from Warsaw. Dąbrowski stopped in Kutno, passing three days there to complete the organization of his corps. While there he was joined by reinforcements sent to him by General Woyczynski from Thorn. This reinforcement consisted of the 3/10th and 3/11th Infantry Regiment and six cannons. The Governor of Thorn had also dispatched the 3/12th Regiment to Plock, where it joined General Haucke, who occupied that city with a battalion of light infantry raised in the Department of Pock. Haucke, now commanding two battalions, crossed the Vistula on 25 May and advanced on Sochaczew in order to coordinate his operations with those of General Kosinski, who was moving on Lowicz and who occupied that city on 31 May. The same day, Kosinski occupied Boli and Major Uminski, at the head of two squadrons of cavalry, entered Blonie. General Dąbrowski found himself commanding a division that consisted of:

3/10th Infantry Regiment		Each battalion had about 700 men,
3/11th Infantry Regiment		bringing his total to 5,600 men
2/1st Infantry Regiment	Formed in Posen	
2/2nd Infantry Regiment	Formed in Posen	
Light Infantry Battalion	Formed in Posen	
Light Infantry Battalion	Formed in Kalitz	
	Total 8 Battalions	Total 1,660 men

1st Cavalry Regiment	Newly formed	
2nd Cavalry Regiment	Newly formed	
8 guns served by foot gunners		200 men
Train and ambulance		100 men
		Total 7,500 men

The Austrians attempted to cross the Vistula, near Modlin, during the night of the 27th/28th. Their force consisted of 3,000 men, but they were repulsed with losses by the 3/3rd Infantry Regiment under the command of Major Krukowiecki, who had been sent from Modlin to the crossing point. Emboldened by this success, General Zajączek ordered Colonel Neuman to put himself at the head of several newly raised forces and to chase the Austrians from Obory Island, situated two miles above Warsaw. Neuman attacked on 31 May, at 2:00 a.m., and threw the Austrians back, inflicting 200 casualties, capturing 88 prisoners, and seizing the island.

The archduke, whose headquarters were in Mokotow, near Warsaw, received successively the news of the raising of the siege of Czenstochowa, the progress of Dąbrowski, Schauroth's check at Sandomierz, and the occupation of Obory Island. Threatened on all sides, he decided to evacuate Warsaw and abandon the duchy. He sought to unite his forces between the Piliça and the upper Vistula in order to act from a central position against the Polish Army, which spread from Lowicz to Sandomierz, formed a semi-circle around his army. He gathered in the detachments of Egermann and Grammont, which were posted near Krakow, and completed his regiments with new recruits that he found in the depots in New Galicia. This permitted him to deploy a force of 30,000 men and gave hope of future success. However, in order to achieve this success, it was necessary for him to concentrate his forces, not spread them out as he did. This being so, he left the vicinity of Warsaw on May 30th and marched in parson towards Sandomierz, where General Geringer had preceded him with a force of 6,000 men. He also intended to have Schauroth join him before this fortress. Mondet, at the head of 13,000 men, remained in the duchy to block the progress of Zajączek and Dąbrowski. The army of the archduke was, as a result, divided into two corps. One corps operated against Sandomierz and the other withdrawing over the frontier into Galicia.

Conforming to his instructions, Mondet evacuated Warsaw during the night of June 1st/2nd and advanced on the Piliça in two columns. The first column, which was the larger, marched on Nowemiasto and the second on Bialobrzegi.

When Zajączek learned of the evacuation of Warsaw he ordered Colonel Neumann, who, as we have said earlier, occupied Obory Island, to cross over the Vistula and move on Wilanow. Neumann executed this order on June 2nd, during the afternoon, and when arrived in the

Warsaw suburbs he engaged in a number of skirmishes with the Austrians. Zajączek followed quickly behind him and upon his entry into Warsaw found large quantities of supplies and 1,000 wounded who had been left in the Uyazdow military hospital. His lead elements gathered in several hundred stragglers in the city and its vicinity. The population of the capital of the duchy abandoned itself in its joy at the appearance of national troops. Soldiers and citizens kissed and greeted each other in their joy. The city was spontaneously illuminated. The enthusiasm was overflowing. On 3 June Zajączek issued a proclamation to the citizens of Warsaw in which he said, "The had of God has avenged us. A thankless aggressor, forgetting the good acts of our ancestors, not content with the double despoliation, which they have already imposed on Poland, sought to ravage those parts of our territory that the great Napoleon has restored to us. The hour of vengeance has arrived. Our enemy has fled before our troops and evacuated the capital during the night."

The forces on the right bank of the Vistula were no longer threatened, so Zajączek left only a newly formed regiment, some infantry depots, and some artillery detachments[1] to garrison and drew together his forces around the city.

3/1st, 3/2nd, 3/3rd & 3/8th Infantry Regiments	5 battalions, 2 companies
2 Cos, 3/6th Regiment[2]	each battalion had about 700 men
Light Infantry Battalion from Luzwa	
Approximate Total of Infantry	3,740
1 newly formed cavalry regiment	800
2 artillery cos drawn from forts with 12 cannon	280
Train and Ambulance	80

Total   4,900 men

Dąbrowski learned of the evacuation of Warsaw during the 2nd and on the 3rd he sent General Kosinski to Warsaw where he assumed the function of governor. Kosinski held this position for only a few days when Colonel Kosecki, chief of staff to Zajączek, received him. The Council of Ministers returned to Warsaw on 8 June and took up the reins of government.

While these events were occurring in the North Prince Poniatowski recalled the various detachments he had dispatched into Old Galicia and prepared for the vigorous defense of Sandomierz. On 31 May he received from Berthier a letter dated 18 May which was delivered by Captain Malczewiski. This letter ended saying,

"His Majesty is satisfied with the operations of the army and the good spirit that has animated the duchy. It is presumed that you have reentered Warsaw, which was abandoned by the archduke. Now that you hold it you can move on Olmutz or throw yourself into Silesia. The principal goal of your operations should be to hold in check a corps equal to that of yours and to close with the armies of the emperor. His Majesty shall cross the Danube with his army tomorrow to fall on the

---

[1]General Piotrowski, who commanded Modlin, deployed a garrison that was so weak that he feared a revolt among the Austrian prisoners of war every time another large group of them arrived at his fortress. He considered blindfolding them as they entered Modlin and keeping them so until they went into their casemates.
[2]Four companies of this battalion had been sent to Sierock to join Poniatowski on the San.

debris of the enemy army that had saved itself by moving to the left bank of the Danube.[3]   It is presumed that when you have received this letter we will be closer to you. Arouse an insurrection in Galicia, which will form useful battalions; recruit; augment your army by all possible means. This is of the greatest importance. Regarding the Russian army, the emperor has received letters from Saint Petersburg dated April 28th and the same day the order was given to the Russian Army to enter Galicia. We have made common cause with the Russians, so you have nothing to fear on that side."

After the victories of Ratisbonne, Napoleon had marched on Vienna and entered it on 10 May. The bridges over the Danube were destroyed and he was obliged to take several days to prepare his assault over the river. On the date of this letter from Berthier, his preparations were completed. He was about to move 100,000 men to the far bank of the Danube and counted on an assured success over the archduke's army, which had been broken by the defeats it had suffered. In Italy, Eugène had pushed back the Austrian army into the Alps. On 16 May he was at Pontebba and on the 18th at Tarvis, following his adversary [the Archduke John] as he withdrew on Graz. In the Tyrol, Marshal Lefebvre had defeated the insurgents and by 19 May the pacification of the entire province was complete.

In consequence of the letter from the Emperor Napoleon, Prince Poniatowski issued the following proclamation to his troops at Trzesia:

Soldiers!

Because of your success in Galicia and the manner in which you have been received, it has come to the attention of the emperor, who has, in the middle of his victories, witnessed to me that he is content with you and the spirit that animates you. The capture of Sandomierz, of Zamosc, the conquest of almost all of Galicia, assures us of new proofs of his good will and the capture of Leopol will prove to him that you have not been blinded by the shadows of your laurels. This sit has opened its gates to us; your comrades here have been received with the same sentiment that has met each of our steps on this hospitable land of our brothers is a recompense or an encouragement for us to fly to a new success. Already those successes you have gained have given your brothers the ability to join our ranks and to join you in deserving the protection which gave you existence and which has placed you at the side of the invincible cohorts, which are universally praised. Already the incontestable proves give me certainty that your Galician brothers are deserving of our common fatherland.

In such little time, their numerous battalions have augmented our forces and shared our defeats and glory, contributing to the destiny prepared for them by your courage and the protection of victorious heroes.

The Galician government, presided over by Zamoyski, occupied itself with the formation of many new units, which operated at the expense of the inhabitants of the province. He

---

[3]Editor: The pending assault across the Danube of which Berthier speaks was the battle of Aspern-Essling. The Austrians were not quite the "debris" that Berthier suggests they were. In fact, it was a terribly hard fought battle and Napoleon suffered his first major defeat. He crossed the Danube and fought with it at his back, which is a very dangerous thing to do. It has often been suggested that Napoleon attempted this dangerous enterprise with so little preparation because of his misperception of the remaining strength of the Austrian army. Berthier's comments here are indicative of that misperception.

ordered the organization of a militia in the various cities and asked that each village provide an armed cavalry trooper, a process, which would provide 4,000 to 5,000 horse. A new regiment of infantry was organized at Lublin. Another formed at Pulawy under the command of Prince Constantin Czartoryski. A third, formed in large part from forestry guards of the Majorat of Zamosc, was organized in Zamosc. Zamoyski announced his plan to put himself at the head of this corps and to leave the presidency to take part in the operations of the Polish Army. However, Poniatowski did not wish to consent to this and asked him to continue in his administrative functions.[4] As we have mentioned earlier, Adam Potocki formed a cavalry regiment at Leopol. Four other cavalry regiments were formed in Austrian Podolia. Notable citizens of Russian Podolia, Mssrs Ryszczewski, Tarnowski, Rozwadowski, and Trzecieski recruited and organized at their expense regiments that they led. These units were formed not only with Galician volunteers, but with more than 1,000 patriots from Podolia and Wolhynia who crossed the Russian frontier, armed and mounted, seeking to serve the fatherland.[5]

At the same time Poniatowski received a dispatch from Galitzin, carried by Lépin, an ordnance officer of Napoleon, and in this it announced that the Russian general planned on entering Galicia. The Prince understood his secret intentions and instead of supporting the insurrection he sought to shackle it. He ordered the central government, which was in Lublin, to administer the country in the name of Napoleon in order to cover, with the shield of his protection, the formation of the new Galician units. This measure was later, approved by Napoleon and confirmed in the orders he sent to Vienna on this subject.

Ferdinand arrived before Sandomierz during the evening of 4 June and reviewed his troops, now numbering 13,000 men. Wishing to confirm the strength of the Austrians and to reconnoiter their position, Poniatowski ordered General Sokolnicki to move out of the fortress and to move before the Austrians. Sokolnicki, who was soon to be reinforced by a few cavalry squadrons, commanded 5,000 men. He began his movement at 3:00 a.m., on 5 June. The 2nd and 5th Cavalry Regiments began the march and had orders to march on Lipniki in order to attract the attentions of the Austrians in that direction. Sokolnicki followed them and moved to Roszki with the 3rd and 12th Infantry Regiment, one squadron of both the 1st and 6th Cavalry Regiment, and 12 cannons. He stopped there and reviewed the archduke's dispositions, then withdrew slowly on Sandomierz. The Austrians began to pursue them and using their superior number of cavalry and artillery, attempted to turn their flanks while charging them frontally. However Sokolnicki's troops did not permit them to succeed in their efforts and returned to the fortress without loss. A squadron of the 5th Cavalry and a peloton of the 1st Cavalry executed a brilliant charge against the Austrian infantry and threw back a battalion of the Davidovich Infantry Regiment, which was regarded as the best in the army. This attack cost the Austrians 500 men killed, wounded or prisoners.

The morning of the 6th passed quietly, but that afternoon the advanced works and the suburbs were violently attacked. The archduke directed his troops and stimulated by his presence. They were, nonetheless, repulsed on all points and again with considerable losses. The Poles took 50 prisoners and lost only 3 dead and 8 wounded. However, they also had to mourn the death of the brave Chef de Bataillon Gayzenbach, of the 3rd Infantry Regiment, who was among the dead.

---

[4] See Appendicies.

[5] The emigration of the young Polodian men was so great at this time that the bureaus of the civil government of Kamienic was deserted by its employees and the functioning of the government had ceased.

The archduke, convinced of the uselessness of his direct attacks on Sandomierz, formed the project of crossing the Vistula and maneuvering on the San to force Poniatowski to abandon his position and recross the river. He believed this would permit him to invest Sandomierz on both sides of the river. He began his movement on 8 June. General Schauroth moved, at the head of 8,000 men, against Polaniec, where he crossed the Vistula and then advanced on Wisloka, extending his right to Dembica. General Egermann, who had joined Grammont's detachment to his forces and occupied the line of Dunayec, marched with 4,000 men on that place. General Geringer, with 3,000 others, took up a position between Bogorya and Szydlow, on the left bank of the Vistula in order to cover the movement of the archduke. Poniatowski had established his army behind the Wisloka. This river was fordable along most of its length, so it was not capable of stopping the Austrians. Poniatowski did not believe it appropriate to dispute their passage. He expected the Russians to arrive the following day and hoped to maintain himself with their support. He remained with the bulk of his forces in his position by Trzesnia, where was joined by the 2nd Infantry Regiment and three companies of the 8th, which had been relieved by new Galician levies raised in Lublin and Zamosc. He contented himself with moving his advanced guard before the Austrians. This advanced guard, under the orders of General Rozniecki, consisted of the 2nd and 5th Cavalry Regiments, four companies of the 8th Infantry Regiment, and four cannons. It advanced via Baranow on Tuszyn, where it encountered, on 9 June, Schauroth's cavalry. The Poles charged the Austrian cavalry repeatedly forcing it to withdraw. It was in this charge that Chef d'Escadron Kurnatowski was taken prisoner. The Prince, learning of the Austrian progress from Rozniecki, and learning that they advanced in force, looked to abandon his position and take another, more concentrated, before the San by Wrzawy. This position was covered by dikes, hedges, and ditches, which could easily be defended and the Polish army could manage the superior Austrian cavalry there. However, in executing this retrograde movement, Poniatowski was forced to raise the bridge at Sandomierz. He sent the boats to the mouth of the San and cut his communications with the fort. As we have said earlier, if the bridgehead had been reestablished, he could have put himself under the protection of its entrenchments, and by being able to cross the river at will he could have attacked the two parts of the Austrian Army separated by the Vistula, defeating each separately and in detail. However, in the actual state of affairs, this was impossible. The central position was not fortified and he could only seek to maintain himself on the San.

While these events occurred in central Poland, Zajączek vigorously pursued Mondet's troops as they fell back on the Piliça. Hauck joined him on the 7th at Warka where he had moved and formed his advanced guard. Reinforced by 1,400 men, Zajączek crossed the Piliça and advanced on Radomka, crossing the immense forests that covered the interval between the two rivers and extended to within a half mile of Iedlinsko. If he did not appear until he arrived at the edge of the woods, he had nothing to fear from Mondet who crossed, at that time, the Piliça at Bialobrzegi and at Nowiemasto. However, he imprudently advanced into the Iedlinsko plains and took up a position on the 9th, occupying the dikes that ran from that city to Random, threatening that city, which was occupied by only 2,000 Austrians. On the 10th he moved his advanced guard to Iankowice, on the road to Przytyke. Mondet united under his command 11,000 men, on this point, and found himself in a favorable position to attack the 6,300 Poles. Dąbrowski, who found himself at Lowicze, where a flying corps observed him, received orders from Poniatowski to join his movements with those of Zajączek. He advanced on the 10th to Skierniewice and on the 11th to Rawa, chasing before him the Austrians. His advanced guard, under the orders of

Major Uminski, occupied Nowemiasto that same day and captured 500 Austrian wounded. The bridge at the Piliça was cut so Uminski was unable to advance further. Zajączek found himself abandoned. Mondet would be able to attack and destroy him by virtue of his superior forces.

On 11 June, at daybreak, Mondet's advanced guard, commanded by Gartemburg, attacked Hauke's brigade. One of his battalions, under the command of Major Swiderski, was chased from the village of Iankowice. Hauke, heavily pressed, retired in disorder on Iedlinsko. The news of this check reached Zajączek, who advanced with his division, leaving only a battalion of the 3rd Infantry Regiment and two cannons under Major Krukowiecki, to guard the dams. The Polish infantry advanced in column, its artillery leading, and a newly raised cavalry regiment on its left. Hauke rallied his troops behind this force as it advanced to his aid. Gartemburg was driven back in his turn and the Poles occupied Iankowice again. This position, however, was dominated by the hills behind which Mondet had deployed all his forces. Zajączek advanced and found himself confronted by the Austrian masses that assumed the offensive with vigor. The Polish cavalry was driven back and driven off the battlefield. In vain Major Rostworowski attempted to rally them, but failed. Mondet turned the Polish left that was uncovered by this check. His cavalry struck the Polish infantry in the rear as it was engaged to the front. General Zajączek, nonetheless, did not lose his courage. He ran through the ranks, harangued and animated his troops by his words and example. The Austrians, though redoubled in their valor and audacity, could not break them. The Polish infantry formed in square and retired slowly and in good order on Jedinsko. The 3/12th Infantry Regiment particularly distinguished itself on this occasion, driving back the Austrian cavalry with a fire by files and inflicting heavy losses on them. The cavalry, however, retained the two Polish cannons that it had captured. The Lomza light infantry, supported by some platoons of the 3/8th Infantry Regiment, threw themselves against the cavalry and forced them to abandon the guns. As night fell, Zajączek fell back to his position at Idelinsko.

Major Krukowiecki, attacked on the Iedlinsko dikes, stood equally firm. General Mohr, at the head of the Austrian columns, vainly attempted to force passage to Radomka. Showered by cannister, each time that they presented themselves, they were unable to take the bridge and had their formations disordered. The day, however, was still hard on the Poles. Six hundred Polish dead and wounded covered the battlefield and 400 were taken prisoner. The Austrian losses were lower, not exceeding 500 men. General Zajączek withdrew during the night on Kosienice, arriving there on the 12th. On the 13th he marched on Gniewoszow and on the 14th he took up positions at Gora, vis-à-vis Pulawy. He had no bridge over the Vistula and stood with his back to the river, running the risk of being destroyed. However, the Russians occupied Pulawy and he thought that he might be able to count on their support. This was, however, a terrible error. He would have been much better served had he moved up the Vistula and found security in the Iedlonka Forests. At the same time he could have covered Warsaw. If the Austrians had followed him to Pulawy, they would have been able to drive to the Vistula and destroyed his division. The Austrians could have reached Zajączek in two days' marches via Radom and Zwolen. Fortunately, Mondet, who had united his forces at Radom, was ordered to march on Sandomierz, in order to invest it from the north.

As Zajączek marched on Pulay, Dąbrowski marched on Lubochnia, which he occupied on the 12th. He remained there two days, chasing the Austrians from Uiazd and Wolbroz. He then advanced on Piotrkow, which he entered on the 16th. His advanced guard, consisting of a squadron of the newly raised 1st Cavalry Regiment and a company of light infantry, presented itself before Suleiow. A force of Austrian cavalry occupied this post. The Polish cavalry squadron charged it, pushing it, in disorder, through the city to a convent where it was taken under fire by a force of Wallachian grenz. The fire of the Wallachians shot down 20 Polish troopers. However, the Polish light infantry rushed to their support, threw themselves on the Austrians, and drove them back to Konskie.

The check suffered by Zajączek gave rise to severe criticism. Some attribute it to a malicious rivalry, a rivalry with Dąbrowski that would not stop, no matter what the disaster. However, sentiments do not merit discussion. The calculation of distances clearly demonstrates that criticisms of Zajączek were unjustified. It was possible that Dąbrowski could have marched on Radom during the 13th, but he had no idea that the disaster had occurred, and justifiably he had no desire to march into open terrain where the Austrian superiority in cavalry could spell disaster, which would bring him criticism. He logically then assumed that Zajączek could find a secure refuge in the woods that extend towards the Piliça.

Prince Poniatowski, who we have left in positions near Wrzawy, counted on the pending arrival of the Russians and did not stop Galitzin to support him.

Despite the repugnance that the Russians had for their alliance with the French, Alexander persisted in his commitments to Napoleon. He had no sympathy for the cause of the French Emperor and had little desire to reduce the power of the Austrians. However, he also feared the enlargement of the Grand Duchy of Warsaw, which might grow as a result of Poniatowski's conquests. The levy of soldier sin Galicia, which arose because of their sympathy for the Grand Duchy, was also odious to him. He resolved, as a result, to march forward and give the appearance of support to Poniatowski, but in reality he sought to break the spirit of the Galicians as well as to control their armament. In order to accomplish this, he sought to double the size of the army under Galitzin, but Napoleon, seeing his duplicity, refused this offer.

As Galitzin entered Galicia, he issued a proclamation that contained the following phrase. "The Austrian war with France cannot be a point of indifference to Russia, who is intimately tied by treaties with the Emperor of the French. Russia attempted to prevent this war, but when its representations and counsels were produced no effect, Russia broke off relations with Austria." The Russian Army occupied the following positions: Souvorov's division was in Wlodawa, and extended towards Dubno. Lambert's division (formerly under Gorchakov) occupied Wlodawa and Brzesc. Lewis' division stood in Bailystok and Brzesc. Finally, Doctorov's division occupied Bailystok and Grodno. This army should be estimated as having a strength of 35,000 men.

On 2 June the Russian troops began marching and crossed the frontier at four points. Souvorov entered Galicia via Uscilung, and them moved via Krasnystaw on Ulanow. On the 11th one of his detachments occupied Zaklikow. Lambert's division, after crossing the Bug at Terespol, marched on Kock, which it occupied on the 10th, and then it moved on Lublin. Lewis' division crossed the Bug at Drohiczyn, traversed Siedlce, Garwolin, and advanced on Bobrowniki, where it crossed the Wieprz over a bridge the Poles had built for them. Finally, Doctorov's division united at Gialystok, crossed the Bug at Brzesc, and moved on Lublin. Galitzin followed Doctorov's division.

In reporting to Napoleon of the Russian Army's advance, Poniatowski stated, "The attached letter, which I found in Galitzin's writing case, shall give to Your Imperial Majesty the personal opinions of this general, as well as the delays that, according to all reports, they seek to put to any active cooperation, as well as shortening the marches, by lengthening their rest periods, while at the same time giving one division a line of march that was entirely unnatural to what should be expected of it. The representations contained in this letter appears to give some impression of Galitzin's spirit, and he has just informed me, following information that I gave him about our position, that one of his division's is marching on Purlawy and that another will join my force without delay."

Reassured by Galitzin's promises, Poniatowski continued to believe in the immediate cooperation on the part of the approaching Russian Army in his fight with the archduke. The Austrians had marched down the length of the Vistula, via Baranow, with Schauroth's division, some 6,000 infantry and 2,500 cavalry, while Egermann marched directly on Leopol. On the 11th Rozniecki had joined the Polish Army at Wrzawy, which was deployed as follows: The 1st Infantry Regiment, supported by two horse guns was placed where the San and the Vistula joined, along the dikes constructed by the inundations of the river. This position was covered by the old bed of the San, which was now dry, but formed a deep ditch that would be difficult for cavalry to cross. A detachment of this regiment occupied the village of Wrzawy, where it supported its left. Four companies of the 1st Regiment were posted in the woods that covered the San's ford, situated a half-mile below the main position. The 2nd Infantry Regiment was deployed in columns by battalion, behind the 1st Regiment, with four cannons deployed in front of it. The 2nd and 5th Cavalry Regiments, with two cannons, part of Rozniecki's advanced guard, were placed in reserve in front of the bridge. The 8th Infantry Regiment, four companies of the 6th, two squadrons of the 3rd Cavalry Regiment, the 1st Cavalry Regiment, and six cannons, occupied the position by Pniow, a village situated on the right bank of the San and positioned themselves on a hill with dominated the surrounding terrain. The forces under the Prince came to six battalions and four companies of infantry, eleven cavalry squadrons, and 14 cannons, or about 7,300 men, who were divided into two corps separated by the San and communicating with each over a pontoon bridge which crossed the river at Czekay.[6] This disposition appears strange, but Souvarov's division occupied, during the evening of the 11th, Radomysl and Dombrowa on the left bank. Poniatowski hoped incessantly to be able to take the offensive. Without the presence of the Russians, Poniatowski would have surely awaited the Austrians from behind the San and not exposed two thirds of his forces to be cut off on the far size of the river. Everything appeared to announce that the Russians would arrive momentarily. A detachment of 150 Cossacks arrived in the Polish camp on the 11th and moved down the road to Baranow. In addition, there were frequent communications between Poniatowski and Souvorov.

During the afternoon of the 12th the archduke's advanced guard occupied a position at Gorzyce, a village situated on a hill at not quite a cannon shot's distance from Wrzawy. The Austrian skirmishers moved forward and engaged the Poles. Six cannon were put in battery on the plateau and opened fire, while the two guns supporting the Polish 1st Infantry Regiment replied. At 2:00 p.m., the Austrian army corps under the archduke took up position on the Gorzyce heights and deployed to the right and left of the village. The Austrian infantry columns advanced, covered by a dense skirmish screen, attacking the dikes and the village of Wrzawy, occupied by the Polish 1st Infantry Regiment. The Polish regiment held firm and forced the Austrians to retreat. Not discouraged, the Austrians returned at the charge. Despite the cannister fired by the two Polish cannon and the supporting musketry, a Hungarian infantry company succeeded in crossing the dike to the left of the village. Colonel Malachowski, commander of the 1st Regiment, sent forward his reserve, the grenadiers. They engaged the Hungarians at bay-

---

[6]The other regiments of Poniatowski's corps formed the garrison of Sandomierz and a squadron of the 3rd Cavalry Regiment was detached to Podolia with Strzyzewski.

onet pont and drove them back across the dike. The Poles, however, became overly excited by their success and drove too far forward, only to be charged by an Austrian chevauleger squadron that had hid in ambush behind the houses of the Gorzyce village. Twenty men, including Captain Siemionkowski, were sobered and a further 50 were captured. The remainder returned safely to Wrzawy.

At 4:00 p.m., the Austrians deployed a few squadrons, supported by a battery, on the left of the village and threatened to advance. Poniatowski, who had come at the beginning of the battle, placed himself at the head of the 2nd Infantry Regiment.[7] A battalion of this regiment was ordered to counter the Austrian move, and, supported by the fire of four guns, prevented them from executing their intended movement. If Poniatowski had had some cavalry, he would have been able to successfully charge them, but the cavalry brigade that had been before the bridge had been redirected to the ford that was covered by the four companies of the 1st Infantry Regiment when it was feared that the Austrian cavalry, after crossing the San, might move to take the Polish infantry in the rear.

At 6:00 p.m., the archduke, seeing the uselessness of his efforts to force Poniatowski's position, doubled the artillery at Gorzyce. The subsequent cannonade was very heavy and lasted until 9:30 p.m. The Austrians lost several hundred men hors de combat and lost 100 prisoners. The Polish lost 30 killed, 50 wounded, and 50 prisoners. The two parties remained their respective positions the following day. The following night Poniatowski sent Pelletier to Souvorov to press him to cross the San. Siever's brigade was ostensibly ordered to cross it. A bridge was thrown over the river at Radomysl, but when it was time to march Sievers found various pretexts to delay the operation. It was "Monday", which he alleged was an inauspicious day and one on which the Russians abstained from combat. The following day he found he had lost his Cross of St. George, which he took as an ill omen. Poniatowski, meanwhile, floated between hope and despair over having such useless allies, eventually abandoned hope and withdrew. During the night of the 13th/14th the Polish forces crossed the San and raised the bridge. The archduke threw a light infantry battalion across the river, which engaged in a skirmish fight with the Polish infantry. An Austrian cavalry brigade moved on Ulanow, and summoned the Russian detachment that occupied the village to allow it to pass, but they refused.

While these events occurred on the San, Egermann reached Rzeszow, then Iaraslow, chasing before him the detachment of new Galician levies that had barred his passage. He arrived before Leopol on the 18th, occupied it on the 19th, and named Wurmser as governor of the city. He had defeated the French eagles before him, reestablished the Austrian authorities, and ordered that the Polish patriots that had been appointed by Rozniecki be replaced by Austrians. He then began a campaign of vengeance and put several in chains. The Russian Army made no movement to delay the Austrian's progress. The Russians looked with pleasure as much of Galicia returned to Austrian domination.

———•———

---

[7]During this battle, Poniatowski sent the ordnance officer Siodolkowicz to Souvorov to ask that he come to their assistance. Souvorov promised to come, but did not advance.

Vivandier   Fusiliers   Sergeant

2nd Infantry Regiment

The 2ⁿᵈ Infantry Regiment in 1809

Ferdinand units Geringer's brigade and Mondet's Division near Sandomierz; Preparations for an assault – Forces of the garrison of Sandomierz, its means of defense – Ferdinand summons the garrison to surrender – He attacks Sandomierz during the night of the 15ᵗʰ/16ᵗʰ – The assault is repulsed with losses – Capitulation of Sandomierz – The Polish Garrison evacuates the fortress and moves on Mniszow on the Piliça – Poniatowski moves to Lublin on the 15ᵗʰ – Conference with Galitzin – Plan of operations is developed by the two commanders – The Russians are to act on the right bank and the Poles on the left – Inaction of Fisher – Retreat of Zajączek, via Pulay, on the San, where he rejoins Poniatowski – Poniatowski learns of the results of the assault and the capitulation of Sandomierz – Letter from Poniatowski to Sokolnicki – Report of Poniatowski to Berthier of 21 May – Poniatowski reorganizes his army corps – The Polish Army is divided into a division of cavalry and one of infantry – Galitzin Poniatowski wishes to send the 1ˢᵗ Cavalry Regiment to Leopol in order to support the new formations – The Russians oppose him – Galitzin's slowness – He finally crosses the San – Egermann evacuates Leopol and retires on Stanislawow – The Russians occupy Czeszow, Leopol, and Sendziszow – They reestablish the Austrian authorities everywhere – Persecutions of the Polish patriots – Galitzin does not wish to recognize the name Poland – The archduke Ferdinand unites his forces around Sandomierz and begins, on 22 June, his movement on the upper Piliça – He reaches it on the 30ᵗʰ – Poniatowski begins his movement on the 22ⁿᵈ, and arrives in Pulawy on the 24ᵗʰ – He throws a bridge over the Vistula and sends his cavalry forward – Report from Poniatowski to Berthier on 27 June – Events that occurred in May and June in Germany, Hungary, and Italy – The communications of the Grande Armée – Sojourn of Poniatowski at Pulawy – Temple of Sibylle – Poniatowski's order of the day – New Franco-Galician regiments – Poniatowski begins his movement on Radom and unites with Sokolnicki and Dąbrowski – His army now has 23,000 men – He establishes is headquarters at Radom and installs a new government there – Patriotism of the inhabitants – They form a force of partisans – Poniatowski's order of the day.

After throwing the Poniatowski's army corps the San, he hastened to profit from this advantage to invest Sandomierz and to attempt an assault. Mondet, who had force marched his troops, arrived before Sandomierz on the 15ᵗʰ and brought Geringer's brigade into his command. Sandomierz was closed to the north and middle. The Archduke arrived on the left bank and deployed his forces for the assault. He assigned his elite forces to attempt the *coup de main*.

On his side Sokolnicki prepares for a vigorous defense. The breaches that had been in the walls of Sandomierz when the Poles had captured it, had been repaired. The advanced works constructed by the Austrians had been perfected, palisades had been erected on them and a new entrenchment had been raised. The fortress was armed with 39 guns, including 21 siege guns and its garrison consisted of the 3ʳᵈ, 6ᵗʰ, and 12ᵗʰ Infantry Regiments, the 6ᵗʰ Cavalry Regiment, and three companies of artillery. The total force came to about 5,000 men.

At 10:00 p.m., on the 15ᵗʰ, General Geringer presented himself before the fortress in the name of the archduke. He demanded that the fortress immediately open its gates and that the garrison lay down its arms. Sokolnicki could not contain his indignation. He turned towards the regimental commanders in his headquarters and asked them what they thought of the presented conditions. They were boring, responded Colonel Sierawski, commander of the 6ᵗʰ Infantry Regiment. When this garrison consents to submit, my regiment will drive them back and make play with them with bayonets. He then left the room and made preparations for the coming battle. The other commanders manifested their intentions to do the same. Sokolnicki responded to Geringer in a manner that dashed any hope of an arrangement and had him lead back to the advanced posts.

When Sokolnicki's refusal was made known to the archduke, he ordered this artillery to open fire. It was 10:45 p.m. Six howitzers and six 12pdrs, emplaced at the bridgehead on the right bank, were then unmasked. Three other batteries were deployed on the heights of the left bank. They began firing and covered Sandomierz with their projectiles. The skirmishers, on their side, pushed into the houses of the suburbs and began a lively fire against the ramparts. This fire lasted until midnight. The darkness was exceptionally deep. The artillery of the fortress, having no ability to spot its targets, responded only weakly. Ten thousand to 11,000 men drawn from the best regiments of the archduke's army were organized into nine attack columns. At their head were engineering officers who knew the local perfectly and served as guides. These columns were equipped with fascines, gabions, and ladders; in a word, everything that was necessary for an escalade.

Little by little the fort's fire became more intense. The first column, which directed its attack against Battery No. 12, was repulsed. This battery, valiantly defended by the brave Captain Zawadzki, of the 3rd Infantry Regiment, was important because it commanded all the right bank of the Vistula above Sandomierz. Colonel Bontems, director of Polish artillery material, made powerful contributions to its success. The second column turned the village of Strachayce, which was defended by three companies of the 6th Infantry Regiment under the orders of Lieutenant Colonel Blumer. The Poles, almost taken in the rear, withdrew at the last minute in good order on Batteries Nos. 2 and 3, commanded by Captain Rybinski, who was quickly assailed by the advancing Austrian columns. Despite their attack, the batteries remained in Polish hands. Colonel Sierawski defended the newly constructed entrenchment. The third and fourth columns attacked the Church of Saint Paul and Battery No. 4. However, their efforts were checked by the tenacity of Chef de Bataillon Bailkowski, who, at the head of 130 men of the 12th Infantry Regiment, defended this post vigorously and refused to allow the Austrians to succeed. Encircled on all sides, it was freed by Colonel Weissenhoff, who, at the head of two companies of grenadiers, charged the Austrians and drove them back.

The fifth column, which advanced on the side of Loiowice, was repulsed by Captain Plonczynski of the 12th Regiment, who, supported by artillery, inflicted heavy losses on them. The gunners were almost all killed or wounded in the battle, so the officers of the 12th Regiment took their places and served the guns. The officers were, in their turn, almost all wounded. Colonel Weissenhoff had his face burned by the powder.

The fifth, sixth and seventh columns advanced on batteries Nos. 6 and 7, and attacked them three times. The gunners were nearly all killed. The garrison of Battery No. 6, commanded by Captain Pogorzelski of the 12th Infantry Regiment, evacuated the battery after overthrowing the guns. Lieutenant Colonel Morawski, of the 12th Regiment, was forced to abandon Battery No. 7, which he commanded. He wished to retake his command, but being encircled by enemy columns advancing from the village of Chwalki, he was overwhelmed and taken prisoner along with his detachment.

The Austrians then directed their principal efforts against Battery No. 11, where Sokolnicki watched the battle. The Austrians occupied an inn and, despite the redoubled artillery fire, maintained that position despite the fire that sought to dislodge them. General Sokolnicki, nonetheless, did not give up. He ordered a sortie. Captain Czeykoski, of the 3rd Infantry Regiment, launched the attack with his company, killing and wounding many, while taking 80 prisoners. Captain Jerzmanowski, an aide-de-camp to General Bieganski, led another sortie with another detachment of infantry, driving back the Austrians and taking many prisoners. The Austrian skirmishers still held the church and convent where they had established themselves. Captain Jordan, aide-de-camp to Sokolnicki, undertook to clear them from their positions. He attacked them with a company of grenadiers from the 3rd Infantry Regiment and 100 voltigeurs from the regiment. He forced them back and took 20 prisoners. This was at the point where the battle was most heated. The ground in front of Batteries Nos. 10 and 11 were covered with dead.

The two last Austrian columns, the 8th and 9th, advanced, one from Zawichost and the other moved up the Vistula. They moved on Battery No. 9 and came close to taking it. Their commanders, speaking Polish, caused their troops to be mistaken for the voltigeurs of the 3rd and 6th Polish Infantry Regiments. This ruse allowed them to approach to within musketry range of the battery. They then drove forward so quickly that they suffered only two discharges of cannister from the battery's guns. As they attempted to climb the parapet they were repelled by the bayonets of the garrison formed from detachments of the 3rd and 6th Infantry Regiments. Except for two squadrons of the 6th Cavalry Regiment, which were in a position below the wall, they found themselves cut off. Colonel Dziewanowski saved them. This intrepid officer slipped through the Austrian forces and into the fortress. One of the squadrons, commanded by Lieutenant Colonel Brzechwa dismounted and repeated what they had done in the assault on Zamosc. On foot and armed with their lances, they charged the Austrians and drove them of the battery.

The nine Austrian infantry battalions that took part in the regiment were drawn from the Davidovich, Weissenfeld, Strauch and Szeckler Regiments[1] and they fought under the eyes of the archduke, who watched their efforts checked by Polish valor. By daybreak the battle had ceased and the assailants had withdrawn. The Austrians left 689 dead and 6 senior officers 20 subalterns, and 986 wounded on the field. In addition, they lost 315 prisoners, including 6 officers. The Polish lost in killed, wounded, and prisoners around 1,000.[2]

The day of the 16th was spent burying the dead and caring for the wounded. The 17th was spent preparing for a new assault. Sokolnicki had only 4,000 men under arms and they were nearly out of ammunition. They were separated from Poniatowski by the Vistula and blocked on the two banks so they had no hope of relief. In this critical position, it was necessary for Sokolnicki to enter into negotiations with the Austrians and a capitulation was negotiated and concluded, ratified on the 18th at 9:00 a.m.

The garrison had twelve hours to evacuate the fortress. They were to retreat with their arms, baggage, and artillery, with the exception of the fifteen cannon that were on the ramparts. The boat bridge, the magazines, and the material were to be surrendered to the Austrians and the Polish troops were to move via Zawichost, Solec, and Kozienice, to Mniszew, and then to the Piliça under the escort of an Austrian hussar squadron. The prisoners of war, made elsewhere and during the assault, were to be exchanged in mass. The Polish soldiers that the Austrians had forcibly inducted into their army and had deserted to the Poles were mixed in with the

[1]Before the attack the Austrians soldiers had received an abundant distribution of cognac.

[2]Editor: D. Smith, p. 317, indicates that the Poles lost around 1,000 and that the Austrians lost 689 dead and 986 wounded, confirming Soltyk's figures. However, and it is extremely strange, Smith indicates that the Austrians took the fortress and then allowed the Poles to leave on the condition that they would not fight against the Austrians again.

prisoners. The Polish convalescents were transported with the garrison in wagons provided by the Austrians. Those that were not capable of being moved were to be treated in hospital in Sandomierz and to be liberated after recovering so they could join their units. Finally, the armistice was to continue 48 hours after they had crossed the Piliça. One additional article stipulated that, in light of the darkness at night, the last Polish column could delay its departure until the morning of the 19th. As for the prisoners of war, which the Austrians suspected having been Poles who had deserted their ranks, they gave their word of honor to General Sokolnicki and declined to pursue any action against them. The Austrians took immediate possession of the Krakow gate and the castle, and occupied the city during the morning of the 19th.

The delays of the Russian army, the equivocations of its generals, the ill will of Suvorov[3] and Sievers, indicated much of what the Polish Army might expect of its allies. Poniatowski, nonetheless, sought to make a new effort. In the morning of the 15th he moved to Lublin in order to reach an understanding with Golitsyn, to penetrate his true intentions, and engage him to make an effort to recover Sandomierz. He explained to Golitsyn the dangers in which he found in the fortress and engaged him to move his forces to the left bank of the Vistula in order to act against Mondet. Golitsyn referred to his orders from Alexander and formally refused to cross the Vistula. Poniatowski insisted vainly. All that he could obtain from then Russians was that they would act on the right bank and the Poles would act on the left. Poniatowski returned to his headquarters. Hearing the cannonade from Sandomierz he set out. The day he arrived at Pniow he learned of the fall of Sandomierz.

General Fisher, who commanded in Poniatowski's absence, should have attempted a movement at the beginning of the attack, at the least to cross the Vistula so as to act as a diversion. He should have crossed the San at the ford above Wrzawy and threatened the Austrians on the right bank of the Vistula, but this unenterprising general remained totally inactive. Poniatowski, unsure of what was happening at Sandomierz, with which he had no communications, doubtlessly thought that it was too late and did not attempt anything.

He left General Zajączek with his back to the Vistula and fearing an attack at any moment from the direction of Zwolen by Mondet's corps. General Lewis had advanced very little, but Zajączek went to his quarters and spoke with him, sending the following report to Poniatowski" "From Gora," he wrote, "I personally went to Pulawy to speak with the Russian General Lewis, who I found with his division. I requested him to move to my support a detachment of 2,000 to 3,000 cavalry on the left bank of the Vistula. I stated the reason for my demand was the danger run by my division, which had no bridge over the river over which to retreat in case of a check. I told him that the Austrians were in force at Zwolen. But the Russian general refused to cooperate, alleging that such a feeble detachment would not be sufficient if the Austrians advanced in force; and if they were less numerous my forces were sufficient to engage them. I declared to General Lewis that I would cross the Vistula myself to join your corps, which I executed without delay on the 15th in the boats prepared by Princess Czartoryska,[4] who worked with great zeal to allow the crossing. All her domestic servants were engaged in the effort."

After resting his troops in Puławy, General Zajączek resumed his march on the 17th and rejoined the prince on the 19th at the San.

Poniatowski acted as if chained to his position at Pniow. The Russians did not move. Poniatowski had Schauroth's division in front of him and he found himself separated from

---

[3]Arkadi Suvorov (1783 – 1811) was the son of the famous Russian general.
[4]The princess was the wife of Prince Czartoryski, Starosteff, general of the Podolia Lands, Proprietor of Puławy.

Sandomierz by the Vistula. He was very perplexed as to the situation in Sandomierz, having received no report. Finally, on the 19th, he received words of the assault and the conditions of the capitulation that Sokolnicki had signed.

Unfortunate as the fall of Sandomierz was, it was fortunate that the garrison was not lost. Nonetheless he indicated his dissatisfaction to Sokolnicki with this transaction. On the 20th he sent him the following letter: "I have received your report, with the capitulation you have concluded, eight hours after it was delivered by Colonel Neipperg.[5] I am as happy to praise the brave defense that you and your garrison have conducted, as I am to see your precipitous resolution. The reasons that you put forward, in your report, are plausible motives, but the recommendations that I have given you, the bravery of the garrison; everything required you to attempt to hold out longer. Continue your march, as you see fit; later I shall send you more appropriate orders."

Poniatowski had severely reprimanded the defender of Sandomierz, which was necessary as commander-in-chief. However, he was more just in his report to Berthier and he rendered justice to the honorable conduct of the garrison and justified Sokolnicki's capitulation. "The troops", he said, "had neither infantry cartridges nor charges for the 3pdr and 6pdr guns, and found themselves threatened by a new assault." Poniatowski complained of the total inaction of the Russian Army, which had two divisions within range of supporting Sandomierz, yet neither moved, despite his pleas. He added that in these circumstances, he thought there was nothing he could do but attacking on the left bank of the Vistula, moving so as to defend the duchy from any actions by Ferdinand, or to follow the archduke if he withdrew into Krakow. Poniatowski ended his letter by observing the following: "If I am only to support the efforts of the enemy, I will at least not be misled in my resources, I will be able about what to always count, and will be able to continue the course of my operations, without to Be stopped by the slowness and ill-will of the Russians."

The arrival of Zajączek raised Poniatowski's army to 12,000 men. Poniatowski occupied himself with reorganizing his army. The third battalions rejoined their respective regiments. The infantry was organized into a single division under the orders of General Zajączek and the cavalry was organized into a single division under the command of General Rozniecki. On 21 May Golitsyn's army finally moved to relieve Poniatowski on the San and extended towards Leopol. The prince wished to send the 1st Cavalry Regiment on Leopol in order to support the formation of Galician troops in Podolia. The Russians formally opposed this and a single company of this regiment, under Chef d'Escadron Strzyzewski, was permitted to operate on that side.

After having employed several days in marching on the San and establishing himself there, Golitsyn decided to send his forces forward. General Muller occupied Leopol on 22 June when Egermann evacuated it in order to move on Stanislawow, behind the Dniester. A Russian division took possession of Rzeszow on the 23rd. The same day Golitsyn established his headquarters at Sendziszow and the bulk of the troops found themselves echeloned on the highway from Krakow to Leopol. Austrian authorities resumed the direction of affairs, everywhere the French eagles were replaced by the Austrian coat of arms. The Russians and the Austrians intended to act. The Polish patriots who had so nobly embraced the national cause, continued to be the target of persecution by their allies and enemies. Poniatowski succeeded, only with great efforts, to maintain the authority that he established in the area of New Galicia, on the right

---

[5]Chief of staff to the army of the archduke.

bank of the Vistula and in Zamosc, which was part of Old Galicia. In his communications with Golitsyn, Poniatowski used the title of "commander-in-chief of the Polish Army" who protested against that title, saying that Poland no longer existed and that his troops were not Polish, but those of the Grand Duchy of Warsaw.

Ferdinand had occupied Sandomierz in the morning of the 19th and was hurried to re-establish a bridge over the Vistula. He evacuated his wounded and material from Sandomierz to Krakow and immediately occupied himself with the destruction of the fortifications at Sandomierz, the fortifications that had cost his army so much blood. After the fortifications were destroyed on the 22nd he immediately set out for Kielee, moving on to Malagoszcz, and then to Przedborz. His advanced guard, under the orders of General Mohr, occupied Piotrkow on the 30th. He sought to move towards Germany and bring his forces closer to those of the Archduke Charles, who was at that time in Marchfeld. He left only weak detachments on the right bank of the Vistula with orders to withdraw if Golitsyn advanced and to offer him no resistance.

On his side, Poniatowski left Pniow the same day. He arrived in Puławy on the 24th and threw a bridge over the Vistula on the 26th, immediately moving his cavalry over it and into Radom and Opatow. In explained the various events and motives for his conduct to Marshal Berthier, Napoleon's chief of staff, in a dispatch dated 27 June. In it he rendered an account of Golitsyn's behavior in crossing the San and of his refusal to cross the Vistula. Poniatowski attributed this to two motives: to facilitate the passage of the Austrians to the left bank and to menace the duchy. This had decided Poniatowski to move to Puławy from where he could observe the Austrian's movements and to move to the left bank of the Vistula where he could coordinate his operations with those of Dąbrowski and Sokolnicki. He ended by announcing that he did not neglect to seize any opportunity to obtain a new success; that he had not lost sight of the archduke and would fulfill the intentions of His Majesty the Emperor, in tying up an Austrian corps stronger than the forces he deployed. He did not conceal that the arrival of the Russian Army had slowed down the formation of new Galician formations, but he hoped that the zeal of the inhabitants would overcome this new problem, and that his army would not be denied the support available from Galicia.

In conformation with the capitulation of Sandomierz, Sokolnicki moved to Mniszew. His brigade arrived opposite Puławy as Poniatowski arrived there. Sokolnicki went in person to receive orders from Poniatowski, who enjoined him to press his march and to join General Dąbrowski, to whom he had sent orders to march on lower Piliça and to cover Warsaw. Dąbrowski, after resting until the 19th in Piotrkow and having spread alarm as far as the gates of Krakow, moved via Inowlodz and Nowe-Miasto, where his advanced guard was engaged, on the 24th, with a small force of Austrians. He them moved via Mogielnicz on Czersk, where he found himself in communication with General Sokolnicki as he came from Mniszew.

Poniatowski had 12,000 men at Puławy and 11,000 men on the left bank at Piliça. These forces were close enough that they could unite at Radom in two days.

Ferdinand's expedition had been checked. He found himself being controlled by the maneuvers of his opponent. He was reduced to holding himself on the defensive and covering the rear of the army of the Archduke Charles as he prepared to give a decisive battle on the Danube.

In order to better appreciate the position of Poniatowski, we will now relate in a succinct manner the events that had taken place up to this point, since Napoleon's occupation of Vienna.

On 21 May the Grande Armée began crossing the Danube, which then began to flood, rapidly growing in size and depth. Archduke Charles came out of Bohemia and took advantage of the situation. He gathered up boats, filled them with rocks and launched them into the river to break the bridges that linked Lobau Island to the right bank. The portion of the French army, which was heavily engaged by Aspern, found itself suddenly cut off. It was separated from Vienna and from its reserves. It was forced to fight desperately foot by foot. Attacked anew on the 22nd, it deployed the same consistency and energy. The Austrians were unable to break the French Army, but they inflicted heavy losses on it. The French withdrew in good order and on the 23rd, at daybreak, they withdrew to Lobau Island. Though he had pushed the French back, he did not push his success too far. He then withdrew and established his army a mile from the battlefield.

The Archduke John, on his side, was in full retreat. On 26 May he arrived in Komorn followed by Prince Eugène who engaged him at Raab on 14 June. Defeated on this memorable day, John withdrew on Pressburg where he crossed the Danube. The Raab fortress capitulated on 23 June.

Napoleon prepared for his revenge for his defeat at Aspern. During the first days of July Marmont had brought two strong divisions up from Dalmatia and Bernadotte had advanced from Linz to Vienna. Prince Eugène had joined the Grand Armée with his victorious troops. Napoleon, at the head of his united forces, prepared to cross the Danube. Prince Charles resolved to oppose the passage, directing that the Archduke Ferdinand close on Krakow to protect the rear of the main Austrian army, which Poniatowski's army could threaten during the upcoming battle.

The check suffered by the French army at Aspern-Essling had raised the hopes of Napoleon's enemies. Schill had seized Stralsund and waited in that village for the support the English had promised him: arms and munitions. His hopes were dashed when, as the British fleet appeared, General Gratien pushed into the city and, after a lively engagement, forced the partisans to put down their arms and von Schill was killed.

Meanwhile, the Austrians had united an army of 60,000 men, of whom 20,000 were ready to enter the field. They moved into the province in several columns into central and northern Germany.

The Austrian General Amande captured Dresden. The Duke of Brunswick, who had penetrated for a second time into Luzace at the head of his legion, joined him in Dresden on the 12th. These two commanders united to move on Leipzig where they forced the King of Saxony to abandon the city to move on Frankfurt am Mein. The duke then moved on his hereditary states and arrived in Halberstadt on 29 June.

Meanwhile, General Radieovich moved through Egra on 14 June, calling the population to arms and threatening the kingdom of Württemberg. The Tyrol, which had been pacified by Lefebvre, rose again. The Bavarians were obliged to evacuate Innsbrück on 25 May. The insurrection expanded. It pushed on one side into the Danube valley and on the other to the Po.

In the middle of Italy there was the greatest tumult. Napoleon, by a decree dated 17 May from Vienna, had united the Roman states to the French Empire. This measure had exasperated the hopes of the Italians. When the inhabitants of the Papal States learned of the results of the battle of Aspern-Essling they ran to arms, attacked the French garrisons, and forced them to pull back on Rome, where they were blockaded. The Pope, who was in the middle of the imperial troops, did not hesitate to issue a bull of excommunication against Napoleon. An English squadron, which appeared off Naples 25 June, captured the Island of Ischia. Stuart attempted several landings on the coasts of Calabria and Romagna, but was repulsed every time. The firmness of Murat foiled every enemy project. The Pope was arrested and sent as a prisoner to Savoy. This vigorous blow ended the risings in Romagna.

One sees by this, that by the end of June the communications of the Grande Armée were threatened on several fronts and insurrections had broken out in its rear. However, Napoleon counted on a victory, which struck at the decisive point, would decide the war, break the plots of the Austrians and end the parade of their partial successes.

Let us return to what occurred in Poland. Prince Poniatowski had established his headquarters in Puławy, in the château of Princess Czartoryska. His troops bivouacked in her gardens. These charming surroundings, which inspired the harmonious verses of Delille, were disturbed by the sounds of war for the first time. The bivouacs were established on the lawns and in the middle of the flowerbeds. Joy and cordiality reigned everywhere. Patriotism lightened all sacrifices. The mornings were filled with reviews and the evenings with brilliant balls, embellished by the charms of the ladies who surrounded Princess Czartoryska.[6]

In Puławy there was a building known as the Temple of Sybille, where the princess had brought together, over a long period, the souvenirs of old Poland. The arms of the heroes who had brightened the nation were housed there along with the trophies of the victories won by the Poles in various centuries. The young warriors of Poniatowski's army visited this sanctuary of national glory with an almost religious interest and it inspired them with a new energy.

Poniatowski divided his time between the pleasantries of the château and the work that was required of his high position. He received in Pulawy new indications of the satisfaction of the French Emperor. He shared this with his soldiers in an order of the day dated 2 July.[7] He announced to them that he had received orders to occupy the country, to render justice in the name of His Majesty the Emperor and King, and to require that the authorities extend to him an oath of loyalty. The Galician army was to be in the pay of France and was to wear the tricolor cockade. The arms and subsidies were sent from France to complete its organization. These troops, as well as the new regiments that were formed in the Grand Duchy of Warsaw, were given the title "Franco-Galician" troops, but remained under the immediate orders of Poniatowski. What follows is a state of these new units with information on their formation.

INFANTRY

1st Infantry Regiment	Formed in Galicia	Formed at the expense of the Circles of Lublin, Siedice and Biata.
2nd Infantry Regiment	Formed in the duchy on the right bank of the Vistula by Zajączek	Formed at the expense of the departments of Lomza and Plock.
3rd Infantry Regiment	Formed in the duchy on the left bank of the Vistula by Dąbrowski	Formed at the expense of the departments of Great Poland
4th Infantry Regiment	Ditto	Ditto
5th Infantry Regiment	Formed in Galicia	Formed at the expense of Prince Constantine Czartoryski.
6th Infantry Regiment	Ditto	Ditto

---

[6]The Princess Czartoryska did not appear at this reception, she sought to continue to be helpful to the Polish army, and was organizing a military hospital at Puławy, where the sick and wounded could receive the best possible care.
[7]See appendicies.

CAVALRY

1st Uhlan Regiment	Formed in the Duchy on the right bank of the Vistula by Zajączek	Formed at the expense of the departments of Lomza and Plock.
2nd Uhlan Regiment	Formed in Galician Podolia	Formed at the expense of Rozwadowski and the inhabitants of the country.
3rd Uhlan Regiment	Formed in the duchy on the left bank of the Vistula by Dąbrowski.	Formed at the expense of the departments of Great Poland.
4th Uhlan Regiment	Formed in Leopol, Galicia.	Formed at the expense of Adam Potocki and the inhabitants of the country.
5th Uhlan Regiment	Formed in Podolia, Galicia	Formed at the expense of Ryszezewski and the citizens of Austrian and Russian Podolia.
6th Uhlan Regiment	Ditto	Formed at the expense of Trzewiecki and the citizens of Austrian and Russian Podolia.
7th Uhlan Regiment	Ditto	Formed at the expense of Tarnowski and the citizens of Austrian and Russian Podolia.
1st Hussar Regiment	Formed in Galicia	Formed at the expense of the circle of Lublin, Zamosc, Biala, and Stanislawow.
2nd Hussar Regiment	Formed in Konskie, Galicia.	Formed at the expense of the departments of Great Poland.
1st Cuirassier Regiment	Formed in Konskie, Galicia	Formed at the expense of Malachowsi and formed later.

The formation of these infantry and cavalry regiments was not charged to the public treasury. All their equipment was provided at the expense of the inhabitants.

The King of Saxony, Grand-Duke of Warsaw, also sent a proclamation from Frankfurt-am-Mein dated 24 June. In it he said, "We make it our duty to employ the first moments to re-establish our government, to express to you the sentiments which excite in us patriotism and the attachment to our person that the nation has displayed in such a brilliant manner in this moment of distress."

"The enemy has entered into our country with a numerous army; with difficulty it seemed possible to resist them; but it soon learned the valor of our troops led by our brave and capable Minister of War, Prince Poniatowski."

"On its side, the nation has shown that the valorous and patriotism of old Poland continues with them. The aggression of a numerous enemy, far from intimidating you, only brought forward volunteers to sacrifice personal fortunes. They have given everything for the defense of the fatherland. The departments have surpassed themselves in their generosity; to augment the line army, to furnish the necessary material support, and to make it stronger to oppose the enemy."

"Our council of state has given proofs of its fidelity and zeal; its wise measures and the care it has taken in its actions, the methods of its different displacements, and the assistance of the other constitutional authorities, has assured the continuance of our government as much as circumstances would permit."

"Polish nation! Tranquility is returned to you and with it the constitutional government. Our greatest concern will be to try to cure the wounds occasioned by this war."

So spoke this good king, this faithful friend of Napoleon, who was expelled from his states, but trusted his destiny in the fortune of his powerful ally, and who did not forget to think of the fortune of the Poles. After a sojourn of eight days at Puławy, Poniatowski set out to follow Ferdinand's army and resolved to unite his forces at Radom. His cavalry, under the orders of General Rozniecki, advanced into the interior of the country and occupied Opatow, Kielce, and Konskie. It captured several hundred prisoners in this march, seizing 500 muskets and 500 sabers abandoned by the Austrians. General Sokolnicki crossed the Piliça and on 2 July took up position at Zwolen. General Dąbrowski, moving through Nowe-Miastro, occupied Radom on the 4th. The Prince's forces, which left Pulawy on the 2nd, joined Sokolnicki at Zwolen on the 3rd and General Dąbrowski on the 4th. The prince then established his headquarters that same day in Radom. From his arrival he instituted a new government in that city for the department of Radom, and established it under Stanislaw Soltyk[8], who represented the voice of the population. The population of the left bank of the Vistula was animated with an enthusiasm as lively as that of the right bank. They ran to arms, partisan forces appeared spontaneously, and Austrian detachments were cut up and taken prisoner by the insurgents.

Prince Poniatowski held a review of his troops at Radom, and struck by the wonderful appearance of Dąbrowski's corps, and expressed his pleasure in an order of the day saying, "I am pleased to acknowledge that the troops under the orders of General Dąbrowski, formed in such a short time, have not only an excellent bearing, but have already proved on several instances their strong spirit and shown themselves equal to the other Polish troops. This happy result is the result of the indefatigable zeal of General Dąbrowski and the officers of his army corps."

———————●———————

---

[8]Father of the author.

Polish lancers against Austrian cuirassiers

CHAPTER VIII

Position of the belligerent armies on 4 July – The archduke moves into Bohemia – Mondet replaces him in command in Galicia – Retreat of the Austrian Army on the upper Vistula – Poniatowski follows their movements – Engagement at Pinczow – Battle at Zarnowice – Encounters at Xionz and Miechow – Battle before Krakow – Convention for the reduction of this city – Movement of the Russian Army – It comes in haste to occupy the city – The Poles enter it in force and occupy it in conjunction with the Russians -- Report from Poniatowski to Napoleon -- Armistice of Znaim following the battle of Wagram – Positions of the adversarial armies – Strzyzewski's expedition into Podolia – March on Zaleszczyki – Battle at Zaleszczki – Strzyzewski's retreat on Tarnopol – Engagement at Zagrobella – Retreat of Biking on Chorostkow, his rear guard is captured – Kessler at Brzezany – Biking moves to join him – He is pursued and attacked at Winiawka – Capitulation – Strzyzewski marches on Mariampol – Cannonade across the Dniester – The two parties receive the news of the conclusion of the Armistice of Anaim – Strzyzewski marches on Tarnopol and sends his Podolian regiments into their cantonments – Poniatowski's sojourn in Krakow – The duchy's army and the Franco-Galician Army are brought to full complement – Napoleon completes its armament – Events that passed at different points in the theater of war – Peace negotiations – Ignace Potocki and Thade Matuszewic are sent to the emperor's headquarters – Treaty of Schönnbrunn on 14 October – Expansion of the Grand Duchy of Warsaw – Commission named for the delimitation – Observations on the campaign.

On 14 July, the positions of the three armies operating in Galicia were as follows: the Archduke Ferdinand, with 24,000 men, straddled the Piliça, supporting its right on the Nida and covering Krakow. Poniatowski had drawn 23,000 men at Radom and moved his advanced guard to Kielce. The Russian Army, under the orders of Golitsyn, slowly marched down the high road from Leopol to Vienna. His advanced guard was in Dembiça, his rearguard was in Rzeszow, and his headquarters were in Sendziszow. His force, not including the detachment sent to Leopol, stood at 30,000 men.

Ferdinand had received orders to take command of the Austrian forces gathering in Bohemia. Mondet was given command of the Austrian forces in Poland and continued its march towards the army of the Archduke Charles and moved up the Vistula. This retrograde movement was executed in three columns. The first followed the main road to Krakow; the second marched on Oswiecim, by the right bank of the Piliça; the third marched on the left bank towards the same point, where both were to cross the Vistula. On his side, Poniatowski left Radom and, on 5 July, moved on Krakow. First he had to cross over the Ste.-Croix Mountains by a difficult and narrow road. He arrived on the8th at Kielce, where he established his headquarters. That same day he sent his troops forward in three columns. The right column, commanded by Kosinski, marched on Koniecpol, detaching a squadron of the 2nd Cavalry Regiment that surprised Przedlbroz, an Austrian post, where it captured 54 infantry. The center column, directed by Poniatowski in person, marched on Chenciny. The left column was commanded by Rozniecki and moved on Pinczow, which it took on the 9th, after a lively engagement with Austrian cavalry.

On 10 July the Polish Army continued its movement on Krakow in the same order. The right column advanced on Zarnowiec, which was occupied by a detachment of General Mohr's troops. Lieutenant Colonel Szembeck, who commanded Kosinski's advanced guard, was sent to observe this position. However, propelled by his warrior spirit, he advanced too far, chased the Austrians out of their post, and occupied it by noon. However, that evening, he was attacked by an Austrian column of around 3,000 infantry, 500 cavalry, and four cannons under the command of Mohr. Szembeck could not maintain his position and was driven back. However, Kosinski presented himself before the city on the 11th at 8:00 a.m., detached a battalion of infantry to his right and turned the position, while he attacked it frontally. This maneuver succeeded. After a strong resistance, Mohr was forced to abandon Zarnowiec and retire on Xionz, after losing 100 men hors de combat and 200 prisoners. Kosinski found considerable supplies, food and forage, in the city. The 3/10th Infantry Regiment, which was engaged in combat for the first time, distinguished itself in this action.

After having allowed his troops two hours rest, Kosinski launched his pursuit of Mohr. He engaged them again that evening, beat them and drove them from Xionz, after inflicting another 100 casualties and taking 50 more Austrian prisoners from Mohr. This success was the result of the Polish light artillery and cavalry, which distinguished itself with its bravery in this engagement. The Austrians, on their side, gave new proofs of their constancy. In the following days they defended their positions foot by foot, forcing the Polish to deploy many times. Poniatowski established his headquarters in Wodzislaw on the 12th. On the 13th he chased the Austrians from Miechow and on the 14th General Rozniecki arrived at Krakow. The Austrians had lost about 500 men hors de combat and a further 1,000 prisoners in their retreat.

Mondet occupied Krakow, placing strong infantry detachments in the suburbs while hiss cavalry defended the streets. Rozniecki descended into the valley around noon. His cavalry executed several charges against the Austrians, driving them back. An envoy, sent by Mohr, presented himself before the Poles and asked for a suspension of arms. A correspondence began between the two generals and at 6:00 p.m., a capitulation was signed.[1] A twelve-hour armistice was signed during which the Austrian Army evacuated Krakow and surrendered it and Podgorze to the Poles. It went on to state that Poniatowski's advanced guard could not pass Podgorze until six hours after the expiration of the armistice, or that the Austrians had the right to take a position to delay their advance. The bridge over the Vistula and the magazines in the city were to be turned over, intact, to the Poles. The Austrian sick and wounded were to become prisoners of war and the administrative employees were to be treated with consideration.

Poniatowski was in Miechow when he received the news of the conclusion of this agreement. At 8:00 p.m., he mounted his horse and rode rapidly to join his advanced guard. He arrived at Promnik-le-Rouge at about 10:00 p.m. This village was situated a half mile from Krakow and he quickly established his headquarters there. On the road he encountered General Rozniecki who was returning from Miechow in order to ask Poniatowski to ratify the convention that he had concluded. Rozniecki greeted Poniatowski on his coming entry into Krakow and assured him that everything was prepared. Unfortunately, Rozniecki had neglected to take control of one of the gates. This failure led to a series of incidents, which Poniatowski reported to Napoleon. The report read:

> I had the honor to speak to Your Majesty in my previous dispatch, of the attack which I had ordered on Pinczow, as well as the disposition made to turn the enemy's position on the Nida. Both operations were successful. The city mentioned was taken on the 9th after a strong resistance, by General Rozniecki, while a body of troops moved on Chenciny,

---

[1]See appendicies.

and another, under the orders of General Kosinski, moved out by Koniecpol. Not only by this maneuver was the position on the Nida taken in the back, but also the corps of the Archduke Ferdinand found itself equally threatened on its flanks. It hastily recrossed the Vistula as soon as it learned of the threats.

The retrograde movement of the enemy was then entirely decided. He vainly attempted to maintain itself near Wodzislaw, Xionz, Zarnowice, and Miechow. However, each of these points was taken during the days of the 10th, 11th, 12th, and 13th. The enemy was equally dislodged from the intermediary posts available to him in every step he made towards Krakow, and, after a series of affairs, which were successfully concluded by our sides, he found himself totally thrown back under the walls of this city.

The multiple obstacles that the nature of the terrain offered did not permit us to concentrate a large part of our troops, I gave orders to attack the position occupied by Feldmarschal Mondet. General Rozniecki executed the attack with as much bravery as intelligence. The first posts, which covered this position, were taken with great impetuosity. General Mohr, in the name of the Field Marshal, a convention for the evacuation of the city.

I was not near enough to lend a hand. After considering the resistance that the enemy could have offered from the city would last longer than 36 hours; that to execute a successful attack would require the arrival of part of our troops that were still marching forward; considering that this delay would give the Russians, who had until that time remained inactive on the Dunaiec, the times to arrive and to concert their actions with the Austrians to take possession of Krakow, I thought these reasons prevailed over all other considerations, when it came to an important military point, I authorized General Rozniecki to conclude a capitulation which I have the honor to submit to Your Majesty. It assures us, in addition to possession of Krakow, also of Podgorze on the right bank.

I entered Krakow the following day, July 15th, to the day, three months after the entry of the enemy into the territory of the Duchy of Warsaw. The Polish troops, to which Your Majesty has confided the defense, had the pleasure of planting their victorious eagles in the capital of ancient Poland, as they had vowed.

The Austrians have lost in the aforementioned engagements, outside of killed and wounded, about 1,000 prisoners. The Polish troops that had taken part in these engagements have distinguished proofs of their valor. The cavalry had launched this morning seven brilliant charges. The affair at Zarnowice brought infinite honor to the coolness and good dispositions of General Kosinski.

I am forwarding by the courier charged with carrying to Your Imperial Majesty the report that I have the honor to address to you, some extraordinary incidents that resulted in a delay of his departure for a few hours and of which he will render an account. At 10:00 p.m. on the 14th a large number of the inhabitants of Krakow, that had left the city to show the Polish troops the joy caused by their arrival, assured several officers that a picket of Cossacks and another of Russian dragoons were in the city.

At midnight, an Austrian envoy presented himself; he was carrying a letter, by which Feldmarschal Mondet stated to General Rozniecki, commander of my advanced guard, that the officer charged with concluding with him arrangement for the evacuation with Krakow, had exceeded his instructions and his capacities, by stipulating the possession of Podgorze, separated from the city by Vistula, by the Polish troops; he invited the honesty of general to rectify in this respect, convention, the original draft of which had been sent to me. I was astonished that, although Feldmarschal Mondet, was holed up in Krakow, and General Rozniecki was within a musket shot distance, a communication of this nature arrived only six hours after the signing, I was nearly resolved to break the armistice; but before realizing that this could be only a trick to save time and to give to the Russians time to arrive; and the possession of Podgorze, dominated entirely by the city, being absolutely irrelevant, I believed, saw the few hours that it still remained until the expiration of the armistice, the duty to take another action: I ordered the Director of Engineers, Mallet, to go to Feldmarschal Mondet, to tell him that I had granted the change that he wished. He was taken, under various pretexts, via the long road, through the many suburbs located on the edge of the city, and it was only after 4:00 a.m. that he managed to see Feldmarschal Mondet. In spite of the proximity of the camp, he did not return until 5:00 a.m.; he advised me that there were several Russian regiments in the city.

These circumstances gave me no doubt of new treacheries. I ordered my troops in the field to march out. At 6:00 a.m., precisely, Chef d'Escadron, Count Wlodimir Potoçki, at the head of a platoon of cavalry, presented himself at the Krakow gate. He found [Russian] General Sievers there, who told him, "I have orders to prevent you from entering the city." Chef d'Escadron Potoçki responded to him, "I have orders to enter in the name of His Majesty the Emperor of France, and I hope that you will not force me to cross lances with you in order to effect my entry." General Sievers did not judge a point to duty to come there and the Polish advanced guard entered the city. General Rozniecki, who commanded, upon learning that General Sievers was in Krakow, went to him. He carried with him an original copy of the capitulation, which he presented to the Russian general, saying him that an arrangement had been concluded the previous day at 6:00 p.m., and that he had entered the city to take possession of the city in the name of Your Imperial Majesty. In passing before the Russian troops he was surprised to find such a large number of Austrian soldiers, completely armed, which took flight at his appearance. He had them pursued, and gathered up 30 prisoners, including two officers taken from the ranks of the Russians.

Things were in this state when I entered the city with my headquarters staff. I saw in the square 12 Russian cannons, which appeared to be aimed at the city hall. Arriving at the road, which leads to the bridge, I found it blocked by a squadron of Russian hussars in line, their back turned to the enemy [Austrians]. They refused to permit me to pass and I was obliged to force my horse through the troop in such a manner as to push back those who opposed me. This done, I directed two cannons through their line and dispatched them to the riverbank. The infantry moved to the bridge and encountered the same difficulties, a dragoon regiment blocked the road and did not permit them to pass until Lieutenant Colonel Blümer, who commanded the first battalion, had them fix bayonets and advanced them at the pas de charge.

The Russian's dispositions caused me to see the necessity of conserving a preponderance of forces: I had General Sokolnicki's infantry brigade enter the city, but it d not encounter the same obstacles and while it deployed to all the gates to assure me entry into Krakow, I invited the magistrates of the city, who had come to me, to pledge to Your Imperial Majesty, in whose name I took possession of the city, their homage and fidelity. They responded to my request with the enthusiasm that Your Imperial Majesty excites in the hearts of all Poles. The verbal process of the act was inserted in the register of deliberations and the French eagles replaced the arms of Austria. It was at this point where I encountered General Sievers. I related to him my astonishment at coming in hast to find the city conquered by allied troops, and the possession of which was assured to Your Imperial Majesty by a convention. He attempted to excuse himself saying that he was entirely ignorant of this arrangement upon his arrival and, that if he had known of it he would have not caused his troops to enter the city, despite the orders he had received from Prince Souvarov; however, this situation was effected and there was nothing he could do to change his new orders.

I do not personally know the circumstances that preceded or accompanied the arrival of the Russian troops. The most distinguished citizens of the country arrived that afternoon and described to me what had occurred. The results of their comments are:

1. While the Austrian generals were negotiating with General Rozniecki they had hastily searched for a Russian detachment to have it enter the city before our troops; that during the evening of the 14th the two aforementioned pickets of Cossacks and dragoons arrived and they were conducted by the Austrian Colonel Latour, who had assigned them the posts they were to occupy.

2. That the Russian troops, spread over several miles from Krakow, had made a forced march in order to enter the city before the Polish troops and that the request for an armistice, offering an evacuation of the city, had been extended solely so the Austrian general could assure that the Russians would have time to arrive.

3. That the Russian troops that found themselves in the city as the Austrian had permitted the Austrians to withdraw undisturbed and had allowed a quarter of their generals to escape.

All these circumstances were repeated in my presence to General Sievers by many distinguished citizens who had witnessed them, among others by Count Grabowski, former lieutenant general in the service of Poland, who had made an effort to observe these movements. General Sievers had no argument to rebut these comments.

There you have it, Sir, the exact account of what took place relative to the evacuation and the occupation of Krakow. The attached documents compose the correspondence, which has arrived in this regard, convincing Your Imperial Majesty, how much ill will the Austrian and Russian generals bear towards us.

According to information, which I have received on the enemy's march, they have taken the road to Silesia. The troops under my orders find themselves united near Krakow. I am ignorant of the actions of the Russians, but the actions of today have sufficiently proven to me how dangerous it would be to get between them and the enemy. My position had become so difficult that it is impossible to pursue them.

Poniatowski established his headquarters in one of the residences that lined the great square of the city. General Suvorov put his in another. It was feared, in light of the exasperation of the Polish troops, that the close contact between the two nations would result in an immediate conflict. However, the two generals displayed a good intelligence. They mastered the discontent and hatred between the two armies. Poniatowski established a provisional government, for the Department of Krakow. Prince Henry Lubomirski was named president, General Sokolnicki was named commandant of Krakow; General Hebdowski became military governor of Galicia. Mondet withdrew into Austrian Silesia and established himself near Biala. Golitsyn, whose army advanced slowly behind Suvorov, established his headquarters in Bochnia.

On the 16th Poniatowski received word of the armistice concluded at Znaim. According to the stipulations of this armistice the belligerent armies were to remain in the positions they occupied at time that the armistice was signed.[2] If Poniatowski had not been taken in by the ruse and the secret agreements between the Russians and Austrians, he would have already found himself on the road to Vienna, and would have at least taken Wieliczka and its salt riches, however, in light of recent events, he was to be to be seen as fortunate to have thwarted the plans of the enemies of the Polish[3] cause and to occupy Krakow.

While the Poles chased the Austrians before them, great events occurred on the Danube. Napoleon crossed the river on the night of 4/5 July at the head of a formidable army without encountering any significant resistance. Archduke Charles was informed of the concentration of French troops on the Island of Lobau took action and ordered Archduke John to join him. During the days of July 5th and 6th the battle of Wagram occurred, bearing the name of the small village on which the Austrians supported their center. After a battle lasting two days victory came to the Grande Armée. Both armies lost about 24,000 men hors de combat, but the French took 20,000 prisoners. Hard pressed by Napoleon, the Archduke Charles withdrew into Bohemia. When he arrived in Znaim he asked for a suspension of arms and hostilities ceased.

It remains for us to give n account of the operations of Strzyzewski in Podolia. This officer left Leopol on 29 May with a squadron of the 3rd Cavalry Regiment and moved on Bukowina, occupying in succession Zborow, Buczacz, Iazlowiec, and Tluste. He established commanders in all these cities and left pickets of cavalry with them. The country, free of Austrians and animated by his presence, abandoned itself to the sentiments that filled them. They all armed themselves with pikes or hunting guns and came to the column that liberated them. In the Circle of Brzezany, Alois Cikowski, who had in the past served in the Austrian Hussars, organized and equipped a squadron at his own expense. Józef Nowicki put himself at the head of the hunting guards of the territory of Brzezany, propriety of the Lubomirski princes, and at the general expense, organized a company of light infantry.

On 8 June Strzyzewski arrived at Zanleszczyki, the principal city of the area of the same name. An Austrian infantry battalion was entrenched there and he could not enter the city. Zaleszczyki, situated on the left bank of the Dniester, is the last Galician city on that part of the frontier. A boat bridge linked it to the right bank of the river and facilitated communications with Czernowitz, capital of Bukowina, where General Biking had drawn together a considerable body of troops. Strzyzewski knew the importance of such a place, but lacking infantry, he could not hope to take it. He took up a position at Zwiniacz, a village at some distance and waited for the insurrection that would bring him the help he needed. His hopes were not unfulfilled. He successively received diverse detachments of light infantry. Dwernicki and Trzeciecki gave themselves to the ardor of the warrior which animated them, crossed the Zbrucz on 10 June and organized in Russian Podolia 400 well mounted and armed volunteers. Finally, Major Rodkewicz arrived with the levy en masse from the neighboring circles. Strzyzewski found himself

---

[2]See appendicies.

[3]The occupation of a great extent of the territory was not only of great importance, under the military rapport, but it would have a greater importance in the political arena, because it was on the basis of occupied territories that the peace would be established.

at the head of 250 line cavalry, 400 mounted volunteers, 300 light infantry and 4,000 levies. He thought this force sufficient and marched on Zaleszczyki on 18 June. He gave to Chef d'Escadron Lanckoronski 30 troopers of the, 70 Podolian troopers, and 100 light infantry. He charged them to cross the Dniester and to threaten Zaleszczyki on the right bank, while he himself attacked the city on the left bank. The levies formed the first line, while the light infantry and the Podolian mounted volunteers formed the second. The line cavalry stood on the wings. After taking a few discharges of cannister, he saw disorder spread through the first line and the levies broke and fled in all directions.

Strzyzewski did not let this check stop him. Far from that, he maintained himself there with the rest of his troops and prepared to attack the city as Lanckoronski struck on the far bank, taking the Austrians in the back. He ignored the fact that Biking occupied Zaleszczyki with 3,000 troops and four cannons and had drawn more troops from Czernowitz, raising his force to 4,000. Lanckoronski crossed the Dniester by swimming at 4:00 a.m. At the point where he crossed the river was a forest that extended towards the city and ended in a planted copse. He crossed it and at 6:00 a.m., moved into the village of Swinice with his cavalry and placed them in ambush in the copse. Alarmed by this movement Biking, sent a strong column against him. Lanckoronski was obliged to retreat and withdraw in good order, moving into the copse where he struck the light infantry hard, taking down many Austrian soldiers. The terrain did not permit Biking to determine the forces against him, though he thought they were significant, and deployed his troops accordingly. Unable to face the forces before him, Lanckoronski withdrew and swam back across the Dniester where he had crossed it earlier, rejoining Strzyzewski at 11:00 a.m. while Strzyzewski was already heavily engaged. At the sound of the first musket shots he marched on the Austrian entrenchments and attacked them with vigor. However, Biking, no longer concerned about the far bank, concentrated his forces on the left and presented such a large force that there was no chance for success. Strzyzewski withdrew to his position at Dzwiniacz and maintained himself there until the evening. He was able to reform only a part of the levies. The rest had dispersed and were gone. The Polish chief learned the following day, of Poniatowski's retreat and the advance of Egermann. He decided to withdraw on Tarnopol, commencing the movement in the morning with Biking following him with 4,000 troops and four cannons. He passed through Tluste, Czortkow, Budzanow, and along the Sered, arriving on Janow on the 23rd, where he was joined on the 24th by Fozwadowski, who brought with him 200 mounted volunteers. Biking crossed to the right bank of Sered at Janow and attempted to push into the city, but Strzyzewski arrived in time to destroy the bridges, which linked the two banks. At this point impassable swamps bordered the river. To the north of Tarnopol there is a lake two miles long, which extended to the village of Biala. Thus covered, Strzyzewski maintained his position and had time to rally to him various detachments. Three hundred light infantry, fifty mounted volunteers, and finally one hundred troopers of the 1st Cavalry Regiment, which had been sent to him by Poniatowski when he left Pniow and joined his column. He now found himself at the head of 1,500 troops, without counting the levies. He left a detachment under the orders of Rozwadowski at Tarnopol, and marched on Biala on 1 July. He passed around the lake and took up a position in the evening opposite Sered, facing Zagrobela.

During the following night, a non-commissioned officer of the 1st Cavalry Regiment, named Yaszczalt, captured Biking at his headquarters. This brave soldier rode into the enemy camp at the head of 20 troopers. He advanced under the obscurity of night into the middle of the village, dismounted, penetrated into the headquarters and captured him along with one of his colonels. However, he was taking them away, the alarm was sounded. The adventurous soldier was forced to release his prize and to escape in all haste with his detachment. Despite the disproportion of forces, Strzyzewski attacked Biking on 2 July at 4:00 a.m. His forces were divided into three columns, the first advancing on Tarnopol. The second, under the orders of Strzyzewski, moved on Kutkowce. The third first marched on Janowka and then moved to the left. All three converged on Zagrobela. Biking's corps was taken by surprise and had little time to take up their weapons when they were attacked. The Polis cavalry executed prodigies of valor and the new levies rivaled their zeal. They charged the Austrian cavalry, broke them and threw then back on the infantry, which they then proceeded to break. The light infantry supported their attacks with a well-directed fire. Biking was chased from Zagrobela and pursued with vigor, falling back to Mekulence at 9:00 a.m. Strzyzewski had him pursued by a cavalry detachment and moved the bulk of his forces into Tarnopol, which he found occupied by a Russian cavalry, which sought to contest the possession of the city with the Poles. The Russians sought to get rid of them as they had sought to get rid of the column that presented itself before Krakow. However, Strzyzewski did not allow himself to be imposed on and pushed into the city. He was joined in Tarnopol by Tarnowski, who brought 200 newly raised cavalry with him, and by Ryszczewski with 150 cavalry and 300 light infantry. On 4 July he set out in pursuit of Biking. He caught him near Trembowla and forced him to retire on Chorostkow. He harassed him incessantly and captured many of his detachments.

At the same time a force of 3,000 Austrians, under the orders of General Kesler, which was part of Merveldt's division, crossed the Dniester at Haliez and occupied Brzezany, the principal city of the circle of the same name. Strzyzewski could not detached a large force against this force, and contented himself with observing it with the squadron formed by Cikowski and by a detachment of newly raised light infantry. Harassed by these units, Kesler was unable to push forward and sought only to maintain himself in Brzezany. On his side, Biking, who was three marches from his commander, sought to rejoin him. He left a strong rearguard in Chorotow and crossed the Sered at Budzanow. Strzyzewski perceived that he had nothing before him other than a battalion of Austrian infantry, attacked and captured it. This coup de main completed, he set off in pursuit of Biking's column, which he caught and drove onto Winiawka in disorder. The troop was now greatly fatigued. Biking seized a salt convoy and formed the wagons in square, establishing himself behind the wagons as if they were an entrenchment. His soldiers lacked water and looked for it in the village of Winiawka. The Polish light infantry defended the entrance to the village. The heat was extreme and both horses and men were soon tortured by thirst.

Strzyzewski was reinforced by 700 light infantry, which joined him from Bursztyn and Skarbek, who attacked them relentlessly, while Dwernicki at the head of 50 cavalry troopers captured a detachment that attempted to join them. An ordnance officer was sent to General Merveldt to ask support from him was driven back by a patrol. The Austrians then began to lose courage. The non-combatants, who had been denied water since the previous day, were in the greatest distress. A crowd of these unfortunates succumbed to thirst. A sutler fainted and died soon after, but died after vomiting a torrent of curses at the general. The soldiers surrounded her and could not resist this frightful spectacle. They began to murmur, discontent began to spread, and threatened to turn into a mutiny. Biking surrendered, a capitulation was concluded that stipulated that the Austrian troops would maintain 200 muskets and 200 bullet pouches, that the remainder of the arms, cannon, and horses would be surrendered to the Poles, who would then escort them to Czernowitz. They would not serve under arms again until the war was ended. Four hours after the conclusion of this capitulation, the Austrians began to move on their destination, but only after surrendering their firearms and cannons.[4]

In the report addressed by Poniatowski to Napoleon[5] dated 23 July attributed this action to Colonel Ryszczewski, and his regiment. This report, written as a result of the first news, was incorrect and justice was done to those who had done the deed. Colonel Ryzczewski, as well as Tzeciecki, Tarnowski, and Rozwadowski, who like him, formed at their expense new cavalry regiments, were present at the affair at Winiawka with their units. However, none of them had the experience of command and all played only a secondary role in the expedition. Strzyzewski was the commander and it was to him that the glory of this brilliant feat of arms would be given.

After the engagement at Winiawka, Strzyzewski marched against Kesler, but Kesler did not await his arrive, after learning of the disaster that had befallen Biking. He left Brzezany and moved via Rohatyn to Haticz, where he crossed the Dniester. Strzyzewski moved to the river and although he knew that Merveldt, who had been joined by Egermann near Stanislawow, had 8,000 men under his command, he did not fear to engage him. He occupied Mariampol on 20 July and in the following night he sent a squadron of the 3rd Cavalry Regiment across the Dniester. He proposed to cross the following day, but the cavalry squadron of the 3rd, in advancing on Stanislawow, found itself in the presence of far superior enemy forces, and was forced to withdraw in great haste. Pressed on all sides, it was obliged to move up the Dniester and could not cross it until night covered them as they swam across it. Merveldt took a position across from Mariampol with 12 cannons and began firing on the city. Strzyzewski had only the four cannons he had taken from Biking and no trained artillerists. Despite this he was not discouraged, so when he lacked cannon balls he had the Austrian balls gathered up and sent them back over the river from where they had come. The news of the s arrived in the middle of this engagement and hostilities ceased.

Since Strzyzewski had appeared on the Dniester, insurrection had broken out everywhere. It extended into the Carpathians and the borders of Hungary. The most zealous patriots put themselves at the head of the mountaineers. Captain Kopestynski and the Siedlecki brothers stood out in their zeal.

Merveldt attempted to contain this movement. The two Siedlecki brothers were killed in their homelands, which they defended bravely. Kopestynski was captured, tried, and executed. He was a man who demanded great consideration, esteemed by everyone, he died for his country for which all supporters of national independence mourned him. Merveldt left Stanislawow after the execution and could not hide from the unrest he caused. His wife, was obliged to flee from Lwow, and moved with her baggage to Stanislawow, where she was captured by a band of Galician partisans. She was treated with great respect, losing nothing but her husband's maps and papers. She was then sent with a safe conduct to the Dniester. Merveldt was aware of the preceding and learned with chagrin the harsh manner in which Kopestynsk had been treated.

During the armistice Strzyzewski returned to Tarnopol. The cannons he had captured were sent to Zamosc. The four Podolian cavalry regiments took up cantonments facing the Russian frontier where their formation was completed by the receipt of 500 new recruits, which crossed the Zbrucz, despite the defense of the Moscovite government.

---

[4]See appendices.
[5]See appendices.

During his sojourn at Krakow Poniatowski turned his attention to the organization of the troops under his command. He held many reviews, distributed medals[6], made promotions, and pressed the training of new units. Poland now had two distinct armies: that of the duchy, at the end of October, contained:

28,367	Infantry
5,908	Cavalry
2,620	Artillery
Total 36,895	

The Franco Galician Army

16,583	Infantry
8,610	Cavalry
Total 25,139	men

Total ….. 62,088 of all Polish forces.

Including 52,192 that were in Poland and a further 9,896 overseas.

However, the armament of these troops was not complete, so Napoleon sent to Poland, at Poniatowski's request, 20,000 muskets drawn from arsenals in Prussia.

Despite the conclusion of the armistice, hostilities continued in the Tyrol. It was not until the end of August that Lefebvre chased out the Austrians and the Bavarians that the province was brought under control. At the end of June the Austrian General Keinmeyer took command of the Austrian forces in Saxony and Franconia, which united the corps of Am-Ende and the Duke of Brunswick, under his commandm, raising this force to a total of around 15,000 men. Junot and King Jérôme opposed them. He defeated the first and forced him to retire on Amberg. Keinmeyer then marched against Jérôme and forced him back on Erfurth. However, Keinmeyer, learning of the armistice of Znaim, returned to Bohemia. Only the Duke of Brunswick refused to cease hostilities and continued his bold movement towards the north with only 4,000 men. He sought to join the English who had landed at Kuxhaven and started an insurgency in the country. Brunswick defeated the Westphalians and returned to his duchy, but soon he was surrounded by superior forces and was no longer able to maintain himself. He embarked on ships at the mouth of the Weser on 7 August and sought refuge on Helgoland Island until peace was restored.

After the ratification of the armistice by Emperor of Austria, on 18 July, negotiations for the peace occurred at Schönbrunn Palace. There the fate of Austria was decided. It was, so to say, at the discretion of Napoleon, but he could not destroy it without arousing the anger of Russia and perhaps an immediate war with that empire, a war that would surely cause a rupture with Prussia and result in a coalition of all the great European powers against France. As a result, Austria's political existence was continued and he contented himself stripping it of territories to reduce its power. The Poles hoped to receive a considerable aggrandizement of their territories as the price for their bravery and services rendered to Napoleon. However, they

---

[6]Editor. Original manuscript said he passed out "crosses of honor" (croix d'honneur).

feared the intrigues of their enemies. They were not represented at Schönbrunn, but they still wished to plead their case to Napoleon, the cause of their country. Ignace Potoçki and Thaddeus Matuszewic, the first, formerly grand marshal of Lithuania, and the second, a member of the provisional government of Galicia, both distinguished men and zealous patriots, went to the Imperial headquarters where they found General Bronikowski. All three sought to take advantage of the circumstances, all three presented Napoleon with strong presentations. However, despite the favorable attitude of this prince, he could not reunite more than the territories then occupied by Polish troops to the Duchy. It was impossible to obtain anything beyond that.

The treaty concluded on 14 October contained the following article:

His Majesty the Emperor of Austria cedes and abandons to His Majesty the King of Saxony, to be united with the Duchy of Warsaw, all of Eastern Galicia or New Galicia, a district around Krakow, on the right bank of the Vistula, which shall be determined later, and the circle of Zamosc, in Eastern Galicia. The district of Krakow, on the right bank of the Vistula, in front of Podgorze, the radius shall be everywhere the distance of Podgorze to Wieliczka. The line of demarcation shall pass via Wieliczka and reach to the west to the Skawina and on the east to the stream that joins the Vistula at Brzegi. – Wieliczka and all the territory of the salt mines held in common by the Austrian Emperor and the King of Saxony. Justice is rendered here in the name of the municipal authority. There shall be no troops other than police and they shall be of equal numbers from the two states. The Austrian salt at Wieliczka may be transported on the Vistula, across the Duchy of Warsaw, without paying any tariff. Grain from Austrian Galicia may also be exported down the Vistula. There shall be negotiated between His Majesty the Emperor of Austria and His Majesty the King of Saxony a fixation of limits, such as the San, from the point where it touches the Circle of Zamosc to its confluence with the Vistula to serve as a limit between the two states.

Russia was given the Circle of Tarnopol as the price for its cooperation, or more accurately, its neutrality. Commissioners were named from both sides to establish a line of demarcation. For the Grand Duchy, the commissioners were Generals Pelletier and Rozniecki, as well as Prince Henri Lubomirski. For Austria they were Generals Mayer and Wurmser. The part of the two Galicias assured by this treaty was formed into four new department: Siedlce, Lublin, Radom, and Krakow. The constitution of the Grand Duchy was extended to these new territories and 5,000,000 Poles received their independence.

———————•———————

The events that we have presented outline the efforts, the sacrifices of which the Polish nation is capable. Poland entered the fight with 22,000 combatants, it constantly increased its forces, and despite the consumption of troops on the battlefield, despite the shackles imposed on its élan, it contained 52,000 men under its flags when peace was established. This development of forces under such enormously unfavorable circumstances was an enormous undertaking, but patriotism supported it. The treasury was empty, but voluntary donations filled it. The arsenals lacked weapons, so scythes, pikes and hunting rifles were used in their place. Artillery was insufficient, so the army equipped itself with guns taken on the battlefield.[7] New units formed on all sides, as the elite ran to arms from all parts of the nation. The richest citizens, those who

---

[7] During this war the Polish Army captured 68 cannons from the Austrians.

had the most to lose, were those who showed the greatest abandon. The inhabitants of the duchy who came to recover their independence, those of New Galicia, who fell under foreign domination as a result of the last partitioning in 1795, and those of Old Galicia who were part of the Austrian Empire since 1792, all showed the same patriotism, the same enthusiasm. In vain a Russian Army advanced, more to paralyze the efforts of the patriots than to fight the Austrians. The self-sacrifice of the Poles overcame these shackles, and the Russian government saw hundreds of volunteers pass over its frontier, despite their rigorous efforts to block them, to join the Galicians. It was certain, this exceptional spectacle in a nation, abandoned to its own forces, surrounded by enemies, attacked by a veteran army that was superior in numbers, accepted the danger along its entire length, not only defended its frontiers, but also threw back the enemy and extended its conquests into its territory. In vain, 60,000 Austrians successively presented themselves on the battlefield.[8] Some were lost or surrendered their arms. The other part, humiliated, vanquished, only regained the borders of Germany and Hungary with the greatest efforts. These efforts, these sacrifices, were not the only made by Poland at this time. Eighteen thousand poles fought simultaneously in Spain and German, or formed garrisons in Prussian fortresses.[9]

After the check at Aspern-Essling, Napoleon suspended his plans and reunited new forces before resuming the offensive. Germany and Italy were agitated, insurrections erupted at many parts, and all parts of the coalition grew and presented their forces. The rear of the Grande Armée was threatened. Prussia appeared to be taking up arms. Russia, a disloyal ally, could not wait for the moment to strike. On all sides a tempest rumbled. Ferdinand, master of part of the duchy, advanced towards the frontiers of Prussia to light a spark to popular discontent, but the Poles had marched on the San. The Galicians rose up, the fortresses which defended the country was taken, and Poniatowski took up a position in the rear of the Austrian army, while Dąbrowski and Zajączek prepared to attack it frontally. The archduke was forced to retreat, abandon the duchy and to renounce his project of joining the dissidents in northern Germany and provide incouragement to their insurrection. The service rendered by the Poles was significant and Napoleon did not look to underestimate it. Far from that, he praised and exalted in it, having a great desire to form a powerful state on the banks of the Vistula. However, his intentions were blocked by circumstances. He had come to learn from experience the value of alliances. England, victorious in the peninsula, prepared for landings on the continent.[10] He had to temporize with Russia, putting off the restoration of a people whose courage and constant patriotism he esteemed. The Poles did not receive, as a result of the Treaty of Schönbrunn, anything more than the territories that they had conquered. However, in revenge, they could flatter themselves with the knowledge that they had rendered great services to the sovereign who was their greatest friend, their natural ally, who appreciated their political importance, to be resolved to resurrect their fatherland, and regarded, from then on, Poland as the key to the continued existence of his empire.

END

---

[8]The army of the archduke contained 40,000 men at the moment hostilities began. 5,000 reinforcements arrived from Hungary and Bukovina and a further 20,000 recruits were raised, of whom 15,000 Galicians reinforced their ranks.

[9]This force included the Vistula Legion, consisting of three infantry regiments and a cavalry regiment, and the Polish Guard Lancer Regiment that accompanied Napoleon.

[10]Editor: This is probably a reference to the British landings at Walchern that occurred shortly after the Austrians surrendered.

Horse artillery in 1809 by Chelminski

1.

Warsaw, 12 April 1809

To His Excellency the Duke of Auerstadt
Marshal of France, Commander of the Army of the Rhine

According to reports and information that has arrived since my last dispatch, the movements of the Austrian troops in Galicia have taken on a more serious character. Without adding faith to the thousand and one stories that come to us daily on their forces and projects, it is without a doubt that a corps has been put in movement and approaches us.

The frontier is so exactly closed over its entire length and with such severity to intercept all communications, not excepting the mail, from which it is impossible to obtain notions on the effective measures taken, and to distinguish the stories, which are always so common in such parallel occasions. However, by combining the continuous circumstances in different opinions with the positive advertisement that the Archduke Ferdinand is already or will arrive from at any moment at Konskie, to establish his headquarters there, it appears obvious that Austrians intend to establish their line of operations on the Piliça, and that they will take one of the positions that I had the honor of mentioning to Your Excellency in my preceding dispatch. I say one of these positions, because, in spite of their fanfares and their threats, they do not have the forces to occupy them all. A great number of deserters, who arrive to us every day at Krakow, all agree on the number and the names of the regiments which are there; and it appears, according to their reports, that in addition to the corps I mentioned earlier to Your Excellency, the Mitrowski and Ballot Regiments, infantry, and a Hungarian regiment whose name I do not know have arrived. It is generally understood that the Archduke Ferdinand's corps has but 30,000 men, but it is hardly probable that he can advance against us with more than 15,000 to 18,000 men, and the corps which at the time must act on Piliça, would be intended rather to observe our movements that to carry out the invasion of the duchy since so long announced.

At all events, I believe to have, according to the movements of Austrian troops, been more to bring closer the cantonments that the cavalry occupies, and to cover them with infantry and artillery. I have, consequently, ordered the following movements:

The 6th Cavalry Regiment moved from Blonie to Nadarzyn; the 3rd Infantry Regiment moved on Raszyn with 4 cannons; these troops are under the command of General Bieganski, the 3rd Cavalry Regiment took position at Piaseczno; the 1st Cavalry Regiment at Gora; the 5th Cavalry Regiment is moving from Napoknet to Blonie; a company of the 2nd Cavalry Regiment is moving to relieve the posts formed by the 5th; the 3rd Infantry Regiment has been replaced by a battalion of the 6th Infantry Regiment; and a battalion of the 8th Infantry Regiment has been drawn from Serock and Modlin.

In the Strauch Regiment, desertion has greatly increased from before.

Count Potoçki (Stanislaw) believes that the Austrians have a project to enter the duchy; but this word is not official and appears to be to frighten the inhabitants by causing them to be uncertain.

I am, etc.,

Signed, Prince Josef Poniatowski

————●————

APPENDIX II

CONVENTION

Between Prince Poniatowski and the Archduke Ferdinand

Demands	Responses

Your Imperial and Royal Highness, having manifested the desire to establish and recognize the neutrality of the city of Warsaw, and this neutrality cannot be effected except by the free evacuation by the of the allied troops combined under my orders, this arrangement shall be reaffirmed in the following articles:

Demands	Responses
Art. 1. There shall be a suspension of hostilities for ten days.	Art. 1. There shall be a suspension of hostilities of twice 24-hours, to begin this evening at 5:00 p.m.
Art. 2. During that time the army corps shall evacuate, with its personnel and material, the city of Warsaw.	Art. 2. During this delay all the combined combatant army shall evacuate the city of Warsaw; it is accorded, to date from the same time, a delay of five times 24-hours for all the employees and non-combatants of this army, to leave the city. Prince Poniatowski wishes to communicate this
Art. 3. During this delay, the Austrian army shall remain in the same positions it currently occupies and to eliminate all pretexts to break the harmony, only parliamentary officers of the Austrian Army shall come to Warsaw.	Agreed
Art. 4. After this delay there shall not be imposed on the city any extraordinary contribution.	Agreed
Art. 5. The persons, the properties, and the religion shall be respected.	Agreed
Art. 6. The sick and convalescent Saxons, Poles, and French shall be confided to the custody of	Agreed

the Austrian Army; and, upon their recovery, they will receive travel papers and the means of transport to join their respective units.

Art.7. There shall be accorded by His Imperial and Royal Highness the archduke commanding the Austrian forces to the resident minister of France accredited to the Duke and the government, passports and safeguards for his person, his papers, his effects and the persons attached to his mission, to go where he judges it convenient to go.	Agreed
Art. 8. The officers, soldiers, and employees of the French who find themselves in France shall be free to follow the French resident, with their effects and baggage, and shall receive passports and means of security, as well as food, forages, and transportation.	Agreed
Art. Addit. At the moment of the exchange of the present articles, there shall be given on one part and the other senior officers as hostages, until the expiration of the armistice.	Agreed

Made and agreed between the undersigned, generals in chief of the two armies, on the line of respective advanced posts on April 21st, 1809.

The general commanding the army corps of allied and combined troops in the Grand Duchy of Warsaw.	The general commander-in-chief of the Austrian Army.
Signed Józef Prince Poniatowski	Signed: Archduke Ferdinand

APPENDIX III

Headquarters at Okuniew, 3 May 1809

To Major General Prince Neufchâtel

Sir,

I hurry to bring word to Your Highness *à la suite* of the report that I had the honor to send you on the operations in the Duchy of Warsaw, which after several partial advantages taken by the Polish troops on the right bank of the Vistula, the corps that the enemy has moved to this side has been seen to concentrate his forces in the bridgehead that he has constructed at Gora to cover the bridge that he proposes to establish over the Vistula. Not wishing to give them time to complete this operation, already quite advance, and by the success that the enemy would acquire by the ability to move his forces, quite superior to ours, to either bank of the river, I gave the order to attack, which General Sokolnicki, commander of the advanced guard, accomplished with good fortune and intelligence. Today, at 2;00 a.m., the bridgehead, after being summoned to surrender, was carried at bayonet point by 1,200 men, despite a heavy fire, supported by cannon from the far bank. A colonel[1] , 50 officers, and 1,500 men were made prisoner. We have taken two flags and three cannons. General Schauroth barely had time to escape in a boat. One boat, filled with 300 men, sank. We are masters of the entire right bank of the Vistula, and in consequence a part of Galicia.

In view of the triple number of the enemy, I am unsure if I can maintain myself. However, if one considers that the combat which just took place cost the enemy at least 4,000 dead and wounded, and that we have in our hands around 2,500 prisoners, that he has also surely lost heavily through desertion; and our losses in killed, wounded and prisoners is not more than 1,500 men: It is perhaps impossible to assume what is correct, and it shall then be necessary for me to know the intentions of His Majesty the Emperor relative to this province and the manner with which I should comport myself with the inhabitants.

Their sentiments are known to Your Highness, but it shall not a little possible to make use of it without giving positive assurances to them that reunion with their fatherland shall be the price of their efforts. The guarantee of His Majesty the Emperor is the sole assurance of their future, and it would suffice to give the good will of the Galicians all the flight of which it is capable. I await an order from Your Highness to cause me to know how I can respond to the requests that surely will not lack in this regard.

Sincerely,

Signed, Prince Józef Poniatowski

PS. The number of prisoners[2] number about 2,000 and have probably grown yet higher, because more are taken in every moment.

---

[1]Czerwinka, commander of the Latour-Baillet Infantry Regiment.
[2]The prince speaks, without a doubt, of the prisoners made on 3 May.

According to the convention signed with the Archduke Ferdinand, the officers made prisoners of war, designated in the attached list, can be exchanged against French or allied officers, who are in the enemy's power. It is with pleasure that I send to Your Highness, Général de brigade Pelletier, as well as other French officers, authorized to serve in the Polish Army, the justice of having rendered the greatest services in directing the artillery and engineers.

———•———

APPENDIX IV

Headquarters at Wionzonwa, 5 May 1809

To His Majesty the Prince de Neufchâtel,

Colonel Stufflet brought me the order today to enter Galicia.

I have foreseen the wishes of the emperor and the Circles of Stanislawow and Siedice are occupied.

The troops are filled with enthusiasm; they have occupied 42 to 45 Austrian miles. Just to today the Polish Army has not lost more than 1,500 killed and wounded, and the Austrians have lost 6,000 men, including 2,800 prisoners.

The Austrian Army, with 30,00 men, is placed between Warsaw and the mouth of the Piliça; it is pushing parties as far as Kalisz and Plock. The Polish Army, with 11,000 to 12,000 men, has united between the mouth of the Wieprz and Karcew; two cavalry regiments are spread along the Wieprz, pushing detachments s far as Konstantynow on the Bug.

The garrisons of Praga, Sierock, Modlin and Thorn are formed with conscripts. The new levies observe the Vistula.

The occupation of Warsaw has paralyzed the Austrian forces. A garrison of 6,000 men is in danger of being forced to lower its arms, if the inhabitants rise up. The garrison has to be so strong that the Archduke is too weakened to accomplish anything decisive other than occupy Warsaw.

1. The enemy army can move via Sandomierz. In this supposition, I will await it on the San or the Wieprz, to attack it as it crosses or I shall cross the Vistula at Modlin and attempt to gain Teschen and to align my operations with those of the Grande Armée.

2. The enemy can move to Hungary or Moravia, abandoning the Duchy. I can, in this case, move by the right bank of the Vistula down the high road from Leopol to Krakow and follow his movement.

I ask advice of Your Majesty on these subjects: I have informed Prince Galitzin of the victories of the French army; he responded politely, but without revealing what he intended to do. If the Russians act hostilely against us, it will not be possible for me to do more put garrison in the various fortresses and withdraw on Danzig.

Sincerely,

Signed Prince Poniatowski

APPENDIX V.

Posen, 29 April 1809

Letter from Wybicki, Lieutenant of the government in the
Department of Posen, to Prince Poniatowski,
Minister of War

The Austrian advanced posts are at Lowicz and Klodawa. General Kosinski commands the Posen *arrière ban.* He sends word that volunteers from Silesia, dressed in Austrian uniforms, have crossed the frontier and entered into the district of Piotrkow on 26 April.

Mr. Seras, the French ambassador to the Grand Duchy, passed through Posen on 27 April with Colonel Saulnier and the Ordonnateur Mr. Desirat, enroute to Berlin. An Austrian accompanied them. They sang a Te Deum in Posen for the victories of the Grande Armée.

———————•———————

Lubartow, 11 May 1809

To His Majesty the Prince de Neufchâtel,

Sir,

Since the last report that I had the honor to send to Your Highness, dated the 6th of this month, there has been no serious engagement with the enemy. I continue the movement, which I had mentioned and I hope in a few days to find myself on the San. This position will give to the corps under my orders the ability to direct itself on the point where it will be most useful to act, I shall regulate my subsequent movements on those of the enemy, be it to engage him if he moves towards us, be it to move on Krakow and make myself master of the passes to Hungary, if he gives us time to gain them.

Until this moment it has been little possible to judge the projects of the enemy. After the latest information that we have received, the garrison of Warsaw consists of just a few infantry companies; the corps of the Archduke Ferdinand is concentrated near Łowicz and is entrenching itself. It is supposed that he intends to move on Posen. This assumption appears so strange to all military views, that I have difficulty believing it. If, despite this, it should be realized, it cannot be justified except to see if the Russians declare themselves against France and in the cause of the Prussians, which only await a favorable moment to act with hostility and, while waiting, demonstrate their intentions by arming, raising men, and all the secret support that they can pass to the Austrians, while they interrupt the simplest communications that we attempt with the Polish troops that are in Custrin and Danzig.

I am unaware if one can count on the Russians, but so far their actions have not been favorable. It is positively known that Russian officers have been seen in the Austrian camp and last night an aide-de-camp to General Lewis, commander of Bialystok, known to be employed on a secret mission, was brought to my headquarters. He was in possession of a passport for Warsaw where he says he was going for particular affairs. He pretended to be ignorant of what we do in Galicia and of the Austrians in Warsaw, though I had kept the Russian generals, and above all Mr. Lewis, current on my operations. All the indications are not certain, but it appears to me that if the Russians act in concert with France, the result would only be victories for the emperor. Whatever the intentions of this power, I shall act so as to not be taken at a disadvantage should things not be favorable for us. A general levy, ordered in the departments, is organizing rapidly. Already several strong infantry forces guard the right bank of the Vistula, the Narew, and the Bug, and detachments of cavalry, deployed in front, observe the movements of the Russian troops and assure that the army corps will not be surprised on that side. I have given the command of the levies to General Dąbrowski and General Zajączek commands the line infantry.

All the numerous affairs to date have been entirely to our advantage and augment each day the confidence of the Polish soldiers and his ardor to take the measure of the enemy. A picket of five men, led by Lieutenant Kremski of the 1st Infantry Regiment, ventured to cross the Vistula a few days ago and captured an Austrian post of 35 men and one officer, which the brought back as prisoners with their arms and baggage.

Around 400 men of the 6th Cavalry Regiment of Colonel Dziewanowski took part in the advanced guard under the orders of General Rozniecki, sent in pursuit of a transport escorted by 1,000 infantry and took 700 prisoners and the entire convoy, consisting of cloth and shoes to the value of one million Polish florins. They are in pursuit of the rest of the convoy and expect to capture it tomorrow. Around 2,000 recruits were dispersed and put at liberty. This success promises some consistence in our operations. They have produced a full measure of good will from the inhabitants of Galicia, who still fear the return of Austrian troops. Many press to stand under our flags and only the lack of means bounds the growth of the forces we could raise. Prince Constantin Czartoryski has sacrificed all considerations and has arrived at my headquarters to take service with our troops. Simply stating the word "fatherland" to the Galicians has augmented our forces by 20,000 men raised at the expense of the proprietors. A deputation of citizens from many of the circles presented itself to me yesterday to ask me to transmit to His Majesty the Emperor their desire to participate in the blessings and protection, which he might accord to the national existence of their compatriots. This ardent voice, so long suppressed, can I give them the hope to see it granted?

     Signed Prince Poniatowski

P.S. At the moment that I ended this dispatch, I was brought an interesting letter from the Russian General Prince Gorchakov to the Archduke Ferdinand. It appears to be to very important in these circumstances that I have thought it my duty to place the original under the eyes of His Majesty the Emperor.

———●———

APPENDIX VII.

Ulanow, 19 May 1809

Report of Prince Poniatowski
To His Majesty the Prince de Neufchâtel

Sir,

According to the dispositions that I had the honor to make known to Your Highness on the 11th of this month, the corps of Polish troops under my orders found itself on the San today, where the advanced guard and a party of cavalry had been for a few days.

Profiting by the inaction of the enemy, who, for reasons unknown, took up position on the Bzura, I had thought it appropriate to attack the bridgehead at Sandomierz and I ordered at the same time a probe on the city, where the enemy had erected strong entrenchments. This operation was as successful as one might desire. The bridgehead was, yesterday, taken at bayonet point by Chef d'escadron of artillery, Count Włodimir Potocki, at the head of a detachment drawn from the corps of General Rozniecki, and the city of Sandomierz, after a vigorous attack, an attack effected by three battalions of General Sokolnicki's advanced guard, which had crossed over to the left bank of the Vistula, was occupied today, at 5:00 a.m., by a capitulation which I have just received. This operation cost the enemy around 1,000 men killed and around 1,200 prisoners, 20 cannon and considerable munitions. This victory assures us of a point on the left bank of the Vistula where it is possible to debouch, to cross the measures of the enemy and impede him if he attempts to cross the Vistula. My cavalry has extended from the side of Leopol as far as Krakow.

I currently await information from Zamość, which I had attacked by a force under the orders of General Pelletier. I hope to soon learn of the capture of this fortress. The cavalry has delivered 3,000 to 4,000 conscripts already assembled; many officers have distinguished themselves, but we have to regret the loss of the brave Chef de Bataillon Prince Marcellin Lubomirski, killed in the assault on Sandomierz. The Polish army is animated by a sublime spirit. It advances with cries of "Vive l'Empereur!" and all those who had the occasion to render real services envy the good fortune of those of their comrades who have received the mark of satisfaction that this august sovereign gives to the brave

Daily the Galicians give proofs of their attachment to the cause of their ancient fatherland and cannot wait for the moment when they are permitted to prove that they are worthy to belong to it.

Signed: Prince Józef Poniatowski

APPENDIX VIII.

Headquarters at Ulanov, 21 May 1809
Report of Prince Poniatowski
To His Majesty the Prince de Neufchâtel

Sir,

As I had the honor to inform Your Highness on the 19th of this month, I caused Zamość to be attacked by two battalions of the 2nd Infantry Regiment, two companies of voltigeurs of the 3rd Infantry Regiment, 80 voltigeurs of the 6th Infantry Regiment, with six cannons under the orders of General Pelletier. This enterprise had the greatest success. The fort was taken by assault yesterday at 2:00 a.m. The enemy has lost 3,000 men killed or prisoner, several colonels and senior officers, 40 cannon and considerable provisions of every type.

The troops were conducted in the most brilliant manner. I cannot speak too highly of the good dispositions of General Pelletier.

The fortress of Zamość commanded, by its location, a great expanse of country and puts in our power all the part of Galicia between Leopol and Brody. General Kaminski is marching with the 6th Cavalry Regiment to push as far as possible. Our advanced posts are, today, two miles from Leopol.

I believe it my duty to go to Sandomierz.

Signed: Prince Józef Poniatowski

APPENDIX IX.

Operations of the garrison of Fort Częstochowa
from the beginning of hostilities

On 14 April the commandant of the Fort Piliça was informed by Austrian General Bronowacki that the troops under his orders would penetrate into the duchy 12-hours after the receipt of this declaration. On the 17th General Bronowacki arrived before the force, at the head of his corps, consisting of 5,000 infantry, 300 cavalry, and 10 cannons.[1]   On the 18th this general was summoned to surrender the fort. Nothing important happened on the 19th and 20th. Detachments of Austrian cavalry penetrated the previous day into the city of Częstochowa, but they were all driven back, losing a few men killed and wounded. On the 21st the enemy left the vicinity of the fort and moved on Warsaw via Radom, Kaminsk and Piotrkow. Up to May 2nd we did not see the enemy. On that day, at 10:00 p.m. an Austrian column of 1,600 Szeckler infantry, 200 Emperor Chevaulegers, supported by seven cannon and commanded by Colonel Grammont occupied the old city of Częstochowa. On the 3rd the enemy established his camp near the village of Kamien, about 700 toises from the old city, and 2,000 from the fort. He established strong infantry posts in the old city and in the village of Wyczerpy. The same day, at 2:00 p.m., the enemy attacked the Church of Saint John, situated halfway between the old city and the fort. This church ws occupied by a post of our infantry; not only did the enemy not capture it, but he was chased back into the city with a loss of one officer, 20 killed and 50 wounded. On our side we suffered one soldier killed and one officer (sous-lieutenant Kwiakowski) and 10 soldiers wounded. On the 4th, at 4:00 p.m., the enemy attacked the fort with great resolution. They advanced as far as the new city, where they took position, and threw several howitzer shells into the fort. However, his howitzer was soon dismounted by fire from the fort, ably directed by the earlier mentioned lieutenant of artillery Wisniewski. The Austrians had a captain of artillery and nearly all of their gunners killed. Shortly later, the enemy infantry advanced behind the hills, which dominate the new city. Seeing that they were making progress I ordered the guns of the two bastions loaded with canister and commanded that the post occupying St. John Church be withdrawn in order to draw the enemy into the plains where our guns were directed. The enemy, upon seeing the Polish detachment abandon St.-John Church, thought themselves victorious and advanced boldly. As they arrived on the plain of which we have spoken, they were received by canister fire from our guns. Seized by terror and panic, they withdrew in disorder, leaving on the battlefield 40 dead and 100 wounded. We did not suffer, that day, a single soldier killed and only two wounded. The engagement lasted three hours and we remained masters of the battlefield.

Despite the check the previous day, Colonel Grammont summoned me again on 5 May to surrender the fort to him. During the night of the 7th/8th the enemy took position near the village of Stradom, and one of its patrols penetrated as far as the suburb of Saint-Barbara, where it was chased out with the loss of a few men. On the 11th the enemy burnt a third of the old city. During the following night our post, established in the Convent of St-Barbara, was forced. The enemy had one officer killed, 20 soldiers and two cavalry troopers wounded. We had, on our side, Lieutenant Raczynski and two soldiers wounded, and six men taken prisoner.

---

[1]This evaluation should be considered as exaggerated, as Bronowacky commanded only two battalions and eight squadrons. Stutterheim evaluates its strength at 3,000.

During the night of the 15th/16th the enemy opened his first parallel, supporting it on St. Barbara and occupied the suburb of the same name, the garden and the cemetary of the convent. During the morning of the 16th I detached two companies and shortly later supported them with a third, in order to chase the enemy from the positions they had occupied. Despite the fire of three companies, expanded into skirmish order, and supported by the fire of the fortress, the enemy did not cede any ground. However, they could not resist a bayonet attack. I ordered them to break down the gate of the cemetery, which permitted our infantry to penetrate into the interior of the cemetery and the garden, and to attack the enemy with bayonets. The enemy took flight and was unable to recover, as was the practice, their dead and wounded. This day cost the enemy 200 men, hors de combat. We gathered up a large number of muskets and lances (used by their light infantry) that had been dropped by the fugitives. We captured a lieutenant and 14 soldiers. Our losses were seven killed, eight wounded, and five prisoners. Several houses in the Saint-Barbara suburb were burnt.

After this check the enemy lost all hope of taking the fortress, resolved to raise the siege, and effected his retreat during the 16th and 17th via Kozieglowy on Slankow, leaving before the fortress a rear guard composed of 200 infantry, 60 cavalry, and two cannons in order to cover his retreat and to bring hi his patrols which had not yet rejoined their units. This rearguard took up position on a rise in the Mostow woods, and soon followed the retreat of the main body during the night of 20/21 May. The enemy, in his retreat, abandoned to us the magazines of provisions that he had gathered. During the period of the siege I had no occasion to doubt the conduct or courage of the garrison. The following particularly distinguished themselves: Captains Godlewski, Selinski, Szymanowski of the 5th Infantry; Captain of sappers Haan, Lieutenants Raczynski and Bienicki, Sous-lieutenant Kwiatkowski of the 3rd Cavalry Regiment; Lieutenant Rudkowski and the formerly mentioned Lieutenant of Artillery Wisnicwski, and finally magazine attendant Czerno.

The national guard of the old city of Czenstochowa as well as the suburb of St-Barbara nd the villages of Krzepice and Klobucko showed themselves to be very active.

Commander of the Fort of Częstochowa,
Signed: Colonel Stuart

APPENDIX X.

Headquarters at Trzesnia, 7 June 1809.

To His Excellency, M. Zamoyski, President of the
Military, Central, and Provisional Government of the two Galicias,
Under the protection of His Majesty the Emperor and King,
The Great Napoleon

It suffices to be familiar with Polish history, to not doubt that the successor of the illustrious men that the House of Zamoyski has furnished to the fatherland, who have shown on every occasion, worthy of the vertus by which their ancestors have added to the glory of our nation.

Your Excellency had responded to this expectation in a manner beyond all praise.

Not content with putting yourself at the head of government of the two Galicias, to work to maintain the public order and the prosperity of the inhabitants, you have proposed to also raise at your own expense an infantry regiment and bring to yourself the merits of those who serve with weapons in hand.[1]

I have always appreciate the good effects of your actions and now you give new proofs. However, to perpetuate the memory of your noble devotion, I have ordered that the infantry regiment formed at your expense, take the name Zamoyski Regiment.

I desire that all Polish see, in this decree, the proof of the sentiments, which motivated it.

As to the cannons that you have offered to the fatherland that were trophies taken by your ancestors from our enemies, they shall be used for the defense of the ramparts of Zamość where they will be served by the sons of Poland.

Général de division, Commander-in-Chief
Of the Polish Army

Signed: Prince Józef Poniatowski

———————●———————

---

[1]Major Hornowski, commander of Praga, was named colonel of the regiment formed at the expense of Zamoyski.

APPENDIX XI.

Headquarters at Pniow, 10 June 1809

To His Majesty the Emperor and King

Sir,

The ideas which, in my report of the 4th of this month, I had the honor to expose to Your Imperial Majesty on the views that the movements of the enemy gave me pause to suspect have been realized. The Archduke Ferdinand, threatened in his rear and fearing to probably see all of Galicia lost, has united his forces near Sandomierz and appears intended to penetrate Galicia on that front. On the 5th of this month a force of 8,000 to 10,000 men, under the orders of General Schauroth had attempted to approach this fortress, but was repulsed by our troops with a considerable loss in killed and wounded, leaving in our hands several hundred prisoners. A second attack was launched on the 6th, when the Archduke Ferdinand was present, and had no more success. The enemy made no new attack on Sandomierz; and is probably convinced that an assault will cost him many casualties without offering any certain results, so it appears he has abandoned his design for that of dividing our attention by on us by the upper Vistula.

In consequence, General Schauroth abandoned his camp at Opatowiec, and, after crossing the Vistula at Polaniec on the boats that he had gathered there, moved on Wisloka, which he has occupied from its junction with the Vistula as far as Dembica. This little river is fordable at several places, my right flank is not entirely uncovered.

If I ws reduced to only Polish troops, I would not wait a minute to attack the enemy. The good will and courage, which they have displayed on all occasions have given me no reason to be troubled by their superiority of numbers. Though the occupation of two fortresses and a large extent of territory has reduced my corps by around five battalions of infantry and six squadrons of cavalry, the arrival of the Russian troops appears to give me other possibilities and puts me in the situation of putting nothing to risk to obtain the results which their presence must necessarily produce. I had thought, in consequence, to move to the mouth of the San the boats and bridging material established on the Vistula, and, after having brought back my cavalry which I had sent forward to scout the movements of the enemy, to take up a position on the San by Pniow and Czekay.

The part which seems to me most suitable is to conserve the important point of Sandomierz, which gives me the advantage of not only aligning my movements with those of General Zajączek who has already crossed the Vistula and is by Puławy, which

This part appeared all the more suitable to me, that, while preserving the significant point of Sandomierz, it not only has the advantage of linking my movements with those of General Zajączek who, having already passed Vistula, near Puławy, will be necessarily within range to worry the right flank of the enemy forces in front of Sandomierz, on left bank of Vistula, but also to take myself, with the Russians the same line of operations, covered at the two ends by the fortresses of Sandomierz and Zamość.

Such is, sir, the position Polish troops in Galicia. It appears that one can evaluate At 45,000 men the forces that Russia has brought here.

The attached letter, in copy, which I have found in the writing case of Prince Golitsyn, shall make known to Your Imperial Majesty the personal attitude of this general, as well as all the delays, which in all the reports, he has sought to put to the active cooperation of the Russian troops, as well as the shortened marches, the double sojourns, as well as giving columns orders to march in directions entirely opposed to that which was natural for them to take. The representations contained in this letter appear to give an impression of the spirit of Prince Galitsyn and it informs me, after the knowledge that I had given him of my positions, that one of his divisions is moving on Puławy, while an other marches to join my corps and a third marches on Lublin, so as to be able to act on that side where it might be most usefully employed. The division which should support my operations, I hope, will make its junction with the Polish troops tomorrow.

The zeal that animates the Galicians and their good will has in no way diminished. The new levies are pursued with great activity. There are at this moment four infantry and four cavalry regiments forming, all uniformed and equipped at the expense of citizens who offered to form them. Among this number are found the Count Zamoyski, Prince Adam Czartoryski, and the richest men of Galicia. Several battalions are in a state to act in five days and the total lack of weapons, which paralyzes all the efforts of the Galicians, is the only limit of the eagerness that they demonstrate for taking up the defense of the common cause.

Worthy to agree, sir, etc.

Signed: Prince Józef Poniatowski.

———●———

Headquarters at Trzesnia, 7 June 1809

To His Excellency, Prince Golitsyn,
Commander-in-Chief of the Russian Army

Monsieur le Prince,

I have already had the honor of communicating to Your Excellency the motives that caused me to take the position at Sandomierz. This position appears to me to be extremely important, not only to not lost the advantages already obtained over the enemy by the troops under my orders, but also to give the Russian Army the ability to act in a manner conforming to the military situation that presents the circumstances, which I believe it my duty to present again to Your Excellency that, since the enemy stands in force before Sandomierz and occupies Wisloka with a considerable force, it is impossible for me to make any movement without unmasking the point where it is essential that I risk nothing.

The reasons which I had already asked Lieutenant General Pelletier to expose to Your Excellency have engaged me to write that you should direct the column that General Suvorov commands on Sandomierz, and to accelerate its march so as to it into range to cooperate with the Polish Army; however, according to the manner of march, which had just been communicated by the civil authorities, the aforementioned column, instead of going on Sandomierz via

Zamość, which was the shortest way, where no obstacle will stop it, and where I had given the command to provide for all its needs, moves in the direction of Lublin, and, instead of accelerating its movement, which is only of two miles per day, adds to it by this turning four steps and three days of rest.

The orders by which His Majesty the Emperor and King had ordered the operations that I had implemented, were based in large part on the entire cooperation of the Russian troops, relative to which were tied the intentions of their sovereign, his ally, it is impossible to not be able to put him in a state to judge for himself how much in concert our entire movements would facilitate and assure the complete defeat of the enemy; and after having rendered to the Emperor an exact and detailed report, one issue, less advantageous than that which the two sovereigns can expect, will surprise them.

Colonel Paszkowski, aide-de-camp to His Majesty the King of Saxony, who I have charged to carry this letter to Your Excellency shall have the honor of adding verbally from his knowledge observations that are too long to add in this letter; please, Monsieur le Prince, to consider the frankness and the confidence with which I send to these thoughts as a proof of my conviction, how much you are personally disposed in favor of the cause for which we have united our efforts.

Sincerely,
Signed: Prince Józef Poniatowski

APPENDIX XII.

Capitulation of the City of Sandomierz between
General Baron Geringer, Chevalier of the Military Order of Maria-Theresa
And General Sokolnicki, Chevalier of the Order of the Legion of Honor
And the Polish Military Order of Saxony, Commander of the
Fortress of Sandomierz

Requests

Responses

Art. 1. Two hours after the ratification of the articles below, the Krakow Gate and the château shall be placed at the disposition of the Austrian Army, which shall, nonetheless, put there no more than an ordinary police guard.

Agreed

The faith is always the common basis of all treaties that any sign of defiance shall not take place in this circumstance.

The garrison shall leave by the Opatow gate during the day of June 18th, 12 hours after ratification, with its arms and baggage and all the honors of war, so as to rejoin its army. It shall take its artillery, with the exception of the Austrian artillery, the limbers and caissons of munitions found upon the surrender of General Egermann in the fortress of Sandomierz; and on this subject we shall send an artillery officer (at the moment of ratification) into the fortress to take custody of this Austrian artillery and its attachments.

Art.2. The garrison can commence its evacuation from the city it occupies via the Krakow Gate and shall end its evacuation 12 hours later.

The garrison shall leave with the honors of war, carrying its arms, its artillery, its munitions and baggage, and it shall be further accorded to it 100 train horses and wagons for the transport of provisions and the baggage officers who lack transportation. It is understood that the horses shall be returned at the first resting place where they can be exchanged.

At the same moment an engineering officer shall be sent to receifve the wagons and the fortification's tools as well as board with the geometrical instruments and the section of Sandomierz and the surrounds in which it stands; the boats that are on the vistula and which form the bridge shall be faithfully surrendered, as wlel as the furnaces and other affects and materials that belonged to the Austrian garrison of Sandomierz.

Art. 3. The garrison shall have the facility to rejoin the Polish Army beyond the San, crossing the Vistula at Zawichosi, or at some other point below the said city. To this effect, it shall be accorded the boats that it will return to the Austrian commission when its passage is effected, within 48 hours after the definitive evacuation of the city. In the case where this favor cannot be accorded, the garrison shall move beyond the Piliça, in following the most direct road to the Vistula; and then it shall be accorded to the garrison as many days of armistice as there are halting places as might be required to reach its destination, counting three Polish miles for each halt: as it is well understood that General Baron von Geringer will engage himself to not suffer that the garrison be restricted or disquieted during her march during the prescribed period.

The garrison shall move down the postal route, via Zawichost, Solec, Kosinnice, to Mniszew, beyond the Piliça, in the Duchy of Warsaw. The troop shall march three German miles per day and shall be followed by a civil imperial Austrian commissar who will furnish it with halts containing meat and bread, from the moment that the cattle are brought along and led with the Sandomierz troop. General Baron Geringer shall send a squadron with a staff officer for the security of the troop as long as it remains on Austrian territory, under a condtionof no hostilities shall be made by one party or the other until the passage of the Piliça. In return, General Sokolnicki shall be responsible for the secure return of the squadron which accompanied it to the army corps of General Baron Geringer. It is understood that the troops, in crossing Austrian territory, shall camp and not take anything without paying, beyond that which is prescirbed in the halt.

Art. 4. The prisoners of war made in the last affair of June 16th shall be exchanged in mass in part or other, and this exchange shall take place before the exchange of the last column. If, however, it cannot be effected at the prescribed time, there shall be accorded a longer delay for the last until they can reach the rest of their unit; and it is well understood that hostage officers of note shall be given by the Austrian army for the guarantee of this point, in view that the Austrian prisoners remain in the fortress. In this article there shall not be included prisoners of the two nations, taken prior to this affair.

Granted on condition that all the prisoners that are found in Sandomierz, be they officers or soldiers, shall be faithfullly surrendered, without exclusion in which affiar; and if they are found among the garrison Austrian soldiers who were taken involuntarily during the reduction of the fort by General Egermann, they shall be surrendered with the prisoners. For the rest, Austrian faithfulness answers to the completion of this treaty.

Art.5. The Polish convalescents who are in a state to be transported, shall enjoy to be transported shall be accorded transport vehicles beyond those listed in Article 2. For those that are not able to be transported shall be left to the faithfulness and care of the Austrian administration; an officer shall remain to oversee them and they shall be accorded movement

They shall be given sufficient wagons for the convalescent, which shall follow the garrison, as it is impossible at the present to gather such a large number of vehicles.

The rest is granted, with the remark that the hospitals shall be maintained on the same basis as the Austrian hospitals in Warsaw papers to rejoin their units or to move beyond the Piliça when their convalescence is over.

Additional Article: The armistice shall be prolonged by 48 hours after the crossing of the Piliça; at the same time there shall be mutually given hostages to the end of the evacuation of Sandomierz.

The magazines, as well as the prisoners of war, hospital and boats, shall be turned over to the commissioner which General Baron Geringer shall name. The artillery officer is charged with coming to Sandomierz to take possession of the Austrian cannons remaining in the numbers that are found today in the fortress of Sandomierz, which cannot be less than fifteen in number, that is to say:

> 8 18pdrs
> 3 howtizers
> 2 6pdrs
> 2 3pdrs

Beyond this, it extends to all articles of war, the number of which, belonging to the Imperial Austrian army prior to the capture of the fortress by the troops of the Duchy of Warsaw and which were presently found in Sandomierz shall not be removed: they shall be scrupulously and exactly remitted to the commissioner named to this effect.

All agreed to by the undersigned, equipped with full powers necessary by their respective commanders who have been reciprocally communicated with prior to the conclusion of the preceding articles.

In the name and by the order of
Generalmajor B. Geringer

    Obrazow, June 18, 1809

Major of the Chief of staff:

    Signed: Neuman

Ratified at Obrazow, June 18, 1809, at 6:00 a.m.

The Generalmajor of the Austrian Army.
    Signed: Baron von Geringer

By order of General Sokolnicki
Colonel of the 6th Cavalry Regiment

    Signed: Dziewanowski

Ratified at Sandomierz June 18th, 1809, at 9:00 a.m. with the clause stating that the last column shall be allowed not to leave before tomorrow, June 19th, for reason of the darkness of the night, having the wel founded hope that General Baron von Geringer will not refuse this; and in remarking that, when the clause inserted in Article 4 relative to the forced enrollment of prisoners of war, there shall not be exercised any sort of investigation in this regard, I give my word that there are not exist any of these men the corps under my orders, understanding that under no pretext shall our men be forcably enrolled.

Signed: General Sokolnicki

APPENDIX XIII.

Headquarters at Pniow, 21 June 1809

Letter from Prince Poniatowski to the Major General [Berthier]

Sir,

I have the honor of relating to Your Highness in my preceding reports how much the inaction of the Russian troops caused me to fear for Sandomierz; experience has proven that my concern in this regard was well founded. This place was attached during the night of 15/16 June with great obstinacy. Despite the efforts of 10,000 to 11,000 men, deployed during the long assault, the enemy, even though he penetrated into the interior of the works, was completely repelled with a loss of around 2,000 men and 500 prisoners. However, this heavy engagement had completely consumed our munitions and having no more in the fortress, neither infantry cartridges, nor charges for the 3pdr and 6pdr cannons, Général de brigade Sokolnici, perceiving preparations for a renewed attack two days later, which he was not sure of withstanding, evacuated the city in order to rejoin the corps under my orders. Two Russian divisions were, at this time, on the San, a very short distance from Sandomierz; and, despite my pressing solicitations, they made no movement to move to the secure of the fortress. In these circumstances, it appears to me that it is best for me to act on the left bank of the Vistula. If I had only to sustain the efforts of the enemy I should never be deprived of my resources and I would always be sure on whom I could count. I shall cover the duchy from there; and if the enemy forces me to restraint, I shall be able to pursue without being stopped by the slowness and ill will [of the Russians]. The troops under my orders shall march out tomorrow. I have to honor to forward to Your Highness the attached copy of the report from General Sokolnicki, as well as the capitulation and the correspondence that occurred with regards to it with the Austrian General Geringer.

Sincerely, etc.

The Général de division commanding the Polish troops of the IX Corps.
Signed: Józef, Prince Poniatowski

———●———

APPENDIX XIV.

Headquarters at Pulway, 27 June 1809

Letter from Prince Poniatowski to the Major General [Berthier]

Sir,

I had the honor to forward to Your Highness on 21 June, word that, despite the engagement made by Prince Golitsyn to cross two divisions of his army beyond the San, no such action was taken. In effect, under the pretext of lacking provisions, this measure was not effected except in part several days later, with the same slowness that has characterized all the movements of the Russian troops. These delays have given the Austrian corps, which has moved to the right bank of the Vistula, the time necessary to make its retreat with great tranquility, and was in no manner disturbed. The Austrian Army had unquestionable knowledge that, since this time, the army commanded by Prince Golitsyn did not cross the Vistula, caused Archduke Ferdinand's plans to be carried with speed and move the greater part of his troops, that is around 25,000 men, beyond the Piliça, and to threaten in this manner the border of the duchy. This movement caused me on Puławy. The troops under my commands have been there three days. By means of bridge which I had thrown over the Vistula, I could at this point, without leaving Galicia, observe the subsequent march of the enemy, moving as necessary to the left bank, and, while maneuvering on one of the ends of his line, to coordinate my operations[1] those of Generals Sokolnicki and Dąbrowski, who, with around 8,000 men , have taken up position at Gora. All of my cavalry has been thrown towards Zwolin and Radom, supported by infantry, to observe the enemy's movement, and to unite at a point where they might act with the greatest advantage. I have not missed any opportunity and when favorable circumstances permitted the Polish troops have gained new successes to achieve the intentions of His Majesty the Emperor in keeping the Austrian corps, infinitely larger than my corps, occupied. The arrival of the Russian Army in Galicia and the events that it has created have given the enemy the opportunity to disturb the part of Galicia situated on the right bank of the Vistula, this circumstance required the formation of new units and the Russian generals have contributed even more, in installing wherever they are, Austrian employees, who make it a duty to torment the inhabitants and to choke all who act contrary to the interests of their sovereign. I hope however that the zeal proven by all the Galicians shall overcome this new fetter and that we are not frustrated in our means to offer this country the opportunity to add to our forces, if the lack of arms does not limit their desire to deserve a country, and become worthy of the protection of the Emperor.

Sincerely, etc.

The Général de division commanding the Polish troops of the IX Corps.

Signed: Józef, Prince Poniatowski

———————●———————

---

[1]The two generals had between them a combined force of 11,000 men.

APPENDIX XIV.

Headquarters at Puławy, 2 July 1809

Order of the Day

The prince commander-in-chief wishes to make known to the army that His Majesty the Emperor and King is satisfied with the Polish Army and he has ordered it be known to the army that he approves of their conduct. This testimony of the benevolence of this sovereign must be used by them as encouragement so as to in the future to deserve similar praise and protection of which he has given us evidence. Arms and subsidies are already enroute. The commanding prince in chief has received orders to provisionally occupy Galicia in the name of His Majesty the Emperor and king to replace the Austrian eagles with the French eagles, to give the order to all the tribunals to render justice in the name of the French Emperor, and to receive the oath of fidelity of the authorities to this sovereign. As a consequence, the prince orders to all the generals and officers of all grades to conform strictly with this order and to execute it as well as they can. In addition, he informs the army that His Majesty the Emperor has ordered that a Galician Army should be organized on the same basis as the French troops; that they shall have for ensigns the French eagles and that they shall be maintained at his expense, all remaining under the direction of the prince commander-in-chief to cooperate with our troops against the common enemy.

The General, Chief of the General Staff,

Signed: Fiszer.

APPENDIX XVI.

Pieces relative to the correspondence between the
Austrians and General Rozniecki
Relative to the capitulation of Krakow

1

To the Commander of the advanced guard of the Polish Army

Desiring to preserve Krakow from the ravages of war, I have the honor of proposing to you, sir, an armistice of twice 24-hours, after which I will turn over to you the city and withdraw to the right bank of the Vistula. Please indicate to me the lace and the hour where we can concert, at the advanced posts, on the objects and determine the articles of this convention, which have no other goal but to spare the inhabitants of this city.

Krakow, July 14th 1809

General commanding the advanced guard of Mondet's Corps
Signed: Baron Mohr

2

To Général de brigade Rozniedcki, Chevalier of many orders,
Commander of the Advanced Guard of the Polish Army

General Baron Mohr has advised me of the proposal that you have made to him to stop all hostilities over a period of 24-hours under the condition that when this lapse of 12 hours is passed the city of Krakow, on the left bank of the Vistula, shall be evacuated by the troops of His Majesty the Emperor of Austria and that the bridge over the Vistula shall not be destroyed.

I accept, sir, these conditions and after that the hostilities shall not commence until tomorrow, the 15th of this month, 12 hours after the signing of this convention.

Lieutenant Colonel Dressery, of the Wukassovich Regiment, is provided with full powers on my part to sign the aforementioned conditions.

Headquarters at Podgorze, 14 July 1809

Signed: Generalleutnant Mondet

3

Lieutenant Colonel Dressery is authorized on my part, to sign the conditions that were agreed to by the general commanding the advanced guard of the Polish troops, for an armistice.

Headquarters at Podgorze, 14 July 1809

4

To General Roznieci, Chevalier of many orders,
Commander of the advanced guard of the Polish Troops.

Nothing is more clear and more positive than the letter which I had the honor to write to you relative to the armistice; you shall see that there is no question as to the two conditions: the first, that the Austrian troops evacuate the city of Krakow on the left bank of the Vistula; and the second and last, that the bridge over the Vistula shall not be destroyed. It is for these two conditions, sir, that I had authorized Lieutenant Colonel Dressery to sign, on my part, this convention; there was no question retarding Podgorze which is on the left bank on the Vistual, nor of other conditions which were added and against which I protest.

I expect, sir, the faithfulness of the Poles, which you well wish to rectify the convention after the contents of my letter, and to this effect, I attache it, which shall be regarded as not cancelled.

Signed: Generalleutnant Mondet

Convention

Between Général de brigade Rozniecki, commander of the advanced guard of the Polish Army, chevalier of many ordes, etc., and Lieutenant Colonel Dressery, of the Wukasovich Infantry Regiment, in the service of His Majesty the Emperor of Austria, equipped with full powers on the part of His Excellency Generalleutnant von Mondet.

Art. 1. An armistice of 12-hours is agreed to after the present signatures. In this period of time the Austrian troops shall evacuate the the fortress of Krakow with their arms and baggage.

Art. 2. Upon the expiration of this term, the Polish troops shall occupy the cities of Krakow and Podgorze.

Art. 3. Generalleutnant von Mondet promises to not destroy the bridge over the Vistula.

Art. 4. The Polish Army shall not pass beyond Podgorze sooner than six hours after the expiration of the first term accorded, 12-hours.

Art. 5. The present convention shall not impede the Austrian troops from deploying to dispute any movement out of Podgorze.

Art. 6. A commissioner of war shall be charged with taking custody of the magazines.

Art. 7. The sick and wounded who are found in the hospitals shall remain as prisoners of war and shall be placed on a list of names. They shall be accorded all the care due the state in which they are due.

Art. 8. The Austrian administrative employees shall be treated with all the regards due to public functionaries.

Signed at Promnik, 14 July 1809, at 6:00 p.m.
Signed: Général de brigade Rozniecki

Dressery, Lieutenant Colonel of the
Wukassovich Regiment

Original copy:
        Prince Józef Poniatowski

APPENDIX XVII.

Headquarters at Krakow, 16 July 1809

Order of the Day

The Prince, Commander-in-Chief, informs the army that an armistice has been concluded on the 12th between the Emperor of the French and the Emperor of Austria, to extend to August 12th. This armistice was signed at the camp at Zniam, and stipulates, with regards to Poland, that the two belligerent armies shall occupy the positions in which they find themselves; that all hostilities shall cease.

The General, Chief of the General Staff
Signed: Fiszer

APPENDIX XVIII.

CONVENTION

Concluded at the Winiawka Camp between the commander of the Imperial Austrians
And the Poles, Generalmajor von Biking and Pierre de Strzyzewski

Requests	Responses
Art. 1. A complete armistice at the end of negotiations	Agreed
Art.2. Al the corps shall return to Bokovina with cannons, arms and all munitiions and cannot, after arriving in Czernowitz, serve against the troops allied with the Poles until a month after the termination of this obligation.	All units may retire and return to the Bukovina with the obligation to not serve until following the peace with France and its allies. The dcannons, arms of all types, munitiions and armaments shall be surrendered; 200 muskets, bullet pouches, and cross-belts shall be left with the corps for its return.
Art. 3. The equippage and the horses of the officers, including the horses and armaments of the Arnauts, plus those which belong to the customs and the light infantry shall be retained.	Granted for the equipment and property with the horses of the officers; however the horses and armaments of the Arnauts, of the personnel of the customs and the light infantry shall surrendered to the Poles.
Art. 4. The returning units shall be escorted by a Polish officer until they meet the first Imperial and Royal troops and shall provide the food and relay horses necessary.	Granted, with the exception that the corps being returned shall be escorted by a Polish officer only to within a half mile of Czernowitz. He shall look after the provisions and the relay horses as necessary.
Art. 5. It is proposed that General Feldmarschalleutnant Merveldt shall send communication of this convention to Czernowitz.	Refused
Art. 6. It is requested, on the part of the commander of the allied Polish, a list of the names of the generals and officers and the entire troops.	Granted
Art. 7. The present convention shall be effective four hours after an armistice of four hours.	Four hours after the expiration of this convention, the corps shall leave its camp and the occupation of it, as is stated above, shall take place.

Art. 8. All prisoners of war of this corps shall be returned in an exchange (Rewers) for the Count Starzynski, Baron Berlinkowiski and the uhlan Jarikowski. Counter billets shall be exchanged immediately after they are sent and the uhlan taken shall be reclaimed upon entry into Czernowitz.

This copy has been made and signed by the two parties at the camp near Winiawka, 18 July 1809.

Signed: Commandant Strzyzewski   Signed: Generalmajor von Biking

Original copy forwarded,

     Chief of the general staff

     Signed: Count Montion

APPENDIX XIX.

Krakow, 23 July 1809

Report to His Majesty the Emperor and King

I am eager to have the honor to bring to the attention of Your Majesty the news of the successes over the enemy by the Galician troops. A part of the uhlan regiment of Colonel Ryszczewski, which was only a part of his formation, supported by a detachment of the 1st and 3rd Cavalry Regiments, had advanced as far as Brykula towards the frontier of Bukovina, and cut off an Austrian coprs that sought to unite with the forces of Prince Hohenlohe. The enemy, attacked with the greatest impetuosity, could not resist the vigorous attack of this cavalry, and despite a triple rank of forges and wagons, behind which it sheltered, was forced to capitulate. General von Biking, who commanded this corps, a lieutenant colonel, 20 officers, and 1,100 soldiers were [taken and] engaged to not serve again for the duration of this war. The enemy lost about as many dead and wounded. Three cannons and several caissons have fallen into our hands.

This affair took place on the 18th of this month, before the news of the armistice was known by the troops that took part in it.

Faithfully, sir,

Signed: Prince Józef Poniatowski

———●———

APPENDIX XX.

POLISH ARMY ON 14 NOVEMBER 1809

INFANTRY

Regiment	Colonel	Effective Strength	Observations
1st	Caimir Malachowski	2,690	
2nd	Stanislaw Potocki	3,030	
3rd	Edouard Zoltowski	2,647	
4th	Maciej Wierzbinski	2,241	2 battalions in Spain
5th	Michel Radziwill	2,104	
6th	Julien Sierawski	2,673	
7th	Stanislaw Jakubowifcz	1,905	2 battalions in Spain
8th	Kajetan Stuart	2,302	
9th	Antoine Sulkowski	2,050	2 battalions in Spain
10th	Antoine Downarowicz	1,996	2 battalions in Danzig
11th	Stanilas Mielzynski	2,145	2 battalions in Danzig
12th	Jan Weissenhoff	2,614	
		28,367	

CAVALRY

Regiment	Colonel	Effective Strength	Observations
1st	Konst. Pszependowski	937	
2nd	Thadeus Tyszkiewicz	1,163	
3rd	Augustyn Trzecieski[1] Lonczynski	1,015	
4th	Walenty Kwasniewski	687	Detached to Germany
5th	Kasimir Turno	1,097	
6th	Domin Dziewanowski	1,009	
		5,908	

ARTILLERY, ENGINEERS & TRAIN

Foot Artillery	Colonel Anton Gorski	2,620	1 coy in Spain
Horse Artillery	Chef d'escadron Wlodz. Potocki		1 coy in Danzig

Total for the army 36,995

---

[1]The author originally listed Lonczynski as the colonel, Gembarzewski says it was Trzecieski. Bronislaw Gmbarzewski, Rodowody Pulkow Polskich i oddzialow rownorzednych od r. 1717 do r. 1831 (Warszawa: Nakladem Tow. Wiedzy Wojskowej, 1925) p. 59

FRANCO-GALICIAN ARMY

INFANTRY

1st	Augustus Szneider	3,425	Became 13th Infantry Regiment
2nd	Euzebjusz Siemianowski	2,852	Became 14th Infantry Regiment
3rd	Kasper Miaskowski	3,422	Became 15th Infantry Regiment
4th	Jakob Kenszycki	2,338	Dissolved
5th	Konst. Czartoryski	2,561	Became 16th Infantry Regiment
6th	Jozef Hornowski	1,985	Became 17th Infantry Regiment

16,583

CAVALRY

1st Uhlan	Augustyn Zawadzki	840
2nd Uhlan	Kazimierz Rozwadowski	954
3rd Uhlan	Feliks Przyszychowski	936
4th Uhlan	Adam Potocki	899
5th Uhlan	Gabriel Ryszczewski	943
6th Uhlan	Augustyn Trzeciecki	916
7th Uhlan	Marcin Tarnowski	611
1st Hussars	Jozef Tolinski	1,048
2nd Hussars	Jan Uminski	803
1st Cuirassier	Stanislaw Malachowski	610

8,618

Total 25,194

Total Polish Army 62,089

6,265 detached to Spain
3,024 detached to Danzig
686 detached to Germany

APPENDIX XXI.

Schönbrunn, 17 September 1809

The Major General [Berthier] to Prince Poniatowski

I am informing you that the Emperor has given the order that 10,000 muskets be sent to you from the arsenal at Magdeburg via Dresden today. His Majesty has ordered that 7,000 that are in Danzig should be sent to you as well as 3,000 from Stettin, which will provide you with 20,000. You shall find attached a duplicate of the order for the 10,000 muskets that are at your disposition.

———•———

The soldiers who have distinguished themselves in the various actions in the 1809 campaign.

(Drawn from the Orders of the Day)

Engagement at Grzybow, 18 April

Name	Surname	Grade
Osipowski		Captain of the 5th Cavalry Regiment
Czyzewski		Captain of the 5th Cavalry Regiment
Loncki		Captain of the 5th Cavalry Regiment
Radwan		Lieutenant
Urbanski		Sous-lieutenant
Brochocki		Sergeant
Maszewski		Sergeant

Capture of the Gora Bridgehead, 3 May

Name	Surname	Grade
Turno	Kazimiers	Colonel of the 5th Cavalry Regiment
Kornatowski	Zygmund	Chef d'escadron, 5th Cavalry Regiment
Blumer		Chef de bataillon, 6th Infantry Regiment
Suchodolski		Chef de bataillon, 6th Infantry Regiment

Engagement at Strzelno, 11 May

Name	Surname	Grade
Wengerski	Emil	Lieutenant Colonel
Suminski		Captain, ADC to Gen. Woiczynski

Engagement at Częstochowa, 16 May

Name	Surname	Grade
Hann		Captain
Cylinski		Captain
Czerno		Volunteer

Capture of Sandomierz and the Bridgehead, 18 May

Name	Surname	Grade
Potocki	Wlodomir	Chef d'escadron
Szubert		Lieutenant Adjutant-major
Osipowski		Captain, 5th Cavalry Regiment
Michalowski		Captain, 5th Cavalry Regiment
Kurnacki		Sous-lieutenant
Janicwicz		Sergeant Major
Urlanski		Brigader
Tomaszyk		Soldier

Pullert		Soldier
Boguslawski		Chef de bataillon, 6th Infantry Regiment
Rybinski	Marthias	Captain, 6th Infantry Regiment
Strzelecki		Captain, 6th Infantry Regiment
Rulinkowski		Captain, 6th Infantry Regiment
Malczewski		Captain, 6th Infantry Regiment
Wolski		Lieutenant
Czarnecki		Lieutenant
Przezdziecki		Sous-lieutenant
Swirzenski	Albert	Sergeant
Nagorski	Józef	Sergeant
Nielepiec	Albert	Quartermaster Corporal
Bankowski	Michel	Quartermaster Corporal
Biernacki		Captain, 8th Infantry Regiment
Szultz	Christophe	Sergeant
Strymowski	François	Sergeant
Wieliczko	Jean	Corporal
Iedrzeiowski	Charles	Voltigeur
Mantoffel		Voltigeur
Cieplik	Antoine	Voltigeur
Brzozowski	Józef	Voltigeur
Buminski	Michel	Sergeant
Kozlowski	André	Sergeant
Chrzanowski	Jacques	Voltigeur
Owakowski	Antoine	Voltigeur
Dobrowolski	Józef	Voltigeur

Assault on Zamość, 20 May
The following particularly distinguished themselves

Name	Surname	Grade
Gorski	Anton	Colonel of artillery
Potocki	Stanislaw	Colonel, 2nd Infantry Regiment
Strzyzewski		Chef d'escadron, 3rd Cavalry Regiment
Brzechwa		Chef d'escadron, 6th Cavalry Regiment
Krasinski	Ilaire	Chef de bataillon, 2nd Infantry Regiment
Suchodolski		Chef de bataillon, 6th Infantry Regiment
Soltyk	Roman	Captain of Horse Artillery
Daine		Captain, 2nd Infantry Regiment
Jonga		Captain, 2nd Infantry Regiment
Beladowski		Lieutenant, ADC to Gen. Kaminski
Mlocki		Adjudant Sous-officier

Others who distinguished themselves

Name	Rank	Name	Rank
Huisson	Captain	Kozakewiecz	Corporal
Grotowski	Captain	Kancki	Corporal
Slupecki	Captain	Kaminski	Soldier
Krasnodembski	Captain	Bankowski	Soldier
Pawlowski	Captain	Grabowski	Soldier
Boguslawski	Captain	Kierszek	Soldier
Zieleniewski	Captain	Zalewski	Soldier
Gurski	Adjutant-major	Tiurbo	Soldier
Kawecki	Adjutant-major	Iaskulski	Soldier
Kosinski	Lieutenant	Iagielski	Soldier
Hiz	Lieutenant	Przybylowski	Soldier
Klimiewicz	Lieutenant	Iodlowski	Soldier
Dunquert	Lieutenant	Irzeczkowicz	Soldier
Wenzyk	Lieutenant	Koziarowski	Soldier
Dąbrowski	Lieutenant	Piorun	Soldier
Burakowski	Lieutenant	Chwialowski	Soldier
Gzowski	Lieutenant	Grosz	Soldier
Loski	Lieutenant	Mistelak	Soldier
Hornowski	Lieutenant	Cindkowicz	Soldier
Witowski	Lieutenant	Pawlowiz	Soldier
Gembka	Sous-lieutenant	Michalow	Soldier
Budzynski	Sous-lieutenant	Monko	Soldier
Wongrodski	Sous-lieutenant	Bordkiewicz	Soldier
Remiszewski	Sous-lieutenant	Lubodzen	Soldier
Glembocki	Sous-lieutenant	Mikilicz	Soldier
Mlocki	Sous-lieutenant	Stawski	Soldier
Szaniecki	Sous-lieutenant	Borkusizk	Soldier
Thompson	Sous-lieutenant	Barnowski	Soldier
Jelski	Sous-lieutenant	Zyzniewski	Soldier
Ranicki	Sous-lieutenant	Klodzinski	Soldier
Dembski	Sous-lieutenant	Iopowicz	Soldier
Karwowski	Sous-lieutenant	Zuhr	Soldier
Wodzynski	Sous-lieutenant	Zuhr (wife)	Soldier
Pruszinski	Sergeant Major	Myszkowski	Soldier
Falinski	Sergeant Major	Palucki	Soldier
Iedrzeiowski	Sergeant	Ryszkiewicz	Soldier
Baciarelli	Sergeant	Skaldowski	Soldier
Mokrski	Sergeant	Kowalski	Soldier
Krzyzanowski	Corporal	Gajewski	Soldier
Klimkiewicz	Corporal	Swiderski	Soldier
Wisniewski	Corporal	Winkowski	Soldier

Name	Rank	Name	Rank
Borowski	Soldier	Piasecki	Soldier
Rosolski	Soldier	Lipski	Soldier
Bartosiek	Soldier	Andrejew	Soldier
Siarczynski	Soldier	Miaskowski	Drummer

Engagements on the line of Great Poland, 22 May

Name	Surname	Grade
Dąbrowski	Michel	Général de brigade
Biernacki	Józef	Colonel
Bielanowski		Major

Engagement before Sandomierz, 27 May

Name	Surname	Grade
Bieganski	Lukasz	Général de brigade

Engagement at Sandomierz, 6 June

Name	Surname	Grade
Zoltowski	Edward	Colonel, 3rd Infantry Regiment

Engagement of Iankowice, 11 June

Name	Surname	Grade
Krasinski	Izydor	Général de brigade
Kossecki	Ksawery	Colonel of General Staff
Zielinski		Colonel of General Staff
Oskierka		Major
Hofmann		Lieutenant Colonel
Kossecki		Lieutenant Colonel
Radzyminsi		Aide-de-camp to General Zajączek
Yabkowski		Aide-de-camp to General Zajączek

Engagement at Wrzawy, 12 June

Name	Surname	Grade
Kamieniecki	Michael	Général de brigade
Malachowski	Kazimierz	Colonel, 1st Infantry Regiment
Potocki	Stanislaw	Colonel, 2nd Infantry Regiment
Paszkowski	Franciszek	Colonel, ADC to King of Saxony
Wolinski		Major
Redel	Anton	Major of Artillery

Kryzinski		Lieutenant Colonel of artillery
Ostrowski		Lieutenant Colonel, 3rd Cavalry Regiment
Daine		Lieutenant Colonel, 3rd Cavalry Regiment
Soltyk	Roman	Captain of Horse Artillery
Huisson		Captain, 1st Infantry Regiment
Krasnodembskii		Captain, 1st Infantry Regiment
Gavard		Captain, 1st Infantry Regiment
Lonczynski		Captain, 1st Infantry Regiment
Gorski		Captain, 1st Infantry Regiment
Slupecki		Captain, 1st Infantry Regiment
Szweikowski		Captain, 1st Infantry Regiment
Wenzyk		Adjutant-major
Godlewski		Adjutant-major
Klimkiewicz		Lieutenant
Puchalski		Chief Physician
Przybylski		Surgeon Major
Przystanski		Surgeon Major
Koch		Surgeon Major

Assault on Sandomierz, 16 June

Name	Grade	Name	Grade
Sierawski	Colonel, 6th Infantry	Symaniecki	ADC to Gen. Bieganski
Bontemps	Colonel of Artillery	Zawadzki	Captain
Zoltowski	Colonel, 3rd Infantry	Jordan	ADC to Gen. Sokolnicki
Weissenhoff	Colonel, 12th Infantry	Pawlowski	Adjutant-Major
Dziewanowski	Colonel, 6th Cavalry	Koszubski	Lieutenant of grenadiers
Bialkowski	Lieutenant Colonel	Stembert	Lieutenant of grenadiers
Suchodolski	Lieutenant Colonel	Plonszinski	Lieutenant
Kurcynsz	Captain	Dzialkowski	Lieutenant
Wiesiolowski	Captain	Eisner	Lieutenant
Leanski	Captain	Bielski	Lieutenant
Czeraiski	Captain	Lubieniecki	Lieutenant of artillery
Bleszynski	Captain	Tykel	Lieutenant
Kosinski	Captain	Rychlowski	Lieutenant
Zolondkowski	Captain	Szczepanowski	Lieutenant
Plonczynski	Captain	Zdztowiecki	Lieutenant
Poniatowski	Captain	Koricki	Sous-lieutenant
Chmielowski	Captain	Zabielski	Sous-lieutenant
Strzalkowski	Captain	Bulawecki	Sous-lieutenant
Pogorzelski	Captain	Grzelakowsi	Sous-lieutenant
Walichnowski	ADC to Gen. Sokonicki	Tuszczewski	Sous-lieutenant, ADC Gen. Woyczynski

Poniatowski and the 1809 Campaign

Czaykowski	Captain	Ianowski	Sergeant
Skoraszewski	Captain	Bosko	Sergeant
Oskierko	Sergeant	Bogudzki	Sapper
Wieczerski	Quartermaster Corporal	Wasilkowski	Soldier
Rudkowski	Corporal	Zawadzki	Corporal
Fergus	Sapper	Szfraniak	Soldier
Wisniewski	Drummer		

INDEX

Austria *army offensive* 53-55, 115-122; *Austrian Army organization* 44-48

Dąbrowski, Jan Henryk 10, 13, 14, 16,17, 20, 25, 27, 29, 39, 42, 62, 66, 68, 69, 70, 72, 74, 75, 76, 83, 103, 104, 105, 106, 109, 110, 111, 115, 122, 123, 124, 175

Ferdinand, Archduke D'este 34, 44, 53, 54, 55, 56, 58, 60, 62, 63, 66, 67, 68, 71, 73, 74, 75, 81, 82, 83, 84, 85, 92, 103, 108, 115, 119, 120, 121, 124, 126, 128, 137

Galitzin, Dmitry 16, 17, 92, 99, 101, 103, 108, 111, 112, 115, 145

Gorchakov, Mikhail 85, 86, 111, 148

Grand Duchy of Warsaw *creation* 34-40; *Organization* 40-44, 47, 57, 58, 71, 76, 84, 105, 106, 122-123, 135, 139, 170-1; *1809 campaign* 15-18; *1812 campaign* 19-27; *1813 campaign* 21-32

Kaminski, Michał 42, 59, 72, 74, 86, 92, 93, 96, 98, 150, 174

Kosciuszko, Tadeusz 5, 7, 8, 9, 10, 12, 13, 39, 43, 56, 69, 70, 99

Krakow 3, 8, 10, 16, 17, 27, 28, 29, 32, 44, 46, 47, 50, 54, 82, 87, 88, 92, 97, 101, 105, 118, 119, 120, 121, 126, 127, 128, 129, 131, 133, 135, 136, 138, 147, 149, 157, 163, 164, 166, 169

Mohr, Johann von 14, 15, 16, 44, 53, 60, 61, 66, 71, 72, 73, 74, 75, 76, 81, 83, 103, 104, 110, 120, 126, 127, 128, 139, 141, 142, 144, 147, 148, 154, 161, 163

Mondet, Ludwig 17, 45, 53, 103, 105, 109, 110, 115, 118, 126, 127, 128, 129, 131, 163, 164, 182

Pelletier, General 46, 57, 58, 63, 66, 70, 75, 76, 77, 83, 92, 93, 94, 95, 96, 98, 101, 113, 136, 144, 149, 150, 155

Polish Units in Spain 14, 46-47

Poniatowski, Prince Józef 1, 2, 3, 5, 6, 7, 10, 11, 12, 13, 14, 15, 16, 17, 18, 19, 20, 21, 22, 23, 24, 26, 27, 28, 29, 30, 31, 33, 34, 38, 39, 42, 46, 47, 53, 54, 56, 57, 58, 59, 60, 61, 62, 63, 66, 68, 70, 71, 72, 74, 75, 76, 78, 80, 81, 82, 83, 85, 86, 90, 92, 93, 96, 97, 98, 101, 103, 106, 107, 108, 109, 111, 112, 113, 115, 117, 118, 119, 120, 122, 123, 124, 126, 130, 131, 132, 134, 137, 140, 141, 142, 145, 146, 148, 149, 150, 153, 155, 156, 160, 161, 165, 169, 172, 177

Poniatowski, Stanislaw Augustus 1, 3, 4, 7, 11

Potocki, Stanislaw 3, 45

Raszyn, battle of 14, 15, 53, 57, 58, 59, 60, 61, 62, 63, 71, 75, 139

Rozniecki, Alexander 42, 57, 60, 76, 87, 88, 89, 90, 92, 96, 98, 99, 103, 109, 112, 113, 119, 124, 126, 127, 128, 129, 130, 136, 148, 149, 163, 164, 165

Sandomierz 15, 16, 46, 49, 50, 54, 81, 82, 87, 88, 89, 90, 92, 96, 97, 98, 101, 103, 105, 106, 108, 109, 110, 112, 115, 116, 118, 119, 120, 145, 149, 150, 154, 155, 157, 158, 159, 160, 173, 176, 177

Saxony 14, 15, 18, 19, 28, 30, 43, 46, 47, 48, 53, 57, 58, 59, 61, 62, 63, 67, 68, 75, 81, 92, 99, 121, 123, 135, 136, 141, 156, 176

Sokolnicki, Michał 16, 17, 28, 42, 59, 60, 61, 62, 66, 69, 70, 72, 73, 74, 76, 77, 78, 81, 87, 88, 89, 92, 96, 97, 103, 104, 108, 115, 116, 117, 118, 120, 124, 129, 131, 143, 149, 157, 158, 159, 160, 161, 177

Soltyk, Roman 3, 6, 7, 27, 46, 59, 78, 85, 94, 117, 124, 174, 177

Soltyk, Santislaw 3, 21, 32

Warsaw 2, 4, 6, 7, 8, 9, 10, 11, 12, 13, 14, 15, 16, 17, 18, 19, 23, 26, 27, 28, 31, 34, 36, 38, 39, 40, 41, 43, 46, 47, 48, 49, 50, 51, 53, 54, 55, 56, 57, 58, 59, 60, 61, 62, 63, 64, 66, 67, 68, 69, 71, 73, 74, 75, 76, 81, 82, 83, 85, 97, 99, 100, 101, 103, 104, 105, 106, 110, 111, 120, 122, 123, 126, 128, 136, 139, 141, 142, 143, 145, 147, 151, 158, 159

Wrzawy 16, 103, 109, 111, 112, 113, 118, 176

Zajánczek, Józef 14, 16, 42, 69, 74, 75, 76, 105, 106, 137, 147, 154, 176

Zamosc 27, 46, 49, 82, 86, 92, 93, 94, 96, 97, 98, 107, 108, 109, 117, 120, 123, 134, 136

List of Illustrations

Prince Jozef Poniatowski by Jozef Grassi — Frontpage

Roman Soltyk (unknown) — iv

Prince Józef Poniatowski by Franciszek Paderewski — 33

Gen. Jan Henryk Dombrowski (unknown) — 52

The Battle of Razyn by Julisz Kossak — 65

The Battle of Razyn by January Suchodolski — 80

Gen. Jozef Zajączek (unknown) — 91

The Battle of Razyn by Julisz Kossak — 102

The 2nd Infantry Regiment in 1809 by Jan Chełminski — 114

Polish lancers against Austrian cuirassiers by Julisz Kossak — 125

Horse artillery in 1809 by Jan Chełminski — 138

A Map of the Grand Duchy of Warsaw — 179

The Council on America's Military Past, USA, Inc. (CAMP) is one of the leading national military history organizations dedicated to preserving, interpreting and sharing our military heritage.

Our purpose is to identify, memorialize, preserve and publicize America's military history including the structures and facilities used by our soldiers, the living conditions, customs and traditions of our men and women in uniform, and the progress and purpose of United States military organizations.

We produce two publication: Heliogram and JAMP as well as a yearly organizational Meeting

For membership information, please refer to the website:

www.campjamp.org

or contact Nick Reynolds, membership secretary at nereyn@earthlink.net

502 N. Norwood St
Arlington, VA 22203

The Kosciuszko Foundation, Inc
15 East 65th Street
New York, NY 10065

www.thekf.org

Look for more books from Winged Hussar Publishing, LLC – E-books, paperbacks and Limited Edition hardcovers. The best in history, science fiction and fantasy at:

https://www. wingedhussarpublishing.com

or follow us on Facebook at:

Winged Hussar Publishing LLC

Or on twitter at:

WingHusPubLLC

For information and upcoming publications

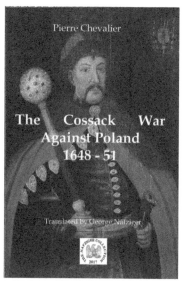

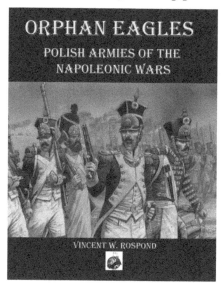

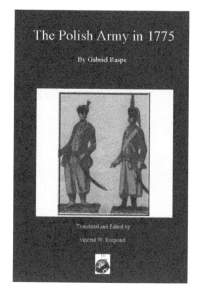

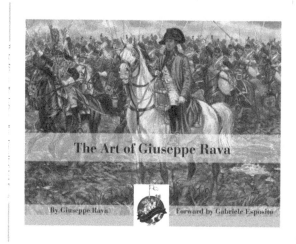